D1526909

To Turid

Human Capital in Organizations

Competence, Training, and Learning

Odd Nordhaug

Human Capital in Organizations
Competence, Training, and Learning

Scandinavian
University Press

Scandinavian University Press (Universitetsforlaget AS)
0608 Oslo, Norway
Distributed world-wide excluding Norway by
Oxford University Press, Walton Street, Oxford OX2 6DP

Oxford New York Toronto Dehli Bombay Calcutta Madras
Karachi Kuala Lumpur Singapore Hong Kong Tokyo Nairobi
Dar es Salaam Cape Town Melbourne Auckland Madrid and
associated companies in Berlin Ibadan

Oxford is a trade mark of Oxford University Press

Published in the United States by
Oxford University Press Inc., New York

© Universitetsforlaget 1993

ISBN 82-00-21807-4

British Library Cataloguing in Publication Data
Data available

Library of Congress Cataloguing in Publication Data
Data available

Printed in Norway by A/S Foto-Trykk, Trøgstad 1993

Preface

This book was written during a two-year research grant generously awarded me by the Norwegian School of Economics and Business Administration where I have enjoyed being at the faculty of the Department of Organization Science for nine years. Part of the fellowship period was spent at the Center for Human Resources and the Department of Management at the Wharton School, University of Pennsylvania. I am indebted to Richard L. Rowan, Peter Cappelli, and the rest of the staff for the hospitality they once again showed me, and I want to thank them all. I would also like to thank Pat and Nick, Carol and Christian, Maria and Raja, Zenzo, and Antoine for the good company I enjoyed while living in the Philadelphian urban jungle.

Several colleagues have given me invaluable comments on earlier drafts of the chapters, and I especially want to thank Åge Garnes, Paul N. Gooderham, Kjell Grønhaug, Peter Lorange, Bente Løwendahl, Torger Reve, and Gunnar M. Økland for their constructive critiques. However useful their comments, none of them bear any responsibility for shortcomings in the book.

The book is dedicated to Turid who has had to put up with a husband whose relationship with the personal computer at times approaches that of a non-platonic one. Her support and sustained encouragement have once again been invaluable. Ingerid and Åshild have contributed with their customary curiosity and very funny (?) jokes about silly fathers writing books instead of playing soccer and bizarre American video games created for monstrously intense piglets just like the two of them.

Bergen, December 1992
Odd Nordhaug

Contents

PART I

Introduction

Chapter 1

Purpose and Background

Introduction

Today, we seem to witness the beginning of an era in which organizations are increasingly reinterpreted from being mainly production-centered economic units to being learning-centered economic units. This does not mean that the significance of productivity and effectiveness will diminish, but rather a comprehension that human capital in the form of competences carried by employees and teams form a decisive basis for both of these performance measures. This is also indicated by the increasingly commonplace propensity to speak about strategic learning instead of strategic planning in firms. That is chiefly a reflection of the requirements confronting firms – requirements stemming from the accellerating pace of economic development. However, it equally mirrors the relatively fresh insight that competences and their growth are at the very core of organizations' future prospects, and that there has in the field of business administration been a silent shift from focusing predominantly on physical and financial capital to focusing on human capital. Furthermore, whilst in the marketing and strategic management literature, the customer base of the firm has traditionally been described as its harvesting ground, it is, however, important to keep in mind that before harvesting on that ground firms must both *sow and cultivate competences* that can create value-added for present and new customers.

The purpose of this book is to outline and discuss important conceptual, theoretical, and empirical aspects of human capital in organizations. Whereas this concept was developed within and is commonly associated with the neoclassical economic tradition of human capital theory, the approaches in this book lie within the administrative sciences, including elements of institutional economics. Focus is set on work-related competences, personnel training, and learning processes in firms and other work organizations. Given the fact that the study of competences in organizations is still in its infancy, there is a strong need to develop conceptual and analytical tools that can be applied in future research and practice.

The book is divided in four parts, and the main parts treat competences in firms, training and learning, and future directions to research and practice.

Background

In many countries, growing amounts of resources are spent on the development of employees' knowledge and skills. Furthermore, investments in competences, through personnel training and learning in work, are regarded as being increasingly important for the success of firms and other organizations as well as for future economic development on a national level (Carnevale, Gainer, and Meltzer, 1990; Carnevale, 1991; Gottsleben, 1991; Hornbeck and Salamon, 1991; Ryan, 1991a, 1991b; Luttringer, 1991).

At the same time, there is a growing consensus within the research community and in work life that human resources are the most crucial of all resources, both within firms and other organizations – and in relation to economic development on the national level (cf., Kuznets, 1966; Anderson and Bowman, 1976; Schultz, 1981; Becker, 1983; Itami, 1987; Hall, 1989; Hornbeck and Salamon, 1991). Yet, these resources have received scant attention compared to physical and financial capital both on the firm-level and the national level.

In spite of the increased attention paid to human resources in work life, only modest efforts have been made to identify and classify different types of such resources. This situation is clearly paradoxical when contrasted with the high and increasing significance of these resources in work life. An indicator of their rising importance is the development of the value of human time, as noted by Schultz (1981:60-61) who argues that the rate of return on investment in human capital has tended to exceed the rate of return on investment in physical capital: "The central issue is the increase in the economic value of human time. This rise in the value of human time is, in large part, a consequence of the formation of new kinds of human capital in response to economic incentives. The most important achievement of modern economic growth is undoubtedly this increase in the stock of human capital".

In human capital theory, focus has primarily been set on investment in human resources and returns on such investment. The *substance* of human capital has been treated predominantly as a black box, although rough distinctions between investments in education, training, immigration, and health-related measures have been drawn (Schultz, 1961). However, it is basically the substance of the *means of generating human capital*, rather than the substance of the human capital itself, that has been discussed. Hence, it is important to supplement human capital theory at this point by endeavoring to illuminate the black box.

Although human capital is important on the level of national economies, it is in a sense even more important to study on the firm level. Developments in national economies depend heavily upon the performance of firms which in turn, to a considerable degree, is a result of the quality and composition of their human capital. Moreover, since most decisions with regard to provision, maintenance, development, and utilization of human capital in a society are made within work organizations, it is paramount to study such resources also at the level of firms.

Despite being a commonly applied concept in the organization theory and organization behavior literature, the generic notion of human resources is an inherently vague and virtually all-encompassing term that does not in itself give much direction to concrete analysis unless being subdivided into dissimilar, specified forms of such resources. This vagueness constitutes a problem for research on the functioning of organizations in general and for research on the impact of different human resources in particular. There is thus a need to identify and define the types of human resources that are particularly important in relation to work performance in organizations.

It is analytically fruitful to distinguish between health and employee competences (defined as knowledge, skills, and aptitudes that are relevant for work) on the one hand and work motivation and commitment on the other. The two former elements together constitute the individual employee's basic capacity to perform tasks; what the person is technically or potentially *able* to do on the job. The two latter elements of human capital influence the actual performance of work by reflecting what the individual employee, given his/her competences, is *willing* to do on the job. Together, the ability and the willingness to perform define the individual employee's capability in work.

At the individual level of analysis, application of the concept of competence allows for a more accurate description of human capital which is crucial in relation to work performance and organizational performance. In practice, this is reflected in the increasing attention and effort that have been directed toward the development of employee competence through learning inside and outside the organization. In most parts of modern work life, the increased weight on learning in organizations has put a pressure on both ordinary employees and, not least, managers. With regard to the former, there is a pressure toward maintenance and development of individual competence. This is, of course, also experienced by managers, who are in addition exposed to a pressure toward stimulating and facilitating competence development amongst their subordinates. An illustration is the fact that some companies have introduced incentive systems which are designed to inhibit managers from being promoted unless they have developed at least one subordinate in their staff who is competent of replacing them when they become promoted.

Concerning the organizational level of analysis, it has recently been suggested in the strategic management literature that the traditional single business unit perspective can be favorably substituted by a perspective in which core competences are the main focus of attention (Prahalad and Hamel, 1990). However, a valid criticism is that the micro level is missing in this perspective. The fact that the significance of individual competences for creation of core competence and organizational competence has not been paid much attention to, uncovers a crucial missing link in this macro approach (see Cohen, 1991). Moreover, it is important to establish this link if the notion of organizational competence is to be developed beyond its present embryonic stage. Before that, however, it is necessary to develop conceptual foundations for the study of individual competences, competence bases, and competence networks in firms. The task in Part II of this book is to contribute to such a development.

Although it is increasingly recognized that human resources are crucial for the competitiveness and economic success of firms, research has paid scant attention to economic aspects of such resources. Major parts of the human resource management literature, and in particular the human resource development literature, have been dominated partly by psychological approaches and partly by prescriptive, practical approaches. These are of course important for the development of the field but only to a limited degree do they allow for investigation of economic aspects of human resources on the firm level. Recently, however, a growing number of researchers have paid attention to such aspects, and the body of literature is growing (see, for example, Williamson, 1981; Nelson and Winter, 1982; Itami, 1987; Naugle and Davies, 1987; Winter, 1987; Flynn, 1988; Hall, 1989; Mitchell and Zaidi, 1990; Nordhaug, 1990b).

One of the main problems in studying economic properties of human resources in firms is the lack of a set of basic concepts that theory development can build on. Even though useful concepts can be found in the literature on human capital theory (for example firm specificity) and transaction cost theory (for example measurability of individual productivity), there is a need to refine and integrate existing concepts as well as to develop new relevant concepts which can be used to form a coherent analytical basis for future empirical analyses of human capital in firms. Furthermore, this especially concerns concepts that are suitable for analyzing economic aspects of the behavior of firms.

In this book, work-related competences are conceptualized as subindividual units of analysis, since each individual normally possesses a variety of them. This has several, both analytical and practical, advantages. Among these are the opportunity to aggregate single competences across individuals and to elaborate concepts such as competence stocks, competence portfolios, competence configurations, team competence, organizational competence, and strategic competence pools (Grønhaug and Nordhaug, 1992, 1993; Heisler, Jones, and Benham, 1988; Naugle and Davies, 1987; see also Chapter 4 and 5). In addition, it makes far more sense to speak of the *types of competences* that an organization needs for its operations than to talk about the amount of human resources required or the mere number of employees that have to be recruited or hired. When tasks are to be performed, it is not employees per se that are needed, but employees who possess certain, more or less specialized and more or less advanced, competences that can yield a high work performance.

Overview of the Book

Chapter 2 provides an integrative perspective on and overview of the management of competences in firms. In order to achieve this, an analytical framework – called the competence chain – is presented. The chain consists of four links: competence planning, external competence acquisition, competence development, and competence utilization. The links are discussed separately, the main weight being put on acquisition, development, and utilization.

Competences in Firms

In Part II the intention is to discuss essential aspects of competences as productive resources in firms. Since this field is, thus far, largely uninvestigated, there is a particular need for conceptual and theoretical building stones making up a foundation for empirical research. The discussion in Part II outlines and revolves around the concepts of individual competences, competence bases, competence configurations, and competence flows in organizations, which are all considered to be central in relation to organizational performance.

Chapter 3 proposes a conceptual basis for future theory development, empirical research, and practical analysis in firms by presenting and discussing a basic conceptualization of individual work-related competences. Furthermore, an analytically based classification is outlined that builds on the three dimensions of task specificity, firm specificity, and industry specificity of employee competences. Six types of employee competence are identified: Meta-competences, industry competences, intraorganizational competences, standard technical competences, technical trade skills, and unique competences. Each of the categories are exemplified and discussed, and their sources of generation highlighted.

The aggregate of competences carried by employees and teams in the organization, its competence base, represents one of its most important resources.

In Chapter 4 competence bases are discussed in depth. Fundamental properties of such bases are identified. Drawing on insights from human capital theory and organization theory, it is argued that competence bases can be fruitfully described and classified in terms of a number of analytical dimensions which can be used as descriptors of important economic aspects of competence bases both in empirical research and in practice. The chapter closes with an outline of implications that derive from the discussion.

Chapter 5 delineates and discusses an analytical framework for the study of competences on different levels in firms. It is argued that the concepts of competence configuration and competence flow constitute fundamental building stones for the construction of such a framework. These elements are believed to have a profound impact on organizational performance, and together they describe competence networks in firms. Each of the two elements are elaborated upon, and an integrated framework is presented. Finally, implications are discussed.

Training and Learning

Part III focuses on competence development in the form of training and learning in work organizations. The significance and amounts of personnel training are rapidly increasing in comtemporary work life, and a growing number of studies of training are reported in the literature. However, the concentration has chiefly been on areas such as needs assessment, recruitment, and evaluation of results from single training activities or programs (cf. Scott and Meyer, 1991). The chapters in Part III supplement these traditional perspectives on training by focusing on determinants of training, the role of training in relation to reward systems in organizations, its role with regard to provision and transformation of human capital, and barriers against employee learning.

In Chapter 6, determinants of personnel training are discussed and a distinction is drawn between rational and political antecedents. Furthermore, factors that are assumed to contribute to determining whether firms and other work organizations choose to carry out personnel training themselves (in-house training) or choose to buy training services from external providers, are discussed. Distinctions are here drawn between economic and political determinants of such choices, and these are discussed separately. Propositions that can be tested through future empirical research, are formulated.

The point of departure in Chapter 7 is that personnel training, in addition to developing competences, may function as a part of the reward or incentive system by providing rewarding outcomes for employees. An empirical study of reward functions of personnel training based on data from Norwegian work life is presented and organizational implications of the findings discussed.

The relationship between personnel training and the fundamental organizational challenges of human capital provision and transformation is the topic of Chapter 8. Possible effects of training on the organizational level that are assumed to contribute in this respect are identified and discussed. The effects include occupational qualification, screening capacity, labor market reputation, enhancement of decision-making capacity, development of learning environments, organizational brain drain, socialization, legitimization, social integration, organizational adaptability, competence mismatch, and generation of internal vulnerability. Research findings relevant to such effects are presented and needs for future empirical research discussed.

A possible approach to analyzing and improving organizations as competence systems is to examine the identification and removal of learning barriers. This is the topic of Chapter 9. A distinction is drawn between factors that serve to inhibit mobility, transfer, and application of competences on the organizational micro level and macro level, respectively. Each of these factors is discussed separately. The micro level factors included in the discussion are current competence, practice opportunities, opportunism, relationships between colleagues, and group functioning. The macro level factors that have been selected, embrace the work system, organizational design, incentives system, organizational culture, human resource development priority, and time perspective. Finally, implications for research and practice are discussed.

Future Directions

In Chapter 10, human resource management in firms is approached on the basis of institutional economics. Based on two analytical dimensions, the firm specificity of competences and the measurability of individual work performance, a theory of determinants of human resource management is developed. An underlying assumption is that firms seek economic rationality by minimizing transaction costs. Propositions about variations in their management of human resources under this assumption are presented. Combinations of high versus low firm specificity of human capital and opportunities of measuring individual and collective productivity are regarded as antecedents of human resource planning, recruitment, development, compensation, and control.

The final chapter contains a discussion of challenges to future research and practice arising out of the presentations in the preceding chapters and out of trends in the development of work life in advanced economies.

Chapter 2

The Competence Chain

Introduction

The objective of this chapter is to provide an integrative perspective on competences in organizations and shed light on the main elements in organizations' overall management of employee competences. This is done by elaborating the competence chain metaphor and discussing its single links. In line with the conceptual outline to be presented in the next chapter, competence is understood as the knowledge, skills, and aptitudes which are used or may be used by employees in the performance of work.

The Competence Chain

Competence development has been assigned great significance in relation to important organizational matters such as reorganization, efficiency, competitiveness, and potential for economic growth. The danger in focussing exceedingly on the developmental aspect is that other, equally important, aspects of competence management are easily overlooked. In addition to being developed, competence must be planned, acquired, and utilized. These stages together comprise what we will call the *competence chain* in organizations. This is illustrated in the model in Fig. 2.1.

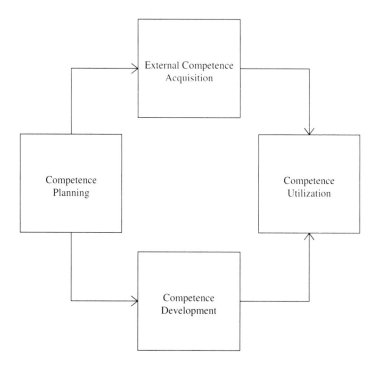

Figure 2.1. The Competence Chain

The individual elements in the model may be regarded as stages in a competence process. The stages are successive, and evaluations carried out at each stage have consequences for the carrying out of tasks in the subsequent stages. In the following sections, the four elements will be discussed separately.

Competence Planning

Many organizations put a lot of work into planning the quantitative and qualitative aspects of competence. The procedure is often that one first calculates future needs and then compares these with the present situation. The result is a *competence gap* which the company will try to fill. The gap is often specified in terms of the number of people to be hired and the areas in which they are needed. A more sophisticated version of competence planning also takes into account the internal mobility in the organization, i.e. the degree to which, as well as how, existing employees can be moved from one position to another. This approach requires active career planning within the firm. Demographic analysis to determine rates of termination, turnover, and internal mobility is also frequently used (cf. Walker, 1991).

It has become increasingly common to emphasize the need for a close relationship between the organization's goals and strategy and the planning of human competence. Yet, it seems that such close relationships are relatively rare. Douglas T. Hall (1984) defines strategic development of human resources as the identification of competence needs and active managing of employees' learning in the long run according to the organization's strategy and maintains that the final element in the definition is the most critical and the one which is most often lacking. Many organizations invest considerable resources in training and development but never really examine how training and development can most effectively promote organizational objectives, or how developmental activities should be altered in the light of business plans. Hall continues to note that a recognition that business plans should be altered because of the portfolio of expected future employee capabilities, is even rarer (Hall, 1984:160).

A study conducted among the 500 largest companies in the United States may further illustrate the significance of a close relationship between strategy and competence. The personnel managers of these companies were asked to rank the importance over five years of a set of tasks related to competence development. The single task which was ranked as extremely or very important by most managers was to obtain comprehensive knowledge regarding the company's corporate and strategic plans (92%). Ranked second was analysis of user needs (88%), followed by evaluation of effects of competence development (65%) (Ralphs and Stephan, 1986:70).

An important part of planning is to determine which competences to acquire externally and which competences can be obtained through development of current employees. In considering this problem, organizations face decisions related to both finances, development of organizational culture, and evaluations of the status of various employees' competence. A main financial question will be whether it is in given situations less expensive to develop existing employee competence ("make") than to obtain competence from the external labor market ("buy"). With regard to organizational culture, investment in a large amount of in-house competence development may reflect a desire to build or maintain an internal labor market in order to create a desirable culture. Concerning the status of available competences among employees, external recruitment is accentuated when development of needed competence within the firm is either very costly or difficult to accomplish.

Competence Acquisition

External acquisition of competence includes recruitment of new employees, purchase of consultant services, and cooperation with other organizations. We shall now take a closer look at these types of competence acquisition.

Recruitment

The most important method to procure competences in organizations is through recruitment of new employees. As the main concern in this section is with acquisition of competence, recruitment through external labor markets is of particular interest, whereas internal labor markets will be discussed under the development phase in the competence chain.

In relation to external recruitment, it is important that the organization monitors the development in external labor markets and finds appropriate channels to reach potential applicants with information regarding vacancies. The company's reputation in the labor market is of importance here: "in the absence of an explicit contract, applicants will seek information from other workers about the employers' past performance. Applicants are obliged to judge the employer, in part, by reputation" (Okun,1981:51; see also Chapter 8).

In other words, it is largely a matter of how attractive the firm is to people who initially have no detailed knowledge about it. The degree to which the firm is known to the public and the degree to which it has a culture that is regarded as attractive are crucial factors. We must assume that certain corporate cultures are more attractive and others less attractive. Maintaining and improving the invisible asset of labor market reputation is therefore an important part of strategic competence management, especially when there is a scarcity of important types of labor (cf. Itami, 1987). If we look at, for example, a field where the demand for highly qualified labor is greater than the supply, the company's reputation as a provider of opportunities for professional and personal development will be of considerable importance for choices made by potential applicants, in addition to purely economic compensation and incentives. Internal mobility and career planning may also have an effect. Potential applicants will often be interested in investigating the career opportunities provided by the organization. The active and direct marketing of positions which many firms carry out at colleges and universities illustrates this point. The competition for labor has, so to speak, moved into the educational system and this is underpinned by the fact that undergraduate students are often hired in advance of their graduation.

In addition to the external and internal labor markets, there is a third type which represents a blend of the two. Here, the search for employees and recruitment is conducted through personal contacts. In the literature, this has been called an "extended internal labor market" because it represents a network extension of a company's existing workforce (Manwaring, 1984). According to Ford and associates (1986:14), there are indications that this type of labor market has expanded in recent years. One of the advantages of this type of recruitment is that screening and selection costs are usually reduced. First, the need to advertise vacancies may either be less or nonexistent. Second, companies may gain more knowledge of the relevant applicants than they would be able to do through regular recruitment procedures. This may, however, be unreliable due to the fact that the information a company receives from employees about relatives, friends or acquaintances who search for employment will often be biased because employees generally want to assist these persons.

The overall recruitment strategies companies choose when it comes to attracting highly qualified personnel may vary substantially. In principle, needed competences may be procured either through external recruitment of well educated, experienced personnel or through in-house competence development intended to elevate employees to more advanced levels of qualification. The latter seems to be particularly widespread in firms having internal labor markets. Other companies invest only small amounts in qualifying their own employees and instead offer highly competitive compensation packages in the external labor market in order to attract personnel whose training has been financed by other firms. National military air forces have, for example, financed very costly educational programs for pilots who have later received job offers with much higher salaries from commercial airlines and who have thus left the air force. Likewise, the tax authorities in many countries have for years trained experts in the taxation of companies only to see them leave for better paid jobs in companies after training and accumulation of valuable experience. Where one organization develops or sows competence, another may harvest it.

External Consultants

In many instances companies hire special competence for a limited period, as when an external consultant is engaged to provide a final or permanent solution to a particular problem. In this case there may be little or no use for such competence later. Examples are consultant support during an acute crisis and selection of a new top manager through a headhunting agency.

A second reason for hiring external consultants may be that they are expected to transfer some of their competence to the company's employees in order that the desired competence thus remains in the organization after the consultant has finished the assignment. Then the objective is not to solve a particular problem but to generate learning that results in durable knowledge and skills amongst the organization's own employees. Organization development and training programs aimed at providing the firm with lasting abilities to meet challenges related to communication and cooperation may serve as illustrations.

Third, external consultants may be used due to internal political games and power relations in the organization. In this context, external experts may be used in two ways. They may be brought in to make it possible to exercise power in a more invisible or seemingly objective way. Furthermore, they may be brought in to legitimize decisions that have already been made and to supply the preceding decision-making process with an aura of rationality (cf. Pfeffer, 1981: 144-145).

A fourth possible reason to engage consultant support is related to considerations of cost-effectiveness. Firms will often face a choice between employing new expertise on a permanent basis or hiring external consultants whenever that is needed. Adding more employees usually involves substantial investments, including discounted future compensation. These are, moreover, largely irreversible investments to the degree that legal protection from dismissal exists or a principle of job security is practiced in the firm. Consequently, firms may in many contexts achieve greater flexibility by hiring required competence on an ad hoc basis.

Interorganizational Cooperation

Most companies base their operations and continued survival on the fact that they have one or more distinctive or unique organizational competences (Prahalad and Hamel, 1991). In order to compete effectively they must, at least in their customers' eyes, have an edge on their competitors in some area. Corporate strategy is hence fundamentally a matter of positioning the firm and its products in order to maximize relative competitive advantages.

Against this background, it does not intuitively seem probable that companies would cooperate with other companies in order to extend their competence base. At the extreme, this is probably true of fiercely competing companies. However, the less strong the competition between two firms that operate in related or complementary areas of business, the higher the probability of cooperation emerging between them. Reve and Stavseng (1984) have pointed out that there are gains to be made from cooperation in at least three main areas. The first is related to the exploitation of complementary resources. The second area is related to economies of scale that may be attained through development of a shared production facility or sales system. Third, transaction costs may be reduced by cooperation, for example, illustrated by a cartel agreement securing a ceasefire in a devastatingly resource-consuming "marketing war".

Cooperation through exploitation of complementary resources

has the advantage that the parties in those cases seldom compete directly with each other. In a study of suppliers to oil companies in Norway, it was demonstrated that complementary resources were the clearest motive for interorganizational cooperation. Almost 40 percent of these companies evaluated access to qualified personnel as important or very important. In comparison, the corresponding percentage with regard to financial resources was below 20 percent (Reve and Johansen, 1982).

In addition to extending their competence base through cooperation with other companies, firms may do so through cooperating with other kinds of organizations. Research and development units, certain government institutions, universities, and other educational institutions are central here, as are professional networks, branch organizations and other business associations. During recent years, we have witnessed an accelerating tendency to develop competence centers, business centers, and "R&D-parks", where companies, schools, and research centers are located together. The chief objective is usually to improve the common utilization of the *relative competence advantages* of these organizations by exchanging expertise and thereby creating organizational synergies.

Competence Development

Development of competence consists partly of planned programs and partly of less systematic activities, such as various forms of informal learning. A variety of areas are included, such as personnel training, job training, management development, employee consultations and career planning, trainee and apprenticeship programs, and internal forms of cooperation such as seminars, work groups, networks, and quality circles. In order to structure the discussion, a way of classifying dissimilar forms of human competence development is presented. The objectives are to note the variety of programs which are carried out, to indicate the degree of participation in various development programs, and to distinguish between active and passive learning activities. The point of departure is an assumption that all development of competence is inextricably tied to learning, which is here defined as processes that lead to changes in one or more of the following dimensions:

knowledge, skills, attitudes, and other personality-related factors. Literature on the subject often maintains that a necessary characteristic of learning is a more or less permanent alteration of behavior. In our opinion this is too stringent a requirement as there may be forms of learning which do not necessarily manifest themselves in individual behavior but yet constitute a latent potential for future behavioral changes.

Figure 2.2 contains a classification of various forms of human learning related to work.

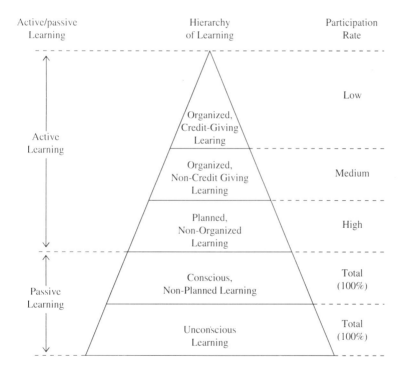

Figure 2.2. A Hierarchy of Learning

The model is constructed as a hierarchy of various types of learning. These are ranked according to how conscious, planned, formal, and result-oriented they are. The pyramidal shape has been chosen to indicate that the higher the level in the hierarchy, the lower the participation rate amongst employees. This is shown to the right in the figure, where the degree of participation is indicated (high–low). In the left part of the model, the degree of passivity of learning is indicated.

Informal Learning

At the bottom of the pyramid, we find unconscious learning which comprises all the impulses individuals absorb without being aware of it. This learning is passive and may be illustrated by the socialization processes all individuals within an organization go through. In the literature on organizational cultures, cognitive maps or models of reality which are unconsciously taken for granted by the members of the organization, are viewed as essential elements in such cultures. These cognitive maps or models have to a significant degree been unconsciously internalized in individuals: "I will argue that the term 'culture' should be reserved for the deeper level of basic assumptions and beliefs that are shared by members of an organization, that operate unconsciously, and that define in a basic 'taken-for-granted' fashion an organization's view of itself and its environment" (Schein, 1985:6).

The next step is conscious, non-planned learning, in which all employees "participate" and that can furthermore be characterized as passive. Much of the on-the-job training occurs without having been planned and can therefore be subsumed under this category. Another example is the learning of cultural values individuals are in retrospect aware of having internalized, but that was not initially planned by them.

The first type of active learning in the model is planned and informal. Here, the rate of participation is necessarily high, albeit not total. Alan Tough (1971, 1979) studied a representative sample of the adult Canadian population and found that during one year 98 per cent had completed at least one self-directed learning project (consisting of at least seven hours of independent study in a specific area). He estimated that these independent, planned learning projects equalled approximately 80 percent of all known completed learning projects. This study was directed at all kinds of learning and therefore cannot be unconditionally applied to learning in working life. There is, however, reason to believe that independent learning is also important within firms, particularly in connection with the job. A considerable percentage of the informal job training that takes place falls into this category of planned informal learning. Personnel programs such as job rotation and job development (extension and enrichment of jobs) are designed to generate this kind of learning. The performance of some jobs is nearly totally based on the completion of independent learning projects. This is particularly true of highly professional occupations. Researchers, teachers, computer experts, doctors, nurses, and engineers are some examples of professions or semi-professions where the members must continuously update their competence through individual study of literature, independent study programs, learning through trial and error, and learning from others' performances, experiences, and judgements.

Formal Learning

The first type of formal learning is not geared toward any examinations or other types of formalized tests. Most of the planned personnel training can be found on this level in the learning hierarchy. The fact that these programs are not directed at exams does not mean that they may not provide some sort of certification at all, as the completion of a course or program is frequently documented through a certificate of participation. We would expect that such documentation is more common in firms having extensive internal labor markets, since such organizations can be assumed to have a particular need for objective standards of evaluation that may be used when making decisions about internal promotions. Among other things, such standards may provide an increased sense of legitimacy to the process of selecting promotees. If motivation to learn and trainability are desired qualities in employees who are to fill vacancies, the individual employee's participation propensity and merits in training might be applied as an approximation to these qualities.

The above argument is probably even more relevant for the top type of learning in the model: formal examination-oriented learning. Although this type is a less common type of personnel training, there are indications that it has become more widely used in larger organizations. Many companies have established their own corporate colleges or universities where employees pursue credit-giving programs (Eurich, 1985). If this kind of training cannot be arranged in-house, it may be purchased outside the firm, for example in the form of professional continuing education offered by colleges and universities. A recent trend in many countries has been for companies to establish college or university level educational programs for their employees in cooperation with educational institutions. Furthermore, commissioned education provided by these institutions is a relatively new area of expansion.

The learning hierarchy provides a tool to classify and rank dissimilar types of learning. It is not, however, a division of different types of learning programs. This distinction is essential because, among other things, specific learning programs may span more than one level of the hierarchy. For example, there are programs in which both organized and unorganized learning activities are included. An illustration is so-called combined instruction that consists of combinations of lectures and group work mixed with periods in which part-time independent studies are pursued parallel to ordinary work.

Competence Utilization

The final link in the chain is the utilization of employee competences. This is the stage at which organizations may reap the fruits of their efforts to acquire and develop competence resources. A crucial question is how rich or poor the harvest really is. This is often very difficult to answer directly, because in many cases isolating and measuring the effects of programs as to their actual provision of new competences is virtually impossible.

An important dimension of competence utilization is the way in which competences are configurated or organized. Knowledge, skills, and aptitudes cannot be utilized isolated from the structures and processes within which they function. In other words, these structures and processes frame and govern competence utilization. This is a comprehensive area of study and fundamentally a question of the division of labor within the organization. All organization is basically a matter of finding the best possible utilization of human competence relative to one or more objectives. Among the broad range of organizational factors that impinge on this, we have chosen to take a closer look at the significance of transfer barriers, organizational form, specialization versus despecialization, involvement and participation, and incentive systems. More precisely, the intention is to discuss important determinants of the competence chain.

Transfer Barriers

As it is difficult to measure directly the effects of competence development on the organizational level, it is often far easier to approach the question indirectly by focusing on aspects of the organization which function as barriers to the transfer of knowledge and skills to the work situation and the organization. If one subsequently manages to reduce or remove some of these barriers, a more effective utilization of the competence is likely to follow. Studies of the conditions for implementation of competence acquired through training have identified a number of barriers to the utilization of competence in organizations. A Danish study defined barriers to implementation as factors which hindered the utilization of the results of training and which were related to the situation in which the utilization was meant to occur (Dylander and Olesen, 1976). The authors applied a systems-theory approach in which the companies were viewed as embracing a social, an administrative, and a technical system. Personnel training was categorized according to its orientation toward developing skills, knowledge, and attitudes. Those who responded to the survey identified 60 different barriers against transfer of competence to work. Most were listed under the administrative system and were related to formal rules, informal rules, and the presence of bureaucratic decision making routines. Sixty per cent of the barriers mentioned belonged to this category. The tendency was the same for all three types of training. Barriers were also identified in the social system, primarily in the form of a lack of acceptance from colleagues, superiors and subordinates, and a general resistance to change. Some people had tried to expand their job territory after having participated in a training course in order to better adjust their tasks to the training they had received. They frequently met with opposition. This illustrates the very important point that it is problematic to develop competence without simultaneously working systematically with job analysis and job development. Extensive improvement of human competence within an organization characterized by a relatively static division of labor may have very unfortunate consequences, such as decreasing job satisfaction resulting from overqualification relative to the job, increased turnover, and higher absenteeism.

Organizational Design

The organizational structure or design has considerable significance for the utilization of competence by partly determining or reflecting the internal division of labor.

One way in which the organizational design can create particularly evident consequences for the utilization of competence is when independent subunits are established. These units are often characterized by having a particular or unique competence relative to the rest of the organization and by being largely self-sufficient concerning human capital. Such establishment and allocation of autonomy may be seen as a way to cut back on internal coordination costs. However, a precondition for efficiency is, then, that integration and supervision may be achieved through indirect methods of control, such as development of an organizational culture with a minimum feeling of solidarity across unit borders and identification with the organization as a whole. If this fails, suboptimization may easily result.

The autonomy of research and development departments is an important element of many large firms' utilization of crucial competence. These companies often face a difficult choice between the demand for results which may be translated into products and services in the short run and the need for long-term investment aimed at producing significant innovations. As far as both of these demands are concerned, it is important that the staff be given the opportunity to participate in external professional networks in order to maintain and develop the employees' competence. This may, in turn, result in future contributions to the organization. Moreover, a certain degree of isolation relative to the rest of the organization is often necessary. Some companies have consciously set out to achieve a so-called greenhouse effect by isolating groups of R&D personnel so that they can work reasonably undisturbed and closely together. A parallel is found in attempts to cultivate "entrepreneurship" within relatively slow and inert organizations, i.e. intrapreneurship. This is a form of internal entrepreneurial activity which is frequently organized through the establishment of small, independent organizational units. Highly innovative competences often cannot be sufficiently utilized in a context characterized by dependence and bureaucratic decision-making processes. Creating loose couplings through the establishment of autonomous intrapreneurial units within an organization will therefore usually be required. If creative persons are put under tight control or are forced to supervise others, the innovativeness and technical enthusiasm may easily wither and their competence steadily depreciate.

Specialization versus Despecialization

While the period after the industrial revolution and until recently has generally been characterized by increasing specialization, we have during the last decade witnessed a strong tendency toward despecialization in an increasing number of areas. The "Cooperative Experiments" in Norwegian work life during the 1960s represent an early illustration of a desire to humanize work and thereby create increased productivity through despecialization (Thorsrud and Emery, 1970). These experiments included job rotation within self-governed groups in which the members themselves allocated given tasks within the group. Thus the employees developed multiskills; their training was no longer limited to the performance of only one single task or a very narrow set of work tasks.

In addition to providing many employees with a more interesting and varied career, job rotation is usually considered to improve the internal integration of the firm: "Although many companies have traditionally developed people up through one department, function, or operating unit, there is a new trend toward greater cross-functional movement. Experiences in different parts of an organization force the person to develop a wider range of skills, a wider network of relationships, and a more company-wide perspective" (Hall, 1984:166).

Earlier, we pointed to job rotation as a type of competence development which may create the kind of results mentioned above. At the same time, letting human competence flow between different parts of the organization is a way of utilizing it. New people with experience from other areas and with other ways of looking at things will often be a valuable supplement and perhaps necessary corrective to a department, staff, or work group. The result may be that the total competence is better utilized and that the overall organizational ability to master change is improved.

Involvement and Participation

Another aspect of the organization which may influence the utilization of competence is the degree of involvement and participation of employees in both work and decision-making processes: "According to research, when people participate in setting goals and get information about their performance two things happen. First, they set goals that are perceived by them to be achievable. Second, their sense of self-esteem and competence becomes tied to achieving the goals and therefore they are highly motivated to achieve them" (Lawler, 1986:30).

The logic behind measures aimed at employee participation is that people are assumed to be more motivated by participating in decision-making and problem solving, and that the collective nature of this kind of work may be conducive to creativity and more effective accomplishment of tasks within the firm.

There is little systematic documentation of the significance of labor unions for competence utilization within companies. We do know, however, that in the Scandinavian countries there is a strong tradition of cooperation between management and labor unions in a number of different areas aimed at increased productivity. This is reflected in Section 9 of the Basic Agreement between the Norwegian Federation of Trade Unions and the Norwegian Employers' Confederation which states the following: "Using their experience and insight, employees shall cooperate in increasing productivity, decreasing production costs, facilitating necessary reorganization, and forming a satisfactory place of work and a work organization which is both efficient and which meets the employees' needs for personal development".

Incentive Systems and Motivation

The utilization of competence depends on the employees' motivation to work, defined as a drive toward attaining the best possible job performance. In cognitive motivation theory, incentives or rewards are of central importance and are considered to be one of the main determinants of individual work motivation.

An important distinction has been drawn between intrinsic and extrinsic rewards or motivation (Porter and Lawler, 1968; Steers and Porter, 1979). The former have to do with the individual's own feeling of having succeeded or failed in something he/she wishes to do, i.e. a type of self-gratification. Improved mastery of work, increased personal competence, greater self-confidence, self-realization, and a feeling of solidarity with others are common intrinsic rewards. Extrinsic rewards are stimuli located outside the individual that are most often controlled by others and that include rewards such as wages, perquisites, promotion, status, and recognition for one's work from colleagues and managers.

It is reasonable to believe that employees' intrinsic rewards may be indirectly influenced by the firm. Job design, the learning environment, opportunities for participation in decision-making, and the social environment in the workplace may all influence intrinsic rewards. In this perspective, a considerable proportion of personnel-related work acts as an indirect part of the incentive system in a company. There are indications that intrinsic rewards emanating from professional and personal development are growing in importance compared with extrinsic rewards, particularly for highly educated personnel. The reason for this is probably partly that personal development is particularly highly valued by such professional groups and partly that the extrinsic rewards they usually achieve are at a comparatively high level to begin with. Moreover, many professionals have, for example, through their education already achieved a lasting extrinsic reward in the form of social status which people with less education do not enjoy. Research in the United States has shown that monetary rewards are rarely among the top three types of reward as ranked by MBAs, engineers, and computer specialists (Devanna, 1983; Roth and Devanna, 1983).

We are hence brought to believe that an increasing percentage of the highly educated in the workforce will encourage or press work organizations to put more emphasis on factors that indirectly affect intrinsic rewards. This is significant both in order to attract highly qualified people and, not least, to achieve a best possible utilization of the competence already present within the company.

Extrinsic rewards will, however, continue to have a decisive influence on the utilization of competence. If employees feel that they are not sufficiently valued in terms of salary and status, the incentive to utilize their knowledge and skills will diminish. This is the main reason why the standard literature in this field emphasizes the importance of designing a reward system which is considered to be fair by a majority of employees (Henderson, 1989).

One aspect of the incentive system which often seems to be overlooked is the extent to which managers are rewarded for stimulating their subordinates to develop and utilize their competence: "Many companies have found that it is fruitless to invest resources in redesigning jobs or in training supervisors to facilitate employee development if supervisors are not rewarded and supported for these activities" (Hall and Fukami, 1979:145).

In order to cope with this potential problem, some work organizations that place a high priority on human resource development have introduced systems in which all managers are periodically evaluated by their subordinates. These managers' careers depend on their results in contributing to the further development of their subordinates. As previously noted, one variant of this principle is when managers are promoted only when they have made sure that at least one of their subordinates has been made fully competent to take over their position once they are promoted.

In addition to including opportunities for development in and outside of work, aspects of the organizational culture may also be influenced. This particularly concerns those aspects of the culture which may affect factors related to the employees' intrinsic rewards. An example is when such values as creativity, courage, curiosity, and challenge are presented as ideals to strive for.

"Human resources development at Toyota has, of course, a motto: it is 'creativity', 'challenge', and 'courage', the three C's which express a sloughing off of personal readiness for self development" (Financial Times, 1986:11).

In organizations where experimentation and learning by trial and error are encouraged, a number of mottos expressing similar values have been put forward: "It is better to ask for forgiveness than to beg for permission", "Everyone can make a mistake, try again", "Don't ask in advance, go ahead". Mottos of this sort may serve to enhance the utilization of competence in that they legitimize attempts at innovation and reduce expected personal risks or costs of error through trial.

Concluding Comment

We have in this chapter presented and discussed the organizational competence chain which consists of planning, acquisition, development, and utilization of work-related competence. Moreover, each element in the chain was discussed separately.

To conceive of organizations' work with competence resources as a process involving different stages with dissimilar characteristics and demands, is regarded as analytically useful. First of all, it implies an integrative perspective on the available or potentially available competences in the firm. It may, furthermore, facilitate strategic competence management by enabling decisionmakers to assess the comparative importance in their firm of the different links in the competence chain. This especially applies to the relative usefulness of external acquisition versus internal development of competences. Trade-offs between these two stages or options are, of course, thoroughly considered by managers and personnel staff. However, viewing and analyzing these stages also in relation to planning and utilization of competence can add a more holistic dimension to the organization's general management.

PART II

Competences in Firms

Chapter 3

Individual Competences

Introduction

The purpose of this chapter is to discuss the concept of individual work-related competence, propose a typology of such competences, and outline implications for research and practice. A conceptual basis for future theory construction, empirical research, and practical analysis within the field of human capital in organizations will be delineated. The point of departure is a conception that work-related competences are fruitfully described in terms of their idiosyncrasy with regard to possible applications, and competence idiosyncrasy is defined in terms of combinations of task specificity, firm specificity, and industry specificity. On this basis, a typology of individual competences is constructed, exemplified, and discussed. Finally, implications for research and practice are suggested.

Individual Competences

The concept of employee competence has been assigned highly different meanings and is among the most diffuse in the organizational literature.

In a recent review, Collin (1989:20) states that, given the central role of competence in worklife, surprisingly little attention has so far been paid to its definition (cf. also Fagan, 1984). The term originates from the latin verb *competere* which means to be suitable. Whereas having been developed within psychology as a concept characterizing individuals' ability to respond to demands placed on them by their environment (White, 1959), it has in more recent, work-related versions been applied to describe an underlying characteristic of a person which results in efficient work-performance (Klemp, 1980; Boyatzis, 1982; Hornby and Thomas, 1989; Woodruffe, 1992; see also Davies, 1973; Fagan, 1984; McClelland, 1973; Pottinger and Goldsmith, 1979; Training Commission, 1988). It is, however, considered necessary to elaborate and apply a more precise definition which emphasizes the status of competences as *independent variables* in relation to job performance.

One attempt at defining the substance of work-related competence or "skills", which is often used as a synonymous term, has been made by Nelson and Winter (1982:73). They define skills as "capabilities for a smooth sequence of coordinated behavior that is ordinarily effective relative to its objectives, given the context in which it normally occurs". Skills are described as programmatic, involving a sequence of steps with each successive step triggered by and following closely on the completion of the preceding one. Furthermore, the authors note that the knowledge underlying a skillful performance is in large measure tacit knowledge. The performer is not fully aware of the details of the performance and finds it difficult or impossible to articulate a full account of those details. Thus, the authors distinguish between skills and knowledge and, moreover, view knowledge as a prerequisite for skills. Stinchcombe (1990), maintaining that the skills of the individual members of an organization form the foundation for organizational capabilities, compares such skills with computer programs, noting that parts of an individual's skills are routinized to an extent where higher faculties are not activated when these skills are used.

Work-related competences are in this book defined as the composite of human knowledge, skills, and aptitudes that may serve productive purposes in organizations. Usually, the concept of ability is included instead of the aptitude concept. This is, however, often used synonymously with the term skill, whereas applying the concept of aptitude places the focus on the significance of natural talents as a part of competences. While other definitions have included attitudes, motivation, and commitment, there is good reason to separate these from knowledge, skills, and aptitudes. This is not to say that such factors are unimportant, it is rather due to a conception that they constitute intermediary variables in relation to the causal connection between competence and work performance.

As pointed out, work-related competences are viewed as consisting of three elements which also need to be clarified. Knowledge is defined as specific information about a subject or a field. Skill is defined as a special ability to perform work-related tasks. Aptitudes encompass natural talents that can be applied in work and that form a basis for the development of knowledge and skills. Furthermore, knowledge is a necessary, although not sufficient, prerequisite for the possession of skills. On the other hand, knowledge about a subject may be possessed without the presence of any underlying skills connected to that subject. The conceptualization is delineated in Figure 3.1.

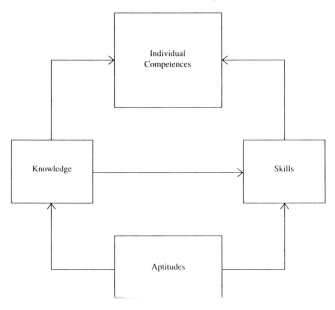

Figure 3.1. A Conceptual Model of Individual Competences.

According to the conceptual model, two classes of knowledge are included in competences. The first forms a basis for skills and is thus conveyed through these skills (cf. McKnight, 1991). The second class is not mediated through any specific skills, hence the direct line from knowledge to competence. For example, possessing knowledge about the conditions of the industry the firm operates within and the markets that are served, is often vital. Likewise, being knowledgeable about the internal organization and interpersonal networks in the company is paramount for the functioning of most employees. In order to accomplish a skill successfully, individuals must usually have some prior knowledge about how to perform this specific skill. The knowledge may be tacit or it may be articulable by the individual possessing it. In addition, many skills require some amount of aptitude, i.e. natural talent, that distinguishes the skilled from the unskilled. Two persons may be on an equal level with regard to their knowledge about how to perform a skill, yet their performances may differ substantially. This difference emanates from variations in aptitude. Let us give two examples of this. The first relates to the mastering of a foreign language. Two persons may have the same level of knowledge about its vocabulary, idioms, pronunciation, and grammatical structure. Still, one of them may be far better than the other in speaking it, because of good intonation and a lack of accent. The art of speaking without an accent colored by one's own native tongue would in Winter's (1987) terminology be "tacit knowledge". This has nothing to do with knowledge, but it has to do with aptitude or talent, e.g. in the form of a sort of "musicality" related to the spoken language. This does not imply that there is no tacit knowledge involved in mastering a foreign language. For example, the skills of persons who learn a language by speaking without writing and studying grammar, are predominantly based on tacit knowledge. Likewise, two individuals may possess equally substantial amounts of knowledge about the history and choreography of a specific dance. Yet, one of them may be an excellent dancer whilst the other is a highly mediocre dancer, and this variance can be attributed to variance with regard to the possession of rhythmical sense, i.e. the relevant natural talent.

A characteristic of aptitudes is that they cannot be developed at all or are at best very difficult to develop. This has important implications for firms. It implies that to the degree they need special types of aptitudes for the performance of skills related to specific tasks, they will often have to search for persons who already possess these talents or who may have a potential for developing them if that is considered a possibility. One cannot just arbitrarily select and then train someone for the task, as is often possible when certain knowledge is the primary prerequisite for successful performance of tasks.

Previous Classifications

The distinction between general and firm specific knowledge and skills is a cornerstone in human capital theory (Becker, 1983), that has later been extensively applied also in theories on internal labor markets and transaction cost theory. The concentration has primarily been on technology-related firm specificity, the logic being that the presence of unique technology in firms requires firm specific skills to be developed among employees (cf. Flynn, 1988, 1991). What has largely been overlooked in the literature employing the concept of firm specific competences, is the fact that such competences do not necessarily have to be linked to the execution of concrete work tasks associated with the technology unique to the firm. There also exists an important class of firm specific competences that are not connected to single tasks, but that are broadly applicable across a number of different tasks. Stated differently, all firm specific competences are not related to the technology of the firm. Some are related to organizational aspects, such as political processes, organizational culture, and interpersonal networks that are, by definition, always firm specific. There is hence a need to supplement the notion of technology-related firm specific competences with the concept of organization-related firm specific competences, i.e. firm specific competences which are *task nonspecific*. This will be done in the classification that follows.

   In addition to the distinction in human capital theory between general and firm specific skills and knowledge, a variety of different skill typologies has been presented, some founded on purely practical grounds and some on more systematic analytical foundations. Among the latter is Habermas' (cited in Bigelow, 1991:xi) distinction between three dissimilar knowledge domains: Technical knowledge which is derived from the empirical-analytic sciences, practical knowledge derived from historical-hermeneutic sciences, and emancipatory knowledge derived from sciences that are critically oriented. These broad categories are developed primarily for macro level analysis but also lend themselves to categorizations on the micro level. One example is provided by Bigelow (1991:xi): "In Habermas' framework, universities have tended to emphasize technical knowledge more and the other two less. This observation is quite consistent with critics, who generally concede that business graduates rate high in their technical abilities."

It is also consistent in that they generally rate these same graduates lower in their practical abilities."

Another general skills typology, considered relevant particularly for the study of organizational learning was proposed by Normann (1985:226), who distinguishes between the domain of interpersonal skills, the domain of analytical language skills (cognitive frame of reference), and the domain of ecological positioning.

One of the most detailed classifications is the recent "SCANS Report" published by the U.S. Department of Labor. The report distinguishes between a "three-part foundation" and five competencies that build on these parts. The three-part foundation encompasses the categories of basic skills, thinking skills, and personal qualities. Basic skills encompass reading, writing, arithmetic/mathematics, listening, and speaking. Thinking skills embrace creative thinking, decision making, problem solving, seeing things in the mind's eye, knowing how to learn, and reasoning. Personal qualities consist of responsibility, self-esteem, sociability, self-management, and integrity/honesty. The five competencies that build on the foundation include the following:

* Resources: Identifies, organizes, plans and allocates resources
* Interpersonal: Works with others.
* Information: Acquires and uses information.
* Systems: Understands complex interrelationships.
* Technology: Works with a variety of technologies.

A complete representation of the classification is shown in Appendix A.

It can be objected that this typology is confounded in that some of the categories describe competence requirements related to work tasks (for example acquires and uses information), whereas others describe competences (for example understands complex interrelationships). Rather than being an analytically consistent competence classification, it is basically a descriptive listing of skill requirements.

In the research on managerial work, a standard approach has been to break managerial jobs down into critical skills that have to be mastered if high performance is to be achieved (e.g., Katz, 1974; Mintzberg, 1980; Robbins, 1989). Furthermore, probably the most widespread typology includes three types of such skills or competences: Technical, interpersonal, and conceptual (Yukl, 1989:191). The first comprises knowledge about methods, processes, procedures, and techniques for conducting a specialized activity – and the ability to use tools and operative equipment related to that activity. Interpersonal skills embrace knowledge about human behavior and interpersonal processes, empathy and social sensitivity, ability to communicate, and cooperative capabilities. Finally, conceptual skills include analytical capacity, creativity, efficiency in problem solving, and ability to recognize opportunities and potential problems. In summary, this threefold typology distinguishes between individual skills in coping with things, people, and ideas and concepts (Yukl, 1989:192). An extended version of the typology, consisting of conceptual, technical, human, and political skills, was proposed by Pavett and Lau (1983). Whereas the two first categories are equivalent to the correspondingly labelled categories in the threefold classification referred to above, human skills relate to the ability to work with, understand, and motivate others – and political skills include the ability to build a power base and establish favorable network contacts.

Focusing on generic management competences, Thornton and Byham (1982), makes an effort to embrace all competences that are important to top managers. However, their comprehensive list of universal competences, counting thirty single items, is a mix of work tasks and personal skills and traits (the list is shown in Appendix C). This is also the case with the classification of "supra competencies" for middle managers provided by Dulewicz (1989)(shown in Appendix D.)

The competence or skill typologies presented in the literature on managerial work have been developed on largely tentative grounds. Furthermore, it is important to note that the typologies concentrate on and emphasize the significance of competences which are *firm nonspecific*. Thus, whereas parts of the human capital literature is characterized by a focus on competences linked to the execution of tasks as defined by the technology applied, in the literature on managerial work focus has been on firm nonspecific knowledge and skills that managers, regardless of the nature of the firm they manage, need or possess.

The core idea of this chapter is that the limitations of

competence classifications as presented in human capital theory and research on managerial work can be overcome by combining the analytical dimensions of work task specificity, firm specificity, and industry specificity, thus forming an analytically fruitful conceptual framework for the classification of employee competences. However, first it is necessary to lay out the conceptualization of work-related competences which constitutes the basis of the subsequent classification and discussion, and which will be applied throughout the remaining chapters of this book.

Competence Idiosyncracies

The concept of human resource idiosyncracy or specificity has been developed by economists focusing on the relationship between employees and employers. Originally elaborated as a part of human capital theory (Becker, 1983; Schultz, 1981), it has been further developed and applied within transaction cost theory (Williamson, 1983; 1985). The notion of firm specificity is a cornerstone in these theories. It is useful concerning the question of financing of human resource development in companies, and it is also an important element in the description of external and internal labor markets. However, the classical distinction between firm specific and general or firm nonspecific knowledge and skills is generally too unrefined to identify the complexity of competences in firms and it should consequently be supplemented. There is a need to add dimensions that make it feasible to obtain more subtle classifications. We shall in the following attempt to do this by discussing competence idiosyncracy that is not only related to the firm level but also to the micro level of tasks and the macro level of industries.

An important dimension of competences relates to whether they can be utilized to accomplish one task only, a few tasks, or a wide range of tasks in the firm. Task specificity is defined as the degree to which competence is related to the execution of a narrow range of work tasks. Low task specificity is characteristic of competence that is not particularly relevant to any one concrete task, but that may be highly relevant to a wide range of different tasks. Examples are analytical skills, competence in cooperating with others, problem-solving capacity, and the ability to delegate work. When task specificity is high, the competence is related to one single work task or very few tasks and is less relevant or irrelevant for the execution of other tasks. For example, the skill of typing on the basis of the "touch-method" can only be applied to the separable task of operating a standard keyboard. In contrast, cooperative competence may be utilized to accomplish or facilitate a wide spectrum of tasks. In the first case, the competence is highly task specific, and in the latter task specificity is low.

If a competence can be used in one firm only, it is firm specific and, by definition, has no value in external labor markets. All competences that are not firm specific, are general or nonspecific and can be sold in external labor markets. Firm specificity is thus fundamentally different from the dimension of task specificity in that it is defined relative to an element of the external environment of the firm. Moreover, it is generally assumed that high proportions of firm specific competences in the labor force of the firm leads to long-term contractual arrangements between employees and employers, since an enduring relationship is normally in the interest of both parties.

Finally, competences may be more or less industry specific, i.e. tied exclusively to one particular industry and not applicable in others.

Classification

In Figure 3.2, the dimensions of task specificity, firm specificity, and industry specificity have been combined to form a typology. The four cells represent different degrees of *competence idiosyncracy* and, thus, dissimilar types of competence. Besides presenting and discussing the competence types, we will give concrete examples of each of them and, moreover, provide illustrations from recent organization and social science literature.

		FIRM SPECIFICITY		
		LOW		HIGH
		INDUSTRY SPECIFICITY		
		LOW		HIGH
		I	II	III
	LOW	Meta-Competences	Industry Competences	Intraorganizational Competences
TASK SPECIFICITY				
		IV	V	VI
	HIGH	Standard Technical Competences	Technical Trade Competences	Unique Competences

Figure 3.2. A Competence Typology.

Meta-Competences

The first competence type is firm nonspecific, industry nonspecific and can furthermore be utilized in the accomplishment of a variety of different tasks. This type can be called meta-competences, and examples are the following:

* Literacy
* Learning capacity
* Analytical capabilities
* Creativity
* Knowledge of foreign languages and cultures
* Ability to perceive and process environmental signals and events
* Capacity to tolerate and master uncertainty
* Ability to communicate
* Ability to cooperate with others
* Negotiation skills
* Ability to adjust to change.

The importance of certain meta-competences for managerial work has been heavily stressed in the management and leadership literature (see Collin, 1989; Morgan, 1988; Training Commission, 1988;). The focus has predominantly been set on interpersonal and conceptual skills, i.e. competences related to managing people and symbols, as well as analytical problems (Katz, 1955; Mann, 1965; Yukl, 1989). However, the threefold typology comprising these skills plus technical skills has been based on an implicit understanding of the significance of only the task specificity of competences. The dimension of firm specificity has not been included, thus limiting the analytical potency of the classification. Emphasis has largely been on the transferability of competences across managerial work situations and not on their transferability across firms or industries.

As noted by Rasmussen (1991:179), communication skills have been repeatedly emphasized as important elements of management practice and skill-training programs (see also Bond, Hildebrandt, and Miller, 1984; Golen et al., 1989). He goes on to point out that a variety of communication skill clusters have been developed that are based on organization research analyzing the skills managers use to conduct their work (e.g., Ghiselli, 1963; Livingston, 1971; Mintzberg, 1975; Flanders, 1981; Boyatzis, 1982). With reference to Cameron and Whetten (1983), it is furthermore noted that "skills related to listening have been repeatedly identified as essential in their own right or as key components of broader skill clusters, such as interviewing, counseling, performance appraisal, and assertiveness" (Rasmussen, 1991: 179).

Another important subcategory of meta-competences that is increasingly emphasized in the literature on organizational behavior is cooperative competence. As pointed out by Katz (1974:33), cooperative competence (skill in working with others) ".. must become a natural, continuous activity, since it involves sensitivity not only at times of decision making, but also in the day-to-day behavior of the individual. Human skills cannot be a 'sometime thing'. Techniques cannot be randomly applied, like an overcoat. Because everything which an executive says and does (or leaves unsaid or undone) has an effect on his associates, his true self will, in turn, show through. Thus, to be effective, the skill must be naturally developed, and unconsciously as well as consistently demonstrated in the individual's every action. It must become an integral part of his whole being". This illustrates an important aspect of many types, although not every type, of meta-competences: they are closely related to fundamental personality traits and may hence, if totally absent, be very difficult or impossible to develop.

In a discussion of career development in organizations, Hall (1986:348) notes that employees need career competences, not just job skills. Furthermore, he calls these career competences "meta-skills" because they are skills in acquiring other skills. As examples, he mentions adaptability (routine busting) and tolerance of ambiguity and uncertainty. Thus, his conceptualization deviates from the one presented in this article, in the sense that his meta-skills constitutes one of several subcategories of meta-competence as we have defined it.

Hornbeck (1991) observes that few manual laborers will be required in the future and that there will be greater need for people who can think, who can formulate a moderately complex thought and express it coherently both verbally and in writing, for people who can solve problems and relate well to a team of others: "Moreover, given the expectation that workers will increasingly change not only jobs, but occupations as well, it will be necessary for the new worker to learn to learn for a lifetime" (Hornbeck, 1991:360). Similarly, Pines and Carnevale focus on the issue of basic workplace skills and note that whereas reading, writing, and math deficiencies in the work-force were the first to surface, increasingly, attention has been directed toward skills such as problem solving, listening, negotiating, and knowing how to learn (Pines and Carnevale, 1991: 243).

A final illustration of meta-competences relates to the work of internal and external human resource consultants. In a competence study conducted by the American Society of Training and Development, such consultants concluded that human resource responsibilities require, among other things, ability in oral communication, presentation, and giving feedback, ability in model building and preparing written materials, as well as ability in performance observations and questioning (Harris, 1985:114).

It should be emphasized that meta-competences, albeit involving low task specificity, are not irrelevant for the accomplishment of concrete tasks. Their importance lies in the fact that they represent a sort of genuinely basic or underlying infrastructural knowledge and skills that are broadly applicable and form a crucial foundation for work performance in general. The facts that they cross-cut different tasks and constitute a potential for the mastering of emerging and future tasks, make them especially critical for organizational performance and change.

Due to their broadly applicable nature, meta-competences are thus especially important in regard to the adaptability of firms. Because they are not specific to any particular context, they constitute a potential for facilitating organizational and strategic change (e.g. learning ability, mastering of uncertainty, ability to tolerate change). Moreover, they are, in general, just as easily applicable after a change as before (for example analytical skills, cooperative abilities, communication skills). Consequently, they are crucial not exclusively for managers but also for subordinate employees at all levels in firms that have to accomplish organizational change. Carnevale (1991:154/157) illustrates this by the trend toward replacing machinists with technicians, and notes the following: "In order to manage the greater scope of action on the job, the technician needs a broader set of skills than the machinist. To operate beyond his or her work station, for example, the technician needs a new set of interpersonal and organizational skills. To cope with change and variety, he or she needs learning and problem-solving skills". Furthermore, he adds that flexibility in varied and changing environments of the "new economy" requires a solid foundation in reading, writing, and computational skills, as well as the capacity to learn, solve problems, and be creative.

Traditionally, the formal educational system has been viewed as the main transmitter of firm nonspecific competences. However, it is important to point out that this to a much lower degree applies to meta-competences. Creativity, analytical capability, and social abilities, for example, are likely to emanate, to at least, an equal degree, from other sources, such as heredity, primary and secondary socialization processes, work experience, and various leisure activities. As noted by Morrison and Hock (1986:242): "Training and education can provide the knowledge necessary for many specific formal job tasks and the elementary level of skills required for many motor and simple cognitive tasks. The knowledge, skills, and behaviors required for informal and interpersonal roles and complex managerial functions, such as those of "power broker" or "priority setter" cannot be learned via formal training programs. Although these latter knowledges, skills, and behaviors are not even reflected in job descriptions, they are essential to effective performance and reflect the need for a great deal of learning – learning that occurs as a result of job experience."

Moreover, many forms of developmental activities contribute to creating meta-competences. One illustration is management development programs, which are often explicitly aimed at generating communication skills, ability to manage conflicts, capacity to handle uncertainty and stress, and creativity in decision-making. Other examples are in-house literacy programs for employees and language courses for immigrants, such as "English as a Second Language" programs. Knowledge of and proficiency in using the native tongue is crucial for the possibility to cope across virtually every organization and work task in any national setting.

Industry Competences

The second competence category is characterized by low task specificity, low firm specificity, and high industry specificity. It thus embraces what may loosely be called familiarity with the industry, and will be refered to as industry competence. This type of competence is thus not completely general in human capital theory terms, since it cannot be applied across industries. However, it is not tied to any one firm within the industry. The following are illustrations of industry competences:

* Familiarity with the history of the business
* Knowledge about the industry structure
* Knowledge about the current development of the industry
* Ability to analyze the operations and strategies of competitors
* Knowledge about key persons, networks, and alliances in the industry
* Capability to form cooperative ventures and alliances with other companies in the industry

An illustration of industry competence is provided by Porter (1980:

4) who notes that the goal of competitive strategy for a business unit in an industry is to find a position in the industry where the company can best defend itself against competitive forces or can influence them in its favor. As the strength of the forces may be obvious to all competitors, the key for developing strategy is to delve below the surface and analyze the sources of each: "Knowledge of these underlying sources of competitive pressure highlights the critical strengths and weaknesses of the company, animates its positioning in its industry, clarifies the areas where strategic changes may yield the greatest payoff, and highlights the areas in which industry trends promise to hold the greatest significance as either opportunities or threats".

The long-lasting debate on whether or not managers need to possess thorough industry specific knowledge and skills in addition to managerial meta-competences is highly relevant in this context. For example, Katz (1955) contended that top-level managers with ample human relations and conceptual skills could be shifted from one industry to another with great ease and no loss of effectiveness. Other researchers have maintained that the transferability of skills for top executives is very limited due to industry specific and firm specific conditions, such as ownership structures, traditions, technology, and organizational culture (Dale, 1960; Kotter, 1982). Yukl points out that different industries have unique economic, market, and technological characteristics, and that familiarity with technical matters, products, personalities, and tradition is a type of knowledge that is acquired only through long experience in the organization. Whereas the general component of conceptual and technical skills can be transferred to a different situation, unique knowledge components of these skills have to be relearned. He also stresses that a period of several years may be needed by an outside successor to develop a network of contacts and reciprocal trading relationships, while an internal successor already has part of the necessary network in place (Yukl, 1989:194; cf. also Kotter, 1982). This view is supported by Whitley (1989:213), who notes that: "...the search for general properties of all managerial work has tended to play down the organizational and industrial specificity of managerial tasks. This specificity means that managerial problems are not easily abstracted from their contexts for solution with general models and procedures. It also suggests that the generalizability of successful practices in one situation to other contexts – across space, time, and cultures – is limited. To illuminate the difference between meta-competences and industry competences one may say that acquiring knowledge of the generic, basic principles put forward in the strategic management literature, including Porter's book on competitive advantage, represents an example of the former, whereas the ability to analyze the specific competitive conditions in the industry the firm operates within is an example of the latter. It is hence also indicated that the industry competences are carried chiefly by personnel in higher-level managerial jobs. However, it may be favorable for the firm if also employees on lower echelons in the organization possess basic knowledge about the industry, the firm's competitors, and their strategies. This is probably especially so in the service industries, where front-line employees encounter dissimilar situations depending on the customer they interact with and often have to make decisions on the spot without having work manuals and the like to consult beforehand. Then, knowing the idiosyncracies of the firm's as well as the competitors' repertoires of customer services may be valuable in guiding work behavior.

Familiarity with the industry is developed mainly through experience gained while working within it and by joining industry associations' meetings and seminars. In addition, such competence can be transferred through external consultants and analysts specializing in this specific industry and its development trends. Moreover, informal contact with colleagues in other firms in the industry may be a valuable source of this type of competence.

Intraorganizational Competences

Type III in the classification depicts competences that exhibit low task specificity and high firm specificity. Since they thus constitute a kind of "internal meta-competence" in an organization, the label intraorganizational competences has been assigned.

The following are examples of intraorganizational competences:

* Knowledge about colleagues
* Knowledge about elements in the organizational culture, such as symbols, subcultures, history, norms, and ethical standards
* Overviews of communication channels, informal networks

and alliances within the firm
* Mastery of organizational dialect or code
* Familiarity with political dynamics in the organization
* Knowledge about the firm's strategy and goals

Yet another illustration is familiarity with different subunits and their working conditions, which is clearly reflected in the aims of trainee programs and job rotation across subunits: "The HRM program (in Philips) is thus designed to develop managers with a broad overview of the company so that they can adapt their generalized knowledge to fluid situations. Cumulative knowledge of all aspects of a product division, from development to marketing, can be acquired through assignments to different areas of activity and levels of responsibility" (van Houten, 1990: 108). The breeding of managerial generalists possessing a substantial amount of intraorganizational competences is particularly well known from many Japanese companies having extensive rotation arrangements.

As for meta-competences, the importance of intraorganizational competences has been discussed in the management and leadership literature but also within politically oriented organization theory concerned with power relations (e.g., Kotter, 1978; Pfeffer, 1981). There, focus has been on skills in internal networking, knowledge of and capacity to manage firm specific symbols, and knowledge of the culture of different parts of the organization, epitomized by metaphors such as "the manager as a political detective" (Yates, 1985:ch.3).

Intraorganizational competences are inextricably linked to the organizational culture of the firm and vice-versa. Although it is common to think of corporate culture as a structural phenomenon, it is partly made up of the organizational interpretations held that are shared by the employees. However, it clearly transcends the level of individuals, which is demonstrated by the fact that knowledge and interpretation systems continue to exist even when key employees are replaced (Weick and Gilfillan, 1971; Walsh and Ungson, 1991:61).

The culturally related intraorganizational competences are also illustrated by Sackmann in her discussion of cultural knowledge in organizations: "... cultural cognitions and knowledge also become *habits* – habits of thoughts that translate into habitual actions. Once they exist the carriers of cultural knowledge apply them without prior reflection when faced with a specific situation. The various aspects of cultural knowledge about past successes and failures are communicated to and *learned* by new members, who may also import cultural variety into the organization. This acquired knowledge becomes generalized in successive communication and reinforcement processes. Eventually its carriers perceive the knowledge as having a higher degree of factuality than originally existed" (Sackmann, 1991:41-42).

In a recent study, Carnevale points out that certain meta-competences may be useless if they are not combined with relevant intraorganizational competences. He particularly refers to the need to blend general leadership skills with knowledge about specific organizational conditions, especially understanding of implicit and explicit power structures: "To be effective inside the organization, the employee needs to understand both. Without this understanding, leadership skills are misplaced; they can even be counterproductive if they become barriers to strategic organizational goals or positive change processes" (Carnevale, 1991:159).

Intraorganizational competences are acquired and developed mostly by everyday learning in the workplace through interaction with and observation of individual colleagues and groups of colleagues. However, when firms take active steps to shape the formation of intraorganizational knowledge and skills by implementing job rotation, trainee programs, mentoring programs, on-the-job coaching, internal executive development programs, and campaigns aimed at disseminating core values and information about organizational goals and strategy, this is often intended to enhance the amount of intraorganizational competence in the labor force. For example, mentoring has been described in the following manner: "Mentors provide advice on how to succeed in the organization. It takes more than knowledge and ability to make it in many organizations; office politics and cultural norms can have an important impact on the graduate's future, and a mentor can give frank and candid advice on these sensitive issues" (Phillips, 1987:174; see also Berlew and Hall, 1980; Kram, 1986).

Probably the most characteristic example of formal training that is geared toward generation of intraorganizational competence, can be found in introductory courses and programs for recently recruited employees. Through these courses, newcomers are frequently expected to become familiar with and start internalizing organizational norms and values and to obtain knowledge about symbols and artifacts in the particular firm.

Standard Technical Competences

High task specificity, low firm specificity, and low industry specificity is characteristic of the fourth type of competences, which can be adequately characterized as standard technical competences. They largely correspond to the notion in leadership literature of technical skills, defined as knowledge about methods, processes, procedures, and techniques for conducting a specialized activity, and the ability to use tools and operate equipment related to that activity (Yukl, 1989:193; see also Katz, 1955; Mann, 1965). However, in an effort to add subtlety to the study of competences, our classification moves further than this by subdividing technical skills into the three distinct categories of standard technical competences, technical trade skills, and unique competences.

Standard technical competences embrace a wide range of generally technical, in the sense of operatively oriented, competences. Examples include the following:

* Typing and stenography skills
* Knowledge of generic budgeting and accounting principles and methods
* Skills in computer programming
* Knowledge of standard computer software
* Craft skills and technical professional skills that can be applied across industries

Important generators of standard technical competences are the ordinary educational system, vocational education and training for adults, parts of in-house personnel training programs, and apprenticeship arrangements. In addition, training that transmits standard technical competences is frequently offered by suppliers of technology as, for example, in the computer business.

Technical Trade Competences

Type V competences are task specific, industry specific, and firm nonspecific. Consequently, they are portable across firms within the industry and can only be used in accomplishing one or a few limited work tasks. This type is illustrated by the following examples:

* Skills in building automotive vehicles
* Skills in building aircraft
* Skills in assembling computer hardware
* Skills in hair-cutting
* Bartending skills

Technical trade competences can be developed through vocational education that is limited to one industry only. Examples are educational programs in banking, training for some crafts (such as hair-dressing and baking), and not the least experience gained through concrete, practical work within the industry. For instance, in Norway, which is a major shipping nation with rich traditions in this industry, there has never been any specialized training or educational program leading to related academic degrees. Recruits into this industry, regardless of their former background, have had to "learn the trade from the bottom". Traditionally, this has also been the case among journalists, especially in the newspaper industry, although some of the skills acquired there are transferable to work in other industries (for example public relations tasks).

Unique Competences

Type VI competences are highly firm specific and task specific, and can be labelled unique competences. They apply to one task or very few tasks within one firm only and include knowledge and skills related to operation of unique technology and routines. Examples are:

* Skills related to the use of specialized tools crafted in the firm
* Knowledge about rationalization devices that have been

developed exclusively within the company
* Skills in repairing tailored technology
* Skills in operating specialized, local filing or data systems
* Skills related to the administration and maintenance of organizationally idiosyncratic routines or procedures.

It is reasonable to assume that the main significance of type VI competences lies more in their contributions to generating congruence between personnel and tasks than in their contribution to facilitating change within the organization. For example, when unique technology is substituted with standard technology, there is no longer a need for the specific competence related to the operation of the unique technology.

Unique competences are, by definition, generated within the one firm only and can be developed through informal learning, in-house training, apprenticeship arrangements, trainee programs, and mentoring processes.

Implications

The proposed typology lends itself to a broad range of possible theoretical and empirical applications in research on competences in organizations, and we shall now suggest some implications for research.

One way to apply the typology is to use it as a basis for analyses of the relationship between market-based and organizational solutions with regard to human resource development activities. It is reasonable to assert that firms, when choosing whether to pursue such activities themselves or to pay others to do it for them, will often put considerable weight on the *types* of competence they want as an output. This explanation offers a theoretical alternative to institutional economists' treatment of "make, buy, or contract" decisions, where choices between organizational and market-based arrangements are assumed to be determined by comparisons of transaction costs related to the different solutions. On this background, an interesting descriptive empirical project would be to investigate which criteria decision-makers actually apply when choosing between make- and buy-options in relation to competence development.

The competence typology may also be utilized in empirical studies of the relationship between firms' competence bases or inventories and their capacity to manage necessary organizational transformation processes induced by changes in the external environment. A reasonable proposition is that meta-competences are particularly important in such processes, because they represent a form of "individual infrastructure" that is probably crucial to employees' overall capacity to cope with change. If this proposition gains support in future empirical research, an interesting *training paradox* would be present: The general impression is that most of the current personnel training financed by employers is directed toward generation of standard technical competences – and, to the degree that they are needed, unique competences. If this is correct, a major proportion of employer-financed training is directed at the creation of *static fit* between employees and current work tasks – and is not aimed at developing individual and organizational *flexibility* through generation of meta-competences and intra-organizational competences. Even though this has not been empirically documented, inspection of the prescriptive professional human resource management and human resource development literature reveals a conviction that creation of congruence or static fit between employees and tasks should be the goal of most types of training (e.g., Goldstein, 1986; Laird, 1986). To the extent that firms actually follow the advice given in this literature, one should thus expect to find that the need for static fit is regarded as more important to cover than is the need for flexibility and adaptability.

The classification of competences has a clear potential in relation to studies of individual career mobility within and across firms. In general, the six competence types outlined may play unequally important roles in different phases of employees' career development and also with regard to the type of career in question. At the early stages, standard technical competences (for example in the form of general professional knowledge), technical trade skills, and some meta-competences (for example ability to communicate and cooperate) are probably the most important ones for a majority of employees. However, as they gain experience in the firm and move up the career ladder, the significance of possessing intraorganizational competences and industry competences is likely to increase strongly along with the importance of meta-competences. At the same time, employees who prefer a professional over a managerial career will have to continue nurturing their standard technical and industry competences and frequently also unique competences in the form of, for example, R&D-related knowledge and skills in using unique and developing technology in the firm. Thus, in general, there is a need to address the issue of changes in competence type requirements and individual competence sets during the career life cycle over time as well as the issue of how the six forms of work-related competences develop over time (cf. Hall, 1986:346).

A paramount challenge in future empirical investigations based on the proposed typology is to produce valid operationalizations of the concepts of firm specificity and task specificity. Delineating a detailed operationalization is beyond the scope of this discussion, but we may provide a brief outline of how this could be achieved. When operationalizing firm specificity, a central criterion will be the degree to which the competence is actually applied or can be applied in other firms. Examples of such measures can be found in studies by Pfeffer and Cohen (1984) and Kalleberg and Reve (1993). The same basic logic can be applied to the concept of industry specificity. Operationalization of task specificity will have to be based on information about the number of distinct work tasks that different competences can be used to perform, that is, their actual range of applicability.

Concluding Comment

Competences were defined as composites of knowledge, skills, and aptitudes that are applicable in work. On the basis of combinations of task specificity, firm specificity, and industry specificity, a classification comprising meta-competences, industry competences, intraorganizational competences, standard technical competences, technical trade competences and unique competences was developed. Both in research and practice, there has so far been a strong focus on generating task specific competences in order to create maximum fit between competences and work tasks. However, when taking into account the externally induced increased demands for flexibility and readiness to alter organizations, additional attention needs to be devoted to task nonspecific competences and their significance for efficiency and competitiveness. This is paramount if the focus is to be shifted from needs for static fit in organizations to needs for dynamic adjustment to continuously changing external conditions.

**

APPENDIX A.

* Resources: Identifies, organizes, plans and allocates resources

A. Allocates time: Selects relevant, goal-related activities, ranks them in order of importance, allocates time to activities, and understands, prepares, and follows schedules.

B. Allocates money: Uses or prepares budgets, including making cost and revenue forecasts, keeps records to track budget performance, and makes appropriate adjustments.

C. Allocates material and facility resources: Acquires, stores, and distributes materials, supplies, parts, equipment, space, or final products in order to make the best use of them.

D. Allocates human resources: Assesses knowledge and skills and distributes work accordingly, evaluates performance, and provides feedback.

* Interpersonal: Works with others.

A. Participates as a member of a team: Works cooperatively with others and contributes to group with ideas, suggestions, and effort.

B. Teaches others new skills: Helps others learn.

C. Serves clients/customers: Works and communicates with clients and customers to satisfy their expectations.

D. Exercises leadership: Communicates thoughts, feelings, and ideas to justify a position, persuades, convinces or otherwise motivates an individual or groups, including responsibly challenging existing procedures, policies, or authority.

E. Negotiates: Works toward an agreement that may involve exchanging specific resources or revolving divergent interests.

F. Works with cultural diversity: Works well with men and women and with a variety of ethnic, social, or educational backgrounds.

* Information: Acquires and uses information.

A. Acquires and evaluates information: Identifies need for data, obtains it from existing sources or creates it, and evaluates its relevance and accuracy.

B. Organizes and maintains information: Organizes, processes, and maintains written or computerized records and other forms of information in a systematic fashion.

C. Interprets and communicates information: Selects and analyzes information and communicates the results to others using oral, written, graphic, pictorial, or multi-media methods.

D. Uses computers to process information: Employs computers to acquire, organize, analyze, and communicate information.

* Systems: Understands complex interrelationships.

A. Understands systems: Knows how social, organizational, and technological systems work and operates effectively with them.

B. Monitors and corrects performance: Distinguishes trends, predicts impacts on system operations, diagnoses deviations in the function of system/organization, and takes necessary action to correct performance.

C. Improves and designs systems: Makes suggestions to modify existing systems to improve product or service, and develops new or alternative systems.

* Technology: Works with a variety of technologies.

A. Selects technology: Judges which set of procedures, tools or machines, including computers and their programs, will produce the desired results.

B. Applies technology to task: Understands overall intent and proper procedures for setting up and operating machines, including computers and their programming systems.

C. Maintains and troubleshoots technology: Prevents, identifies, or solves problems in machines, computers and other technologies.

Source: SCANS (1991). *What Work Requires of Schools. A SCANS Report for America 2000.* Washington, D.C.: U.S. Department of Labor, Secretary's Commission on Achieving Necessary Skills.

APPENDIX B.

"The most widely adopted approach for classifying managerial skills is in terms of a three-skill taxonomy. Similar versions of this taxonomy were proposed by Katz (1955) and Mann (1965). The skill categories were defined as follows:

1. Technical Skills

Knowledge about methods, processes, procedures, and techniques for conducting a specialized activity, and the ability to use tools and operate equipment related to that activity.

2. Interpersonal Skills

Knowledge about human behavior and interpersonal processes, ability to understand the feelings, attitudes, and motives of others from what they say and do (empathy, social sensitivity), ability to communicate   clearly   and   effectively   (speech   fluency, persuasiveness), and ability to establish effective and cooperative relationships (tact, diplomacy, knowledge about acceptable behavior).

3. Conceptual Skills

General analytical capability, logical thinking, proficiency in concept formation and conceptualization of complex and ambiguous relationships, creativity in idea generation and problem solving, ability to analyze events and perceive trends, anticipate changes, and recognize opportunities and potential problems (inductive and deductive reasoning).

It is evident that technical skills are primarily concerned with things, interpersonal skills are primarily concerned with people, and conceptual skills are primarily concerned with ideas and concepts."

(Source: Yukl, 1989:191-192).

APPENDIX C.

Generic competences for top managers (Thornton and Byham, 1982):

* Oral presentation
* Oral communication
* Written communication
* Organizational sensitivity
* Organizational awareness
* Extra-organizational sensitivity
* Extra-organizational awareness
* Planning and organizing
* Delegation
* Management control
* Development of subordinates
* Sensitivity
* Individual leadership
* Group leadership
* Tenacity

* Negotiation
* Analysis
* Judgement
* Creativity
* Risk taking
* Decisiveness
* Technical and professional knowledge
* Energy
* Range of interests
* Initiative
* Tolerance of stress
* Adaptability
* Independence
* Motivation

APPENDIX D.

Supra competences for middle managers (Dulewicz, 1989):

Intellectual

* Strategic perspective
* Analysis and judgement
* Planning and organizing

Interpersonal

* Managing staff
* Persuasiveness
* Assertiveness and decisiveness
* Interpersonal sensitivity
* Oral communication

Adaptability

* Adaptability and resilience

Results orientation

* Energy and initiative
* Achievement motivation
* Business sense

Chapter 4

Competence Bases

Introduction

In this chapter, fundamental properties of competence bases in firms are identified and discussed. The base concept is viewed as consisting of the aggregate of individual competences plus synergies in the form of team competences. An assumption is that organizational performance is determined by how firms solve the two fundamental problems of managing their relationship to the external environment and creating an efficient internal organization. The relationship between competence bases and performance in firms can hence be indirectly approached by looking at how properties of competence bases may influence the solving of these two problems. Drawing on insights from human capital theory and organization theory, it is argued that competence bases can be fruitfully described and classified in terms of their match specificity, industry specificity, task specificity, unit specificity, relation specificity, durability, transferability, transformability, heterogeneity, advancedness, diversity, internal exclusiveness, strategic relevance, extensibility, and distinctiveness. Finally, interrelations between competence base properties and implications for research are discussed.

Background

The study of competences and aggregates of competences in organizations is in an early stage, and the existing literature is both scant and fragmented. There is hence an apparent need to develop basic concepts and theory on the nature of competences and their significance for the functioning of organizations. The point of departure is a belief that the significance of knowledge and skills in firms in respect to creating competitive advantages is soaring and that, accordingly, conceptual development is strongly needed to form stepping stones for theoretical and empirical research in this increasingly important field.

The relationship between human resources and organizational performance has not been much studied in depth, although concepts such as key competences, distinctive competences, strategic skills, and core competences have been introduced to indicate that human resources play a crucial role for such performance (Selznick, 1957; Winter, 1985; Naugle and Davies; 1987; Prahalad and Hamel, 1990). However, the ways in which competences influence organizational behavior and performance have not been systematically investigated. Moreover, the relatively modest amount of research conducted in this area has, to a considerable degree, concentrated on the macro level of firms, by focusing on key or core organizational competences. The core competences of a firm have largely been taken as a given, and few attempts have been made to link employee competences and organizational competence. However, although other resources contribute to creating organizational competence, employees and work teams (including management teams) are the basic carriers of the competence of the firm. Given that organizational competence is in large part made up of employee and team competences, there is a clear need to look at the relationship between the micro level and the macro level. This research problem can be fruitfully approached by elaborating upon the concept of the competence base of the firm.

Resources or Assets?

Competences has by several authors been characterized as a special sort of asset in firms. Itami (1987) includes it in his concept of invisible assets, Winter (1985) characterizes competence as a strategic asset, and Beer and associates (1981) speak about human resources as company assets. These examples reflect the very wide use of the asset concept. Winter quotes two different definitions to the concept: "a useful thing or quality" and "a single item of property". The latter term is clearly in accordance with the way assets are being defined within the field of accounting, whereas the former is not. This may, however, be regarded as a strictly formal and thereby irrelevant argument. Nevertheless, if one defines assets as "useful things or qualities", the concept of resources may just as well be applied to avoid unnecessary terminological confusion. Winter (1985:160) argues that the applicability of the definition of assets as single items of property is uncertain. The reason is that the word item is suggestive of a discreteness that is frequently not characteristic of the skills of individuals and organizations. In my view, the asset concept is not as appropriate to apply to competences, due to the simple fact that competences in firms are contracted or rented and not owned by the employer as would have been the case in a slave economy. Furthermore, the central question in a strategic management context is not whether the firm *owns* the resources it utilizes or not. The crucial question relates to the firm's ability to efficiently *mobilize resources* that can be used to promote its goals, regardless of the legal status of these resources. An essential point in transaction cost theory is that firms may choose whether to make, buy, or contract the resources they need for operation (Williamson, 1983, 1985). The resulting diversity among firms concerning the ways they choose to acquire their resources, implies that the concept of assets is not able to carry us very far analytically, because it automatically excludes resources that are acquired by contractual arrangements.

The Competence Base

In the administrative sciences, the individual employees or members have traditionally been conceived of as the basic building blocks in firms and other organizations. Since each individual is an acting entity, this makes sense in many contexts. However, in the same way as organizations, individuals may also be seen as complex entities that are comprised of a number of different elements. Employee competence, consisting of individual knowledge, skills, and aptitudes, is one such element. Furthermore, from an organizational point of view, individual competence is a more basic unit of analysis than are employees. One may say that an organization has a given stock of employees. However, it is not the stock of human bodies that is interesting but the stock of *properties* embodied in these employees.

Each employee possesses a set of different competences which are relevant to work performance. These sets are unique in the sense that no pairs of sets are entirely equal. On this basis, we may interpret companies' human resources as inventories of competence sets and still be on the individual level of analysis. However, an alternative is to use single competences as the basic unit of analysis and thus operate on the *subindividual* level. Then the human resources in a firm may be described as its *competence base* or *portfolio of competences*. The single competences can theoretically be combined in a large number of ways in order to solve tasks. An important point is that by focusing on competences rather than on individuals, a greater flexibility and creativity in the use of human resources may be obtained. This is, for example, illustrated by project organizations in which the working time of employees is divided between different projects on the basis of needs to tap their dissimilar competences.

Figure 4.1 illustrates the concept of competence base by presenting a fictitious "employee-competence matrix" (E/C-matrix) for a firm. For the sake of simplicity, only the presence or absence of different competences for each employee has been indicated in binary terms.

In addition to the aggregate of individual competences as depicted in stylized form in Figure 4.1, the competence base contains synergies produced by the interactions and cooperation between employees. An especially important class of such synergies is team competences, i.e. the knowledge and skills residing in teams that cannot be attributed to any individual member or the mere sum of members. As the amount of teamwork seems to soar in most organizations, this is an increasingly important part of the total competence of firms.

All organizations control a certain base of sets of single competences that can be combined in a large number of different ways. Among all the internal factors in firms, this base and its configuration can be regarded as being the most critical for the possibilities of future success. Other factors, such as financial resources, organization design, technological level, and work systems, are also important but they all depend ultimately upon and are generated through the application of human competence within those fields. Thus, competence bases are *the* primary resource of

any firm. Without relevant competences, successful action is
feasible by chance only, no matter what other resources the
company controls or has access to.

E/C	C_1	C_2	C_3	C_4	C_m
E_1	0	1	0	1	1
E_2	1	0	1	1	0
E_3	1	1	0	1	0
E_4	0	0	1	1	1
.					
.					
.					
E_n	1	1	0	0	1

Figure 4.1. A Constructed E/C-Matrix for a Firm.

In addition to the internally available competences, the *potential*
competence base of an organization encompasses competences that
can be accessed and mobilized from external sources, such as
consultants, temporary hires, and cooperation or strategic alliances
with other firms. The total competence base of the firm can further
be decomposed into two analytically separable parts – manifest and
latent competences. The former comprises employees' knowledge,
skills, and aptitudes that are known by personnel responsible for
the planning, acquisition, and development of human resources in
the firm (line managers and human resource management staff),
whereas the latent competences are unknown to them. Hence, in

any work organization the planning of competence acquisition and development will be carried out on the basis of limited or biased information. Phrased in the terminology of organization theory, decisions will have to be made under conditions of bounded rationality (Simon, 1957). Furthermore, the discrepancy between the total competence base and the manifest part of the base can be said to represent a cognitive competence gap. The firm has a larger human resource potential than realized, and this cognitively missing part of the total competence base constitutes a hidden reservoir that it could be worthwhile to try to uncover. Stated in economic terms, one monetary unit spent on such exploration may yield a higher return than the same monetary unit spent on recruiting or hiring competence from outside the firm.

It is reasonable to assume that some of the work-relevant employee competences that are organizationally latent, i.e. unknown by managers and human resource management staff, are manifest at the level of individual employees themselves and/or colleagues. These competences are thus, in principle, possible for the management to uncover and include in the firm's competence base through consultations with employees and designated search processes. How much such processes might add to the base is, of course, impossible to estimate, but we are probably in most cases speaking of considerable human resources that are neither known by the management nor being utilized in the firm. Consequently, one course of action for firms that want to expand their competence base will in many instances be to start by searching for hidden competences inside the organization.

However, there is still an analytical class of competences which are unknown both to the management of the firm, the individual employee, and her/his colleagues. Virtually every human being holds hidden knowledge, skills, and aptitudes that cannot be revealed unless the person is involved in specific types of activities where those competences are required for a good performance. This is particularly evident in work life when personnel are moved to new and different assignments and when employees are promoted to managerial jobs. Some succeed and some fail, and the result often could not be predicted simply because these employees entered new work terrain demanding competences that few, if any, knew beforehand if they possessed or not. This leads us to conclude that a work organization which rotates employees between jobs with different requirements and endeavors to keep a high internal mobility, has a much larger potential of detecting latent competences in its labor force than organizations with low scores on these variables. This is supported by Doeringer et al. (1991:189), who state that: "A new job in a new area simply forces the employee to develop new skills, attitudes, and identities. Repeated experience with such mobility engenders higher levels of employee adaptability. The more this internal mobility occurs, when there is no organizational crisis, the more flexible and prepared employees will be to adapt under environmental threat". Thus, having finely graded career paths may not only be functional in order to match the task structure of the firm but also in order to explore unknown competences among employees.

As to the manifest competences, these may either be applied in work or not. In the latter case, the reason often is that the boundaries of the job inhibits application. However, in many instances the reason is that there are various types of barriers that hinder competences in being utilized, such as insensitive or conservative superordinates, rigid colleagues, dysfunctional incentives systems, and bureaucratic rules and procedures that prevent innovative behavior. Firms may have a lot to gain by analyzing inhibitors of competence application in the organization. There is little doubt that in many cases such an analysis may yield more useful results than the traditional evaluations of single pieces of training activities. This is discussed in depth in Chapter 9.

Another distinction can be drawn between the firm's current (organizationally manifest) competence base and the projected base it needs for future operations. The discrepancy between these has in the human resource management and strategy literatures been described as the "competence gap" that must be filled in order to ensure that the firm's strategy can be realized (Grønhaug and Nordhaug, 1992, 1993). In our context, this can be called the realized competence gap, as contrasted with the cognitive competence gap previously introduced.

Managerial perceptions of the firm's competence base probably vary considerably. A conjecture would be that, in most firms, these perceptions are limited to the more or less manifest competences carried by employees within the firm and how these competences can be efficiently utilized. However, some firms have a conception of the competence base as one that is not confined to the boundaries of the organization, but which also includes competences in cooperating firms and competences that can be hired from external sources. This is, perhaps, best exemplified by the increasing number of strategic alliances and joint ventures based on the cooperating partners' complementary competences. Hence, a distinction can be drawn between firms that apply a narrow perspective on their competence base and firms where the management thinks in terms of extended competence bases.

In conclusion, the competence base, whether narrow or extended, represents a potential for the firm that defines what it can be capable of doing in the future. At the same time, it restricts the ways in which competences can be configured in order to obtain efficiency and the ways in which competences flow in the organization. Moreover, it is interesting to note that firms usually have a good overview of their current economic and physical capital resources, whereas this rarely is the case with regard to competences in the labor force. This is even more ironical as these are today considered the most important of all resources in most work organizations.

Organizational Context

Relations between competence bases and the internal organization of firms will be addressed first. More specifically, focus is set on needs to generate flexibility in the organization, to acquire, develop, and retain competences, to facilitate continuous employee learning, and to utilize the available competences. This is done by discussing properties of competences that are assumed to be particularly relevant in relation to these needs.

The task specificity of the competence base is regarded as significant concerning the flexibility of the firm's work-system. The durability of knowledge and skills affects the spendings on procurement and development of competences. Internal competence exclusiveness, defined as the degree to which vital competences are monopolized in the firm, is assumed to generate organizational inertia by inhibiting change and to create organizational vulnerability that may harm the internal efficiency. When competences are, so to speak, locked into specific social relations, whether these are dyadic or exist among several employees, we deal with high degrees of internal relation specificity. The diversity dimension describes the extent to which dissimilar competences are represented in the competence base and is important in relation to work-system flexibility and the potential for specialization in firms. In order to generate individual employee learning, it is crucial that competences can be exchanged between colleagues.thus, the competence base's degree of internal transferability is paramount. Finally, the extent to which competence bases are actually transformable to work performance is seen as descriptive of the firm's capability to utilize human resources.

Task Specificity

Task specificity relates to whether a certain competence can be utilized to accomplish one task only, a few tasks, or a wide range of tasks in the firm. For example, as noted in the previous chapter the skill of typing on the basis of the "touch-method" can only be applied to the single task of operating a standard keyboard. As a contrast, cooperative competence may be utilized to accomplish a broad spectrum of different tasks. In the first case, the competence is task specific, and in the latter, task nonspecific.

The significance of the competence base's task specificity primarily lies in its contribution to creating fit or static congruence in the work system and organizational units. However, this is clearly a double-edged sword in that the internal flexibility, i.e. the capacity to adjust the work system and the organization without incurring considerable costs and time-lags, may be strongly inhibited. The debate in human resource management circles about the status and usefulness of job analysis and the creation of maximum fit between employees and jobs is indicative of this dilemma. It has been pointed out that this way of thinking is virtually absent in Japanese corporations where work teams and their tasks are viewed as being more basic units than individuals and single jobs (Saha, 1987). At the same time, it is argued that the efforts to create short term fit between employee competences and tasks may have negative consequences for the long term fit between employees and careers. For example, a heavy emphasis on short-term fit may imply that employees are not provided with training other than that which qualifies directly for immediate work tasks. When this is the case, they get no opportunity to develop their long term potential for subsequent, more demanding jobs, and their career development is hampered.

Unit Specificity

Unit specificity refers to the degree to which competences can be realized within one specific organizational unit only or can be applied across units. Mastering of a specialized filing system, a unit specific computer routine, or locally tailored technology are examples of unit specific skills.

It can be argued that this dimension is logically parallel to, or even identical with, firm specificity, because organizational units may be viewed as "firms". Consequently, it remains a question of how organizational boundaries, the limits of the firm, are defined. However, given the existence of large companies, including many subunits of considerable size, the dimension of unit specificity provides a necessary supplement to firm specificity. Whereas the latter in our context is treated as a part of the external idiosyncracy of human resources, unit specificity describes an aspect of the internal idiosyncracy.

The competence base's degree of unit specificity directly influences the potential and probably also the actual amount of intrafirm mobility. In the same way as high firm specificity creates a lock-in of employees in the firm, high unit specificity generates a lock-in with regard to organizational subunits. Thus, a second, deduced ramification is that subunit parochialism will often emerge and lead to suboptimizing behavior when the unit specificity of competences is in general very high in a company.

Internal Relation Specificity

Thus far, we have concentrated on specificity associated with more or less formal contexts within firms (tasks, jobs, organizational units). The focus has been on idiosyncracy in connection with identifiable *entities*. However, in some instances the presence of a competence may be contingent on certain interactions between individual employees. In the same way as competences may be strongly related to given organizational entities, they may be inseparably tied to particular *social relations*. As noted by Harre (1981:145): "How are individuals influenced by having their being in collectives? There is an analogous problem in the physical sciences. Are there any mechanical properties which an individual could still properly be said to have if he/she were the only being in the universe? Mach's Principle, defining one form of contemporary cosmic mechanics, asserts that even that most apparently individualistic property, inertia, should be thought of as a relational property manifested by *a* body only by virtue of its location in the system of material bodies. In this and other cases physical scientists are familiar with radical relational analyses of attributes that are, at first sight, unique and stable attributes of individuals, per se. Could we say the same of the important properties ordinarily ascribed to individuals who are members of social collectives? Some properties that are attributed to individuals are clearly constituted by virtue of that individual standing in a certain relation to some other."

This reasoning is clearly relevant also for the individual properties of competences. For example, if an employee who works together with the same colleagues and virtually with none else during his complete occupational career is said to demonstrate a high level of cooperativeness, it is impossible to know whether this is true in general or if the person's cooperative skills are restricted to the specific social relational context in which he/she is embedded.

The term internal relation specificity will be applied to denote the social embeddedness of certain competences. A relation specific competence is hence defined as one that, in order to manifest itself, requires the presence of a particular social relation between two or more employees.

This has implications both on the interpersonal level and on the level of work groups. Some illustrations will illuminate the logic. Stories about managerial succession often contain evidence that subordinates either feel they can perform better or worse under the new leadership. We will contend that this is partly due to the relation specificity of competence. Whatever management style subordinates individually prefer, the relationship between manager and subordinate is always one of a "unique personal chemistry" in that no pair of such dyadic relationships are completely identical.

Some managers are known to be catalysts and to "extract the best" from their subordinates. Another way of putting this, is to say that some of the competences they "extract" have high relation specificity in that most other managers would not be able to accomplish this in relation to the given subordinate.

If we extend the perspective beyond dyadic relationships, the concept of *team competence* emerges. As pointed out by Aoki (1986:25), there exists an important class of competences that can be formed only in an organizational context and embodied only in a *team* of employees. Work groups may collectively possess competences that are inextricably tied to the social context of that specific group and which will consequently vanish if the group is dissolved. These team-related competences represent a sort of synergies or collective goods in companies, since they are not appropriable to individual employees.

For example, when groups of scientists are brought together in isolated environments in order to create an organizational "greenhouse effect", this is done more because of the anticipated synergy effects than because of these scientists' individual competences (which are, of course, not unimportant). The goal is to create a professional and social chemistry, the effects of which exceed the mere sum of the individual competences as much as possible. However, it is important to realize that if this succeeds, it is also because the specific group context or, more precisely, the professional and social *interactions*, contribute to liberating latent individual competences and to the reinforcement of existing ones. If, for instance, the social context exhibits a highly cooperative atmosphere, the emergence of competences that would otherwise have remained latent, is facilitated.

Relation specific competences often represent valuable synergies that may disappear if the firm goes through a restructuring process and when important employees leave the organization. Although they exhibit some vulnerability, these competences first and foremost constitute added resources to the firm. Moreover, these resources can only in rare cases be lost to other firms, since this requires that two or more related employees leave the firm and enter another together. Cases like these can be found in businesses like advertising agencies, consulting firms, and industrial research institutions, where, for example, creative teams may leave to set up their own business together.

To summarize, we can conclude that when the presence of a particular superordinate or colleague, or a group of colleagues, is required for a competence to be demonstrated, that competence is relation specific. An important aspect of such competences is that they are not portable and that they will disappear when the particular social context within which they are embedded is terminated.

Durability

Work-related competences differ substantially with regard to their average longevity. For example, it has been common to describe knowledge in terms of its "half-life", that is the time it takes before one half of the knowledge has become obsolete and hence more or less worthless in relation to work.

The durability of competences can be viewed predominantly as a function of three factors. The first is the frequency of use. Many types of competence will rapidly erode if they are not frequently applied. Examples are intricate manual skills, proficiency in mastering foreign languages, and skills related to the use of complex technology. The second factor is the pace of the development of knowledge and skills in the field that the competences in question are related to; the speed of the relevant technological development. Third, some competences may become substituted by new technology, either in the form of physical equipment or procedures and routines. The history of technology offers many illustrations of human competences that have, so to speak, been materialized by being built into machines or procedures, thus completely or partly eliminating the need for having employees who master them. This has especially been the case for task specific, often manual, competences that have been "taken over" by mechanized or computerized physical equipment. Examples are the competence of typographers becoming automatized and the skills of welders and painters in factories now being performed by robots. Concurrently, new technology exhibiting "skills" that were previously embodied exclusively in employees often generates needs for new competences to be developed, for example, skills in monitoring automated work processes.

The competence base's degree of durability is important particularly due to the time and cost of developing new competences as the old ones become obsolete and superfluous. If the proportion of the competence base having long expected durability is high, the management has little reason to apply other measures than staying alert to the impacts of relevant technology development which can suddenly make previously vital parts of the existing competence base obsolete and that will consequetly call for generation of new or modified competences. If, on the other hand, the proportion of competences having short anticipated durability is high, the firm will have to maintain a hands-on policy with respect to personnel development and invest substantial amounts of money and effort in carrying out such development. In firms where the durability of vital competences is generally very short, for example in the computer business, human resource development becomes a very critical function, since the sustained capacity to continuously develop employees' knowledge and skills is then a crucial determinant of organizational performance.

Diversity

The competence base's degree of diversity describes the extent to which dissimilar competences are represented amongst employees. Conventional thinking has implied that it is rational to have a heterogeneous competence base because low competence variance may lead to problems in carrying out tasks, as a high degree of specialization cannot then be achieved. However, according to more recent insights, a certain amount of overlapping, or similar, competences is considered functional. When more or less identical competences are spread amongst employees, the firm becomes less vulnerable to absenteeism and turnover since employees can replace each other on short notice. This need to create internal flexibility through developing multicompetent or multiskilled employees is the main rationale behind the increasingly widespread incentive system of skill-based pay (cf. Lawler and Ledford, 1986; Tosi and Tosi, 1986). One of the advantages is, moreover, that employees become accustomed to learning new skills and may be able to obtain a broader perspective on the work system and operations of the firm. However, if the amount of duplicate competences exceeds a certain limit, an insufficient capacity to match the division of labor embedded in the work system may evolve. This trade-off is discussed by Cohen and Levinthal (1990:133): "While some overlap of knowledge across individuals is necessary for internal communication, there are benefits to diversity of knowledge structures across individuals that parallel the benefits to diversity of knowledge within individuals. ... Assuming a sufficient level of knowledge overlap to ensure effective communication, interactions across individuals who each possess diverse and different knowledge structures will augment the organization's capacity for making novel linkages and associations – innovating – beyond what any one individual can achieve."

If the competence base is either highly diverse or highly homogeneous, problems may be indicated. In the first case, the organizational flexibility is usually low because quick transfers among different jobs and employees' stepping in for others at short notice are difficult or impossible to accomplish due to the modest amount of multicompetences. Very low diversity may indicate that the range of competences in the firm is too restricted and that little effort is made to meet new challenges and accomplish innovation through extending the competence range.

Internal Exclusiveness

The internal exclusiveness of a firm's competence base refers to the degree to which vital competences are the exclusive "property" of only one employee or a small group of employees, i.e. the extent to which essential competences are concentrated in the organization. For example, if a company employs two computer experts and the knowledge of computing in the rest of the firm is low, they possess internally exclusive competence. If, in addition, their competence is vital to the operation of the firm and the computer experts do not want to share their knowledge and skills with others, the firm's dependency on them may create substantial organizational vulnerability. Such exclusiveness may lead to competence monopolies in those instances where the bearers of the knowledge and skills are unwilling, or unable, to share their work-relevant insights with other colleagues. Crozier's (1964) classic analysis of a French tobacco plant provides an illustration of this by emphasizing the competence monopoly of maintenance workers and their associated power. Likewise, computer departments have in many firms enjoyed a power position based on their possession of internally unique knowledge and skills.

However, the main reason that competences are exclusive probably lies in the fact that the individuals carrying them simply are not encouraged or have no incentive to use their time transferring them to others. As pointed out by Nelson and Winter (1982:115), "... in some cases the memory of a single organization member may be the sole storage point of knowledge that is both idiosyncratic and of great importance to the organization. The knowledge may be tacit – say, an intuitive grasp of the priority structure of the competing demands on the employee's time that are signalled by incoming messages. It may be articulable but not written down – the first names, marital status, and preferred recreations of the important customers in the region, or the action that is called for when a particular machine starts to vibrate too much."

When the degree of exclusiveness in the competence base is high, the firm will be forced to make greater efforts to retain personnel because if employees possessing exclusive knowledge and skills quit, their competence is either lost for good or may be very difficult or time-consuming to substitute. This is, naurally, even more serious if the employees in question possess competences that are vital to the operations of the firm.

Besides making the firm vulnerable to the power position of a small number of employees, the degree of competence exclusiveness inherent in the competence base may hamper the feasibility of organizational and strategic change. The reason is that personnel in such a position frequently will perceive their power potential as threatened by changes and therefore will be inclined to resist changes in order to preserve the competence monopoly which forms their power base.

Transferability

The transferability of competences regards the degree to which they can be exchanged between employees. This is a function primarily of two properties of competences, their degree of tacitness and their degree of complexity.

The concept of tacitness has been employed to describe the extent to which knowledge and skills are articulable (Polanyi, 1962, 1964). According to Nelson and Winter (1982:81-82), the limits on articulation of knowledge may derive from three sources. First, there may not be sufficient time available to transfer the knowledge through symbolic communication relative to the time that is needed. This applies, for example, to manual activities that have to be pursued so quickly that it is impossible to give instruction during the performance of the activity. Second, knowledge of how to perform a skill may be difficult to articulate due to a limited causal understanding of that knowledge. Polanyi (1962) illustrates this by the skill of swimming. Few swimmers have a complete causal understanding of the scientific reasons why they are able to swim and do not sink. Third, knowledge may be difficult to articulate due to limitations in the potential of language to describe the whole and the parts simultaneously: "Efforts to articulate "complete" knowledge of something by exhaustive attention to details and thorough discussion of preconditions succeed only in producing an incoherent message. ...language cannot simultaneously serve to describe relationships and characterize the things related" (Nelson and Winter, 1982:81-82). In general, we will assume that the competence base's degree of tacitness influences the ease with which competences can be transferred from one individual to another. When competences cannot be articulated by the individual possessing them, these are often difficult or impossible to convey to colleagues. However, to the extent that they can be demonstrated in use, transfer may still be feasible through learning by imitation. Hence, transfer may occur even when the instructor is unable to adequately articulate or describe the competence.

The complexity of a particular competence concerns the number of knowledge and skill elements it comprises and the nature of the relationship between these elements. It can be assumed that the more complex the competences, the more time-consuming the transfer between individuals. On this basis, it is reasonable to assert that the transferability of competences is simultaneously determined by their degrees of tacitness and complexity and, furthermore, that the relationship between the two properties is basically multiplicative. Thus, competences which are both tacit and very complex will be the most difficult to transfer, whereas articulable and non-complex competences will normally be easily transferable. The primary significance of the transferability of competences between employees resides in its potential contributions to the learning or, in our terms, competence flows within the firm. When a high proportion of the competence base is easily transferable, the firm possesses a flexibility potential, since the development of multicompetent employees is facilitated. In this way, the firm may become less vulnerable to turnover and absenteeism. Moreover, the career planning system can be made less rigid as employees may to a larger degree be moved quickly between dissilimar positions. However, the extent to which multiskilling will actually occur is also a function of incentives and motivation among employees in relation to transferring their competences to others. Nevertheless, if a large part of the competence base consists of transferable knowledge and skills, one crucial condition for establishing an efficient learning environment is present.

Transformability

After having acquired and developed competence bases, firms face the challenge of converting these into efficient work-performance, that is, to accomplish what we can call "the crucial transformation". Although this applies to all sorts of resources or inputs in organizations, the crucial transformation is especially intricate to achieve for competences. The reason is that employees, who are the bearers of the competence, are also acting subjects. Stated differently, utilization of competence is generally far more difficult to govern than is the use of other resources, simply because the bearers of the competence may themselves also be able to act vis-a-vis the governance system. The tendency to act in order to promote self-interests may be labelled rational behavior, or opportunism if it is "dishonest" in relation to the employment contract (Williamson, 1983:9). The contract is *incomplete* in that it is impossible to specify in exhaustive detail what an employee is supposed to do during every working hour and minute (Coase, 1937; Braverman, 1974). In order that the competence held by employees is to be efficiently utilized in the firm, employment contracts must therefore be supplemented by an informal, often implicit and tacit, social contract "specifying" certain reciprocal moral standards of performance-related behavior and rewards (Okun, 1980). Moreover, research has pointed out that age-earnings profiles in the form of efficiency wages and deferred compensation systems (wage-for-age scales) can be used to reduce shirking, absenteeism, and turnover (cf. Lazear, 1981; Yellen, 1984; Akerlof and Yellen, 1986;Main, 1990).

The firm's competence base may be more or less transformable to the *work situation* depending both on the nature of the competence, the nature of the job context, the technology applied, the objects that are processes in the job, the functioning of work groups, and characteristics of the individual employee carrying the competence. Thus, some competences are manifest, as they are actually used in the job, whereas other competences remain latent, either because they are irrelevant to the job tasks due to external obstacles that hamper application, or because the employee is unwilling to use the competence.

The phenomenon of overeducation in firms provides an illustration of competence irrelevancy (cf. Burris, 1983; Nordhaug, 1991a:ch.10; 1991c). This represents a quantitative mismatch between employees' actual competence and the opportunities rendered by the job design to use that competence. Another illustration relates to qualitative mismatch between competences and jobs. In that case, employees have not received "too much" education and training relative to the current job; they have pursued training that is simply not relevant to the requirements inherent in the job. External obstacles to application of competence can be illustrated by group norms regulating maximum individual work-performance, rigid job-design, and conservative superordinates who oppose the introduction and use of "new" competences. Finally, employees may avoid using their competence due to negative attitudes toward the employer or because they expect that application will either not be rewarded or may even be negatively sanctioned (see Chapter 9).

The transformability of competences constitutes the ultimate test of the firm's efforts and spendings to build an efficient competence base. Thus, if the transformability is low, the firm either does not possess a base that matches its tasks to a sufficient degree or the base is not being sufficiently utilized due to incentive or control problems. However, there is a trade-off here, because firms also have to equip employees with competences that are oriented toward

the mastering of emerging and future tasks and that may thus be
without immediate relevance to current jobs.

Environmental Context

In order to manage their relationship to current and future external
environments, firms have to rely on their competence base. The
question is, then, what aspects of such bases are particularly
important in relation to meeting this challenge. Four assumedly
crucial aspects or properties of competence bases have been
selectedfor discussion. First, the degree of match specificity is
believed to influence the feasibility of pursuing organizational
change. Second, the degree of industry specificity of competences
is similarly considered to have an impact on the external or
strategic flexibility of firms, i.e. their capacity to implement major
strategic changes, for instance, by shifting to another industry.
Third, the competence base's relative degree of advancedness may
have ramifications for the potential costs of replacing key personnel
who leave the organization and thus carry implications for
retainment policies. Fourth, the competence base's overall
relevance for the current strategy is clearly essential. Fifth, its
distinctiveness relative to the competitors' competence bases, has
ramifications for the firm's competitiveness. Finally, the degree to
which existing competence bases can be extended into new
strategic applications, is discussed.

Match Specificity

As originally introduced in human capital theory, the concepts of
general and firm specific knowledge and skills represent polar
dimensions (Becker, 1983). If a competence can be used in one
firm only, it is firm specific and has no value in external labor
markets. All competences that are not firm specific can, by
definition, be sold in external labor markets. The dimension of firm
specificity is thus fundamentally different from the dimension of
task specificity in that it, although sharing the property of being
highly important for the internal organization, is defined relative to

the external environment of the firm.

According to human capital theory, the investment in firm specific knowledge and skills is financed by the firm, whereas investment in general or firm nonspecific competences is financed by the individual, as these competences can be utilized across firms (Becker, 1983). However, it has been pointed out that in reality firms may often to some extent consider it rational to finance development of general competences also, especially when internal labor markets characterized by long term employment relationships prevail (Doeringer and Piore, 1971).

Wachter and Wright (1990:90) have launched the wider concept of match specificity to account for the idiosyncratic relationship between individual employees and the firm: "It refers to firm-specific investments in human capital via on-the-job training, learning-by-doing, etc.; to worker-specific investments; and generally to the case in which a firm and a worker simply have formed a "good match". This match implies a greater expected "surplus" than would result if a new random worker was inserted into the slot, or if the worker was assigned a new random job." This is a constructive extension of the original conceptualization because it pinpoints the reciprocal relationship between individual competences and work tasks, and we shall therefore prefer to apply the descriptor of match specificity. Moreover, it also allows for inclusion of irreversible investments in the firm's labor force in terms of screening and recruitment spendings made by the firm.

The match specificity of competences may be significant in several ways. First, it has ramifications for the feasibility of strategic change. If the firm needs to accomplish a major change process involving implementation of new technology and procedures, match specific competences can create inertia to the extent that they are rendered obsolete or superfluous. Thus, for companies that need to pursue a fundamental reorientation of their business strategy, high match specificity can easily become a hampering factor. However, for firms that are not in such a situation, high match specificity may indicate that there is a tight match between competences and work tasks which secures high productivity. Second, it marks that the firm has a solid potential of retaining its employees, as high match specificity on the individual level usually reduces or eliminates the availability of alternative employment opportunities at a corresponding level of compensation. In general, it can be expected that the higher the match specificity of the competence base, the more efficient the lock-in of its employees.

The positive aspects of firm or match specificity have been extensively covered in the human resource management and labor market literature. One of the advantages emphasized is that it makes employees less mobile in external labor markets, thus facilitating retainment. It has also been pointed out that internal labor markets, which are associated with high firm specificity, create identification with and commitment to the firm amongst employees and that, consequently, the probability of developing a clan-like organization culture is higher in firms comprising substantial amounts of match specific competence.

These arguments are valid only as long as the firm does not need to pursue major strategic changes. However, once such changes are accentuated, the character of match specificity as a double-edged sword becomes highly visible. Employees with more match specific than match nonspecific competences may have a lot to lose through processes of reorganization and strategic shifts. What they will usually fear the most is being forced to leave the firm as they, due to the high match specificity of their competences, are likely to encounter substantial and prhaps even insurmountable barriers when reentering external labor markets.

Industry Specificity

The concept of general or nonspecific competence as developed within human capital theory covers a very wide range of knowledge, skills, and aptitudes. In order to approach a more subtle classification, it is thus important to move beyond the polar case and ask whether there are *degrees* of generality. The dimension of industry specificity, the extent to which competences can be utilized in one industry only, is particularly useful in this context (cf. Perry, 1986; Lengnick-Hall and Lengnick-Hall, 1988, 1990). Industry specific competence is general. At the same time, it is less general than knowledge and skills which can be sold in *any* external labor market.

Besides adding subtleness to the classification of competences, the concept of industry specificity readily lends itself to the analysis of the role of competence bases in relation to economic restructuring processes both on a macro and micro level. For example, skilled manufacturing workers who are laid off possess industry specific skills that may more or less easily be transformed into skills which are applicable in other industries. On the firm level, the amount of industry specificity inherent in the competence base can be a crucial factor in processes of strategic change. If, for example, the firm decides to leave the industry, low industry specificity will be favorable because there is then no strong need for delearning of industry specific skills, and therefore the transferability of current competences is higher. However, if a turnaround is to be accomplished without exiting the industry, industry specific competence will be valuable as it facilitates adjustment to the specific competitive conditions within the industry.

It is reasonable to assume that the competence base's industry specificity is particularly important for the firm's capacity to accomplish strategic changes. If the competence base is highly industry specific, major strategic changes may easily necessitate a substitution of those competences with new competences, either through delearning and retraining of the current work force or through replacement of employees. This will indeed be the case if the strategic change in question involves an exit from the industry and subsequent entry into another industry.

External Relation Specificity

In the same way as internal relation specificity refers to competences that manifest themselves only within certain social contexts, external relation specificity is characteristic of the same logic for social relationships and interactions between employees in the firm and external individuals or groups that are related to the firm. Among these, the customers or clients and employees in firms that are suppliers are usually the most important categories. One would further expect that the more frequent and intensive the interaction between an employee and external persons or groups, the higher the probability that external relation specificity will occur. In the consulting business, for example, employees frequently work very closely with their clients, and in such contexts competences that are specific to external relations are likely to be present to some degree. Strategic alliances, joint ventures and project work across firm boundaries provide other examples of contexts where external relation specificities may emerge – and then disappear when the projects are completed. In his discussion of innovation, von Hippel (1988) has pointed out the significance of tight relationships between buyers and suppliers for learning and innovation. Following up on this, Cohen and Levinthal (1990:134) note that to the extent that an organization develops a broad and active network of internal and external relationships, individuals' awareness of others' capabilities and knowledge will be strengthened: "As a result, individual absorptive capacities are leveraged all the more, and the organization's absorptive capacity is strengthened."

External relation specific competences may represent valuable competitive advantages to firms. As it is the idiosyncratic relationship between customer and employee that contributes to generating a particular competence in the employee, it is reasonable to assume that this may also be the case for the customer or the employee who represents the customer. Consequently, there is a unique relationship that competitors cannot easily, if at all, imitate completely. In strategic terms we are then speaking of a barrier of entry to competitors that is difficult to overcome. Knowledge about the customers and their needs often takes a certain amount of trust to acquire and is time-consuming to generate. Hence, if the amount of externally relation specific competences in the firm is very high, this may cause rigidity problems if the firm has to reorient itself to the extent that new customer groups replace the current ones. Stated differently, if the employee-customer fits are very tight, heavy sunk cost investments have been made in these fits that often cannot be easily recouped if a switch to new customers has to be made.

Relative Advancedness

The degree to which competence bases are highly developed according to external professional and occupational standards describes their level or relative advancedness. One illustration is the density of academic degrees in the organization's work force, which is, however, a formal rather than a substantive measure. Another example is the annual peer ranking of university departments within various disciplines in the U.S. This example is highly illustrative of our conception of competence bases because it is not the competence of individual university professors per se that is evaluated – but rather the joint competence of the entire faculty of each department. One may object that what is measured is actually not competences but performance as measured by external peers' perceptions of the quality and quantity of publications. However, since performance in this context probably is the best available proxy for the advancedness of the academic competence, we may still argue that the rankings provide a reasonable measure for the perceived advancedness of the departments' competence bases.

The primary importance of the advancement dimension resides in the fact that the cost of substituting advanced knowledge and skills is usually much higher than the cost of substituting less elaborate competences. Therefore, the management has a very strong incentive to create arrangements that serve to nurture and retain such competence. Stated differently, it is important to raise exit-barriers or increase employee loyalty in order to protect the base. Thus, the overall personnel policy and human resource management is key. When a high level of advancedness is combined with low overall match specificity, this is even more the case, and the firm may in this situation have to maintain a high level of compensation and create incentives that serve to increase employees' long term commitment to the firm. This is interesting when viewed in relation to the literature on internal labor markets. There, it has been common to postulate that the amount of firm specificity represents the main rationale for establishing such internal markets due to the sunk costs that have been spent on developing firm specific competences (Wachter and Wright, 1990:91). However, if a firm possesses a substantial amount of comparatively advanced, firm nonspecific, competences that are vital for its performance, and the demand for this type of competence exceeds the supply in the external labor market, there is clearly a strong incentive to establish internal labor markets that can increase long-term commitment and secure retainment of key personnel.

Strategic Relevance

The competence bases of firms are made up of a wide variety of different individual competences. Clearly, not all of these are equally important in relation to the firms' current strategies. On the organizational level, this reasoning can be illustrated by concepts such as core competences, key competences, strategic competence pools, and distinctive competences (Selznick, 1957; Itami, 1987; Naugle and Davies, 1987; Hall, 1989; Prahalad and Hamel, 1990). For example, the main strategic tasks of most universities are high-quality knowledge production through research and transmission of knowledge and skills to students. Consequently, the most central competences are possessed by the faculty, which are thus the carriers of the strategically most central competence. This does not mean that the knowledge and skills of other staff, such as administrative and technical personnel, is unimportant for the success of universities. The support staff are essential for the operation of the organization, but in general not as central in relation to the strategic tasks as are the faculty's contribution to the competence base which actually represents the main harvesting ground. This is, furthermore, illustrated by the fact that administrative and technical personnel usually can be more easily substituted than specialized and highly recognized scholars who each have highly idiosyncratic competences. Hence, universities will, in general, need to put more effort in carefully protecting and nurturing its best research and teaching personnel than in protecting and retaining other competence bearers.

Naturally, the question as to which competences are the most strategically relevant depends on the nature of the firm's strategy. A firm that implements an innovation-oriented strategy based on development of new products or services will rely heavily on its R&D personnel who consequently represent key competences that must be protected. If the strategy is based on keeping higher product or service quality than the competitors, the competence of engineers and quality controllers comes to the forefront. If the strategy is based on large-scale provision of low-cost products, the competences of supervisors and cost controllers are especially important.

These illustrations also mark that any major change of a firm's strategy will require acquisition or development of new key competences. At the same time, some competences will substitute others as being the strategically most relevant – and the protection of key competences must consequently also be shifted to the former.

The overall strategic relevance of the competence base is crucial for the firm's capacity to create sustained competitiveness. If substantial parts of the base are strategically peripheral or irrelevant, problems related to implementing the strategy and thus to competing effectively, will arise. This may be illustrated by strategic changes in firms that have not been accompanied by necessary changes of the competence base. For example, the chief explanatory factor behind the grand-scale economic failures of major Norwegian commercial banks during the 1980s is the fact that they changed their strategy and organization without adjusting the competences of their employees in order to make them capable of meeting the expanded job demands. The decentralization of authority to grant loans that resulted from more aggressive strategies triggered by deregulation of money markets and increased competition was not followed up by sufficient competence development among the numerous lower level employees who were delegated authority to make decisions involving large amounts of money. The consequence was a vast number of poor financial analyses and judgments that led to very large losses and brought major banks on the verge of bankruptcy and some technically even beyond (cf. Reve, 1990).

Extensibility

In addition to being more or less relevant in regard to the current strategy of firms, their competence bases will have a varying potential in relation to alternative strategies involving new areas of activity. This concerns the degree to which the existing competence base can be extended into new business areas or industries, and we shall refer to this dimension as the extensibility of the competence base.

Naugle and Davies (1987:39) have pointed out that most new businesses grow from the existing skills of an individual or group. They also note that an examination of the competence pool of the firm may help focus attention on its strengths and the skills it may be able to bring to a new business opportunity. Moreover, two examples were provided: "Citicorp's use of its distributed processing expertise to enter the computer-services business falls neatly into this category. General Electric made a similar move when it chose to enter the jet-engine market by using its expertise in turbines from its power-generation business. Although GE had to develop additional skills to compete in jet engines, it possessed many of the core technical skills required for success before it entered the business".

In practice, assessing the extensibility of the firm's current competence base may be quite intricate, since this requires that one is able to identify potential alternative or added applications of the base. However, the possible gains from developing a capability to explore ways in which the application of the competence base can be extended, are substantial. This is particularly so as the extensibility of the competence base is crucial for the firm's opportunities to create new businesses in related areas. There are a number of examples that companies have been able to diversify their activities and add new, expanding businesses by building on and extending their current competence base. Hence, for most firms pursuing a thorough analysis of the range of the various key competences in the firm, may prove to be worthwhile.

Distinctiveness

The concept of competence or capability distinctiveness has previously been applied on the organizational macro level of analysis in order to describe what the firm is capable of doing better than other firms (e.g. Selznick, 1957; Nordhaug and Grønhaug, 1992). Although it is fruitful to apply the term on a macro level, hence incorporating important synergies, its use should not be limited to this level. It is reasonable to assume that macro distinctiveness is, in most cases, to a substantial degree a result of the aggregation of distinctive individual and team competences. Thus, in order to illuminate competences on a macro level, it is necessary to analyze their constituent parts among which single competences and competence bases are essential. Furthermore, since, per definition, synergies are results of interrelations or interactions between the elements of a system, it is important to note that organizational competence synergies cannot be uncovered unless the other constitutive elements are known in advance.

Several authors have emphasized firms' needs to create and protect core or distinctive competences that create value and generate competitive advantages (Naugle and Davis, 1987; Prahalad and Hamel, 1990; Nordhaug and Grønhaug, 1992). However, developing and protecting core competences on the macro level always translates into protecting and retaining the competences of key personnel on the micro level. Macro synergies are literally rooted in single competences and interactions between the employees carrying these. Hence, the more distinctive the competences of a given employee, the more the firm is expected to invest in raising exit-barriers for this employee. In principle, this is the same logic as for match specific competences in which the firm has made sunk cost investments which are lost for the firm if the employee quits. However, an important difference is that whereas in the latter case the basis of judgment is past investment, future-oriented considerations are governing the protection of individual distinctive competences. It is thus important not only to establish exit barriers but also to raise entry barriers, that is, preventing competitors from gaining access to distinctive competences. Fundamentally, exit barriers for employees are also entry barriers to the degree that employees may leave and go to competitors. But also, when these employees stay, entry barriers must be raised that prevent occurrence of other types of knowledge and skill transfer, for example, through professional exchanges in conferences, industry associations, and journals.

Discussion

So far, we have delineated separate descriptors of competence bases that are assumed to be relevant within the organizational and environmental contexts, respectively. In this section, the intention is to discuss critical aspects of the different properties of competence bases and to outline possible interrelations or interaction effects between them. In order to create an overview that can structure this discussion, the main points in the preceding presentation are summarized in Figure 4.2.

The task specificity of the base is assumed to have its main impacts on the flexibility of the firm's work-system and its readiness for organizational change. It is thus believed that a very high degree of task specificity reflects a substantial amount of organizational ridigity, in the sense that significant alterations of the work-system and technological development eliminating or changing the nature of tasks will necessitate considerable amounts of effort, time, and spendings on delearning and retraining among the employees affected.

The possibilities of establishing and maintaining high rates of internal mobility, for instance in order to promote broader grasps of the firm and develop more general skills in employees, are expected to be dependent largely on the competence base's degree of unit specificity. In the same way as the firm specificity of competences represents both barriers of entry and barriers of exit to potential and current employees, respectively, unit specificity creates such barriers within the firm. Hence, there is an important paradox in that firms wanting to start a job rotation program in order to develop broader competences will be hampered in doing this by the fact that the competences are too narrow to begin with. In some situations, employees will be reluctant to join job rotation programs unless especially attractive career incentives are elaborated that downplay the importance of possessing strong unit specific knowledge and skills and emphasize the significance of broader competences spanning two or more organizational units.

Moreover, a sustained unit two or specificity in the competence base is held to promote suboptimization in the firm because it easily creates high subunit commitment at the expense of commitment to the organization as a whole.

The extent to which competences are inextricably tied to specific social relations between two or more colleagues can be interpreted as an indicator of the amount of competence synergies in the firm. In a stable situation without any needs for reorganizing, this is, therefore, descriptive of added competence resources due to the social configuration of employees. However, when organizational changes involving reconfiguration of the work-system, and thereby also of social interactions, are implemented, high internal relation specificity may imply that important competence synergies are lost, at least in the short term. (Viewed in an extended time perspective, new synergies will be established that may or may not exceed previous ones.)

This reasoning provides a different view of the problem of employee resistance to organizational change than the traditional, psychologically oriented perspective which has stressed emotional and often 'psychologically irrational' factors. Stated differently, employees may not only be generally afraid of uncertainty and potential loss of privileges caused by restructuring processes, they may also fear to lose internally and sometimes also externally

BASE PROPERTIES	MAJOR AREAS OF IMPACT
Organizational Context	
* Task Specifity	Work-system flexibility
	Change readiness
* Unit Specifity	Intrafirm mobility
	Suboptimization
* Internal Relation Specificity	Competence synergies
	Organizational flexibility
* Durability	Frequency of competence development
	Cost of competence development
* Internal Exclusiveness	Competence monopolies
	Organizational flexibility
* Diversity	Work-system flexibility
	Specialization potential
* Transferability	Competence flows
	Learning capacity
* Transformability	Utilization of competences
	Organizational efficiency
Environmental Context	
* Match Specificity	Strategic flexibility
	Employment stability
* Industry Specificity	Strategic flexibility
* External Relation Specificity	Competitive advantage
	Strategic flexibility
* Relative Advancedness	Competence retainment
	Substitution cost
* Strategic Relevance	Organizational effectiveness
	Competitiveness
* Extensibility	Strategic flexibility
	Innovative potential
* Distinctiveness	Competitive advantage
	Competence protection

Figure 4.2. Overview of Presentation.

relation specific competences and judge the probability of creating new such competences as low, unless otherwise persuaded. As argued by Orr (1990:48): "The process of working and learning together creates a work situation which the workers value, and they resist having it disrupted by their employers through events such as a reorganization of the work. This resistance can surprise employers who think of labor as a commodity to arrange to suit their ends. The problem for the workers is that this community which they have created was not part of the series of discrete employment arrangements by which the employer populated the work place, nor is the role of the community in doing the work acknowledged".

The lower the overall durability of the competence base, the more time and economic resources will have to be invested in developing employee competences. This is indicated by, among other things, the substantial differences in the frequency and amount of training between dissimilar industries that have been found in research, although also other factors probably contribute to generating these differences. The efficiency of firms is clearly influenced by the extent to which they actually succeed in continually renewing employee competences. This applies particularly to various types of highly task specific competences, as the durability of these is heavily influenced by the pace of the technological development within the professional field they are part of. Nevertheless, it also applies to higher-level managerial competences, such as knowledge about the industry and competitors, knowledge about the customers, and insights into advances in the field of executive development.

The dimensions of internal exclusiveness and transferability are both related to the competence flow in the firm. In the extreme case of internal competence monopolies, there is no flow between colleagues, except between those who make up the monopoly. Hence, the learning capacity within the firm is restricted. In principle, the same situation occurs when competences are nontransferrable, regardless of whether this is due to their being latent to the bearers, tacit, or too complex to be learned by other employees in the firm. Moreover, in both cases the organizational flexibility may be harmed to the extent that carriers of individually unique competences fear that restructuring of the work-system or the organization as a whole will weaken their position in the firm.

A practical implication is that firms may benefit from preventing or breaking up monopolies that are not rooted in the nature of the competences per se (latent, tacit, or complex) but are based upon deliberate prevention or obstruction of transfer to others.

Ultimately, the efficiency of organizations is dependent upon the degree to which competences can actually be transformed into work-performance and upon the carriers' willingness to do so. The latter is beyond our discussion. The former, transformability, is not related to the other dimensions treated so far, but it is of course strongly linked to the relationship between competences and the work tasks that have to be accomplished in the firm. Knowledge and skills that are not in any way transformable to current or future work, are thus totally irrelevant and therefore not part of the competence base. However, competence bases can be characterized by their degrees of transformability. The higher the transformability, the greater the firm's probability of creating organizational efficiency.

Logically, transformability and strategic relevance are parallel dimensions by being descriptive of potentials of converting competences to organizational outcomes. However, whereas the former relates to the organizational micro level (that is, the relationship between single competences and work tasks), the strategic relevance of competence bases describes the extent to which, on the organizational macro level, knowledge and skills can be converted into externally effective applications. We may say that they depict the same fundamental logic (i.e. transformability of competence bases into task accomplishment), but they apply to different levels of analysis. They affect organizational efficiency (internal standard) and effectiveness (external standard), respectively.

A highly industry specific competence base may create problems for firms wanting to exit the industry they operate within and enter another. Then, substantial parts of the base may suddenly be without any value to the firm. On the other hand, compared to employees with predominantly match specific competences, persons possessing large proportions of industry specific competences are likely to be better off when having to leave the firm, because their labor can be sold to a number of different firms. However, this requires that there is a sufficient demand for labor in the industry, which will often not be the case in declining industries where employment is usually diminishing.

Competences that are both match specific and industry nonspecific, represent the strategically most flexible type of competence since they are neither tied to firm specific tasks, routines, or procedures nor to work that is specific to a particular industry. Competences that are completely nonspecific in relation to tasks, units, firms, and industries were in Chapter 3 termed meta-competences (cf. Nordhaug, 1991a: ch.9). Regardless of the type of strategic change, the existence of meta-competences among employees, such as learning capacity, cooperative skills, and capability to deal with change and uncertainty, are particularly valuable competences in relation to processes of external, strategic reorientation. However, an intricate dilemma is present here. Many firms have an obvious interest in developing meta-competences in employees, since these may often facilitate organizational change by being broadly applicable. But at the same time it will, in principle, not be rational for firms to finance development of such competences due to the fact that they are portable across employers. In practice, this dilemma may be resolved by employers and employees sharing the costs of developing chiefly match nonspecific competences. However, if their knowledge and skills are mainly match specific, the most probable outcome is that the firm finances the whole investment in competences alone due to its strong interest in retaining personnel in which considerable investments through the development of match specific competences have already been made.

The competence base must also to some minimum extent match the competition currently engaged in, by being strategically relevant and at the same time distinctive in relation to the competence bases of rivalling firms. The demands from the environment will most often be reflected in the firm's strategy and hence, given that the strategy is based on fairly realistic perceptions of the environment, we are speaking of degrees of *congruence* or static fit between the competence base and the current strategy. Widespread lack of such fit is one of the reasons behind much of the recent literature and new practices within the field of strategic human resource management (e.g., Tichy, Fombrun, and Devanna, 1982; Dyer, 1983, 1984, 1985; Schuler and MacMillan, 1984; Angle, Manz, and Van de Ven, 1985; Evans, 1986; Schuler and Jackson, 1987; Lengnick-Hall and Lengnick-Hall, 1988; Nordhaug,

1990a). Among the dimensions previously discussed, industry specificity is especially important for external fit, because it is descriptive of a part of the competence base which is directly relevant for the competitive conditions of the firm. Nevertheless, the significance of static fit between competences and strategy has been overemphasized in parts of the strategic human resource management literature (cf. Lengnick-Hall and Lengnick-Hall, 1988:456; Chakravarthy and Lorange, 1992). Similarly, much of the traditional human resource management literature has stressed the importance of internal fit between human resources and tasks. However, in both bodies of literature, the possibility that strong fit is associated with inflexibility has largely been neglected. It is, for example, interesting to note that job analysis, which is predominantly a technique aimed at generating *maximum* fit between current employee competences and current job tasks, has rarely been applied in Japanese firms: "The concept of job analysis and working by the manual has not taken root in the Japanese corporation" (Ishida, 1986:107).

The extensibility of the competence base is related to its strategic relevance, since it (if present) describes a potential to create future strategically relevant applications of the current base. For example, a competence base with low strategic relevance may still be valuable given that its extensibility is high. However, if both dimensions have low scores, the firm is in serious trouble as to its current and future competitiveness.

Concluding Comment

It follows from the discussion of competence distinctiveness that macro competences or capabilities must be decomposed into their constituent parts, namely competences held by individuals and teams, synergies, and competence bases, if firms shall be able to further develop and utilize such macro competences. If the management of the firm identifies its core competences as x, y, and z, no matter how accurate the identification, it has no value unless the management is not able to decompose them. Not until then will the firm be capable of protecting its core competences which are, in fact, macro representations of aggregate micro level elements and the results of their interactions (synergies). Still, knowing reasonably well the constituent elements of core competences is not sufficient. It is equally important to have an overview of how the elements of competence bases that in part make up the core competences are deployed in the organization, i.e. the competence configuration. This is because core competences are not only constituted by a collection of single competences, but also by the way these competences are coordinated, interrelated, and enmeshed in social relations. Thus, core competences are not purely analytical entities that can be easily singled out, but *systems* of parts that have to be interlinked in certain ways to be effective.

Chapter 5

Competence Networks

Introduction

The purpose of this chapter is to outline a framework of competence networks in organizations. Both in the organization science literature and the human resource management field, competences have commonly been conceived of as important *inputs* into processes that determine individual and organizational performance. Hence, human capital including knowledge and skills has been juxtaposed with financial, physical, and technological capital. However, by developing a perspective of competence networks in organizations, it is possible to reach beyond this input-oriented stage and focus on interrelations between competences both on a micro, meso, and macro level. This is particularly important since firms' degree of success in procuring, organizing, and utilizing skills and knowledge is a crucial determinant of their prospects for continued survival.

The following fundamental questions have guided the approach in this chapter to firms as competence networks: How are the available competences in firms' competence bases deployed in the organization (competence configuration)? How and to what degree are competences acquired by and transferred between individuals, groups, and units in the organization (competence flow)?

The intention is to address these questions, thereby outlining an analytical perspective on competences in work organizations that can be a stepping stone for future theoretical and empirical research.

Background

In the administrative science literature, the amount of research on motivation and commitment far outweigh the amount of research conducted on employee competences. Although a number of studies of employees' abilities and skills have been reported, these have mainly been psychologically oriented and largely remained at the level of individuals. However important this research, there is a strong need to study work-relevant competences on the levels of teams, organizational units, and organizations also. Since competences are crucial determinants of individual and group performance, they constitute essential resources that strongly affect organizational performance. Yet, this has not been much studied and there is a general need to develop conceptualizations and theories of how individual competences, team competences, and not least, the configuration and flow of these influence the efficiency and effectiveness of organizations.

As previously pointed out, recent research on organizational competences within the strategic management literature has concentrated on core or key competences in firms that distinguish them from other firms (Grønhaug and Nordhaug, 1992; Prahalad and Hamel, 1990, 1991). This is a continuation of earlier conceptual development in the administrative sciences epitomized by such terms as distinctive and specific versus general or nonspecific competences (Selznick, 1957; Becker, 1983; Williamson, 1985). However important, this research suffers from the shortcoming that no links between the macro level and the micro level in organizations have been established. The point of departure is a notion that firms possess certain competences distinguishing them from other firms but no mention is made about how these organizational competences are constituted. Put bluntly, this corresponds to observing that cars are able to run differently because their performances vary, without exploring their idiosyncratic technical components and the configuration of these. In this way, a somewhat abstract picture of competences on the organizational macro level is drawn that offers only a limited intake to our understanding of differences in organizational performance and thus renders an equally limited knowledge basis on which firms can build their behavior. It is evident that such a basis must also include the micro level since the competence base of the firm is an integral part of what we may call its overall organizational competence and, moreover, serves to condition the types of core competences that can possibly emerge in the organization.

Competence Configuration

The way in which employee and team competences are deployed and combined is highly decisive for the prospects of organizational success. Since firms usually have a substantial number of employees and each of these employees normally possess a wide range of different single competences, theoretically these single competences can be combined in an almost infinite number of configurations. However, in practice, the actual tasks of organizational units, teams, and individual employees – and the restricted opportunities to spread individual employees among different units, projects, and teams in order to disseminate the utilization of their various competences – set limits on this number. Still, the number of possible competence configurations will in most cases be very high.

Charts of formal organizational structures show how employees are configurated in the organization. However, since the informal organizational structure frequently deviates substantially from the formal structure – and since employees possess several dissimilar competences that may be applied within different organizational contexts and formal units – we may rather speak of the way in which these competences are configurated. When, for example, employee X placed in organizational unit A uses all her/his time on the job to work in three different project groups involving personnel from organizational units B, C, D, and E, it is not very informative to know that the person works in organizational unit A. It is far more accurate to say that the employee's competences are configurated across a set of formal organizational units. An important point is, moreover, that the employee is usually placed in the three different project groups on the basis of special competences he/she possesses and which are needed in the different groups. Hence, the employee is not actually selected because he/she is person X but because he/she carries the competences f, k, n, and p, one or more of which are needed in the various project groups.

Thus, in our perspective, it is not primarily employees per se that are allocated to different jobs, teams, and units, but the sub-individual units of work-related competences that are carried by them.

In work organizations the available competences are configured on different levels, and for analytical reasons it is fruitful to distinguish between micro, meso, and macro configurations. Each of these levels will be discussed separately.

On the micro level, employee competences are spread on different jobs in the firm's work-system. This is illustrated in Figure 5.1.

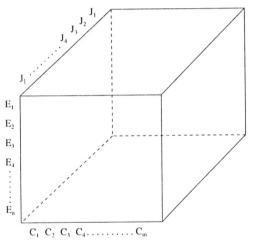

Figure 5.1. The ECJ-Cube

Figure 5.1 is an extension of the competence base that was shown in Figure 4.1. The base has been combined with jobs in the firm to form an Employee/Competence/Job cube. At a given point of time the ECJ-cube provides a representation of how employee competences are deployed within the work-system of the organization. However, the content of the cube is continuously changing, as employees move between jobs, leave, and new employees are recruited.

This micro level perspective on the configuration of competences in organizations is well known as the traditional perspective applied within the human resource management literature and practice. Among other things, it is reflected in the numerous prescriptive statements that firms should make a great effort in careful job analysis and analyses of required incumbent qualifications when filling jobs. Albeit highly important, this perspective is not sufficient in order to grasp the comprehensiveness of firms' configuration of available knowledge and skills. Consequently, it must be supplemented with a meso level and a macro level perspective.

In addition to being distributed on a variety of jobs, single competences are also spread across teams of employees. Although there are individuals who do not belong to any work-team or project-team, most employees usually do. Moreover, many employees located in the same organizational subunit concurrently work within different teams so that their single competences are distributed over two or more teams. Thus, we may speak of the configuration of competences on the meso level in firms.

This configuration is illustrated by the Employee/Competence/Team cube in Figure 5.2.

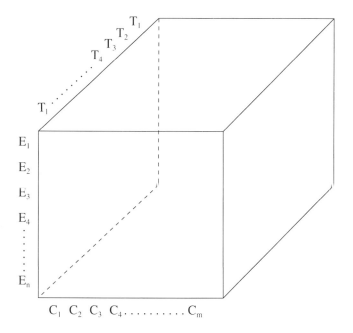

Figure 5.2. The ECT-Cube

This ECT-cube supplements the micro configuration presented above by acknowledging that employees using their competences within one defined job may apply them in two or more team settings. Although useful in regard to recruitment, human resource planning, and compensation purposes, the basic units of jobs have a limited analytical significance since job performance may be appropriated to a number of different group contexts. This is also illustrated by the generally increased attention now being paid to teams and group performance in organizations as well as to project and matrix organizational design. An illustration of the meso configuration of competences is provided by the current tendency within the management literature to focus on executive teams instead of solely on the top manager (cf. Elstad, 1992). The primary entity of analysis, and also to a large degree of modern practice, thus seems to be shifting from the micro to the meso level.

The chart of the firm's organizational structure can be supplemented with a chart showing the distribution of competences within and across formal organizational subunits. However, since the employees who possess the competences also have to be identified if the overview is to make sense, it is necessary to think in three-dimensional terms involving organizational units, employees, and single competences. This is the logic underlying the idea of the macro configuration which is outlined in Figure 5.3.

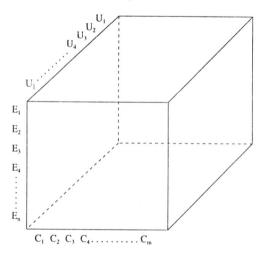

Figure 5.3. The ECU-Cube

The Employee/Competence/Unit cube marks the complexity of any firm's configuration of competences, even in static situations. In principle, the theoretical options for combining single competences represent extremely high numbers, which increase substantially if one adds different work teams under each organizational subunit and project and task groups that gather employees from dissimilar units.

On the other hand, the large theoretical number of deployment opportunities for single competences demonstrates that at the outset firms have generous degrees of freedom as to utilizing their competence bases. It is, moreover, important to note that these degrees are widened when relevant latent competences are detected among the labor force. A recent case that illuminates the reasoning is provided by a Norwegian subsidiary of a French multinational company, Alcatel STK, which has reconfigurated its organization and competence distribution almost completely by applying a zero-budgeting approach. The firm asked the question how the organization would look if it were to start from scratch, and the employees retained during the process were to a large degree assigned to new tasks on the basis of needs in the 'new' organization and the competences they possessed. Besides changing the composition of the competence base through the downsizing, the main result was a comprehensive reconfiguration of the competence base.

However, such reconfiguration occurs less dramatically and more or less continuously in most firms. Kanter (1988) emphasizes the important point that mobility across jobs implies that people rather than formal mechanisms are the principle carriers of information, the principle integrative links between parts of the system. Thereby, communications networks are facilitated, and employees can draw on first-hand knowledge of each other in seeking support. She notes, furthermore, that knowledge about the operations of neighboring functions is transferred through mobility between jobs: "As a set of managers or professionals disperse, they take with them to different parts of the organization their 'intelligence', as well as the potential for the members to draw on each other for support in a variety of new roles. In just a few moves, a group that has worked together is spread around, and each member now has a close colleague in any part of the organization to call on for information or backing" (Kanter,

1988:189). Similarly, Ulrich and Lake (1990) point out that individual competences depend on the structuring of the organization in the sense that communication processes, which include the information flow within the organization, contribute to sustaining such competences. Dealing with the senior management levels, Evans and Doz (1990) indirectly underscore the significance of resources built through competence reconfiguration by noting that multifocalism is facilitated by the interwoven network of contacts created by career mobility and project groups: "Many important environmental alarm bells have been ignored simply because the whistle blower did not have the network, or lacked the influence skills to present his or her case" (Evans and Doz, 1990:236).

The ECU-cube lends itself to a broad array of applications. First, it can be used as a device if the firm wants to apply a portfolio perspective on its competence resources, since the cube allows for a representation of how these are deployed. Second, the cube shows cross-deliveries of competences between organizational units. If these are single business units or profit centers, the firm may choose to introduce an arrangement where units will have to bid for scarce competences in order to channel these to the units that are best able to utilize them economically – in the same way as for financial resources. Many multinational companies have implemented this type of procedure in order to allocate their scarce managerial competence to different subsidiaries (cf. Edström and Lorange, 1986).

In their recent discussion of the absorptive capacity of organizations as to learning from the environment, Cohen and Levinthal (1990:132) provide an illuminating example of the significance of competence configuration: "The firm's absorptive capacity depends on the individuals who stand at the interface of either the firm and the external environment or at the interface between subunits within the firm. That interface function may be diffused across individuals or be quite centralized. When the expertise of most individuals within the organization differs considerably from that of external actors who can provide useful information, some members of the group are likely to assume relatively centralized 'gatekeeping' or 'boundary-spanning' roles".

Viewed in dynamic terms, the ECU-cube will change and, moreover, *change rapidly* due to factors such as organizational

COMPETENCE NETWORKS   123

restructuring, labor turnover and recruitment, and development and detection of new competences. Furthermore, over time single competences will move between different locations in the cube depending on the development of the work system and division of labor. Whereas competence cubes depict the various competence configurations at given points of time, they can also be applied as conceptual tools for the analysis of competence movements within organizations. This leads to the discussion of competence flow.

Competence Flow

The concept of human resource flow has previously been applied by Beer et al. (1984:99; see also Walker, 1992). The authors distinguished between inflow, internal flow, and outflow of such resources in organizations, and applied the flow concept in a way that, from the viewpoint of organizations, makes it synonomous with human capital mobility. In the following, this approach will be supplemented in order to achieve a more subtle categorization of different types of competence flow.

In the context of this chapter, the term competence flow is viewed as consisting of two analytically separable types of competence movement. The first type, competence mobility, which is used in a manner consistent with the approach presented by Beer and associates (1984), is descriptive of changes in the location of competences in organizational space and time as well as competences moving in and out of the firm. The second type of competence flow is far more complex and encompasses learning across dissimilar entities in the organization. Hence, whereas mobility includes changes in the deployment of competences over time, competence transfer embraces the exchanges of competences between colleagues, teams, and organizational subunits in the firm.

Furthermore, instead of letting the formal organizational boundaries of the firm confine the discussion (as done by Beer and associates, 1984), focus will be set on the firm's actual and its potential competence base which extends beyond the boundaries of the organization. As demonstrated in the competence discussion of the base in Chapter 4, the limits of the base do not necessarily correspond to such boundaries since it may include formal applicable competences carried by individuals outside the firm.

Competence Mobility

The competence mobility inside the firm can be defined as the sum of redeployments of employee competences across jobs, teams, and organizational subunits during a given period of time. Stated differently, it reflects the more or less continuous reconfiguration of competence cubes on all the three levels of analysis delineated in the above discussion of competence configuration.

Such redeployments often have a dual rationale. First, the firm wants to utilize its knowledge and skill resources more efficiently by moving them to match changes in tasks. Second, rotating personnel between jobs, teams, and units may in itself be an efficient way of augmenting the competence base, as employees thus acquire broader knowledge and understanding of how the firm functions. In addition to rotation programs across units, development of multiskills provides an example of such efforts. However, as noted by Beer and associates (1984:77/78), the velocity of redeployment is critical. They suggest a curvelinear relationship between such velocity and development of employee competence, implying that slow movement of personnel is likely to result in too few opportunities for employees to broaden their skills and their perspective of the enterprise – hence inhibiting them from developing as generalists. At the same time, it is noted that the type of very rapid movement experienced in swiftly expanding firms can easily lead to individuals'advancing faster than their capacity to develop and demonstrate competences. A consequence may be individual failure and a loss of investment made in competence development and mobility by the organization. The reason is that high flow velocities are more costly, since an employee who has been in a job for a short time is normally not very productive.

However, less rapid advancement can lead employees to question the fairness of the decision-making process in the organization. In addition, the authors point out that high velocity can damage the involved employees' quality of life, arguing that personal stress and higher divorce rates are not uncommon among employees in rapidly growing high-technology companies (Beer et al., 1984:78).

It is worth noting that studies of innovation in organizations have reported that "managers who are broader-gauged, more able to move across specialist boundaries, (and) comfortable working in teams that may include many disciplines are generally more effective in managing change" (Doeringer et al., 1991: 170). In the same vein, Edström and Galbraith (1977) compared the mobility or transfer practices of four multinational firms and found that one of these firms was different from the others by transferring personnel more often, and in large numbers. Moreover, transfers occurred on all organizational levels. This was interpreted as creating a "nervous system" that facilitated both corporate strategic control and the flow of knowledge in the corporation. In this case, the high mobility between organizational subunits generated more efficient communication and increased tolerance across dissimilar units and also a stronger commitment to the overall organizational culture.

Referring to Evans (1975), Evans, Lank and Farquhar (1990:123-124) maintain that a managerial orientation is best developed through mobility across jobs and organizational subunits. Whereas the authority of younger managers is typically based on technical or functional expertise, they later, when cross-functional mobility leads them into posts where they assume responsibility for people with more expertise than themselves, develop the managerial skills and attitudes in "getting results through the expertise of others" which the authors view as indispensible in general management.

Furthermore, the authors argue that experience gained in different geographic regions, functions, and divisions also equip these managers with a broad hands-on feel for their businesses. Similarly Doeringer and associates (1991:189) focus on the generation of flexible and adaptable employees through mobility across jobs and units, noting that new jobs in new fields force employees to develop additional skills, attitudes, and identities.

The influx of new employees is also a part of the firm's competence mobility. This is the traditional way of acquiring knowledge and skills from the external environment. Although recruitment has usually been the sole focus of attention within the human resource management literature, there are several additional and often alternative means of procuring competences from the outside (see Chapter 2). Hiring of consultants and temporary work assistance are common examples. More radical methods are involved when the firm enters into cooperation with other firms in order to exchange valuable competences. These may range from limited collaboration to joint ventures and to competence-based strategic alliances, the frequency of which have increased substantially during the last years. A recent illustration is provided by the cooperation between Apple Computers and Sony in the expanding field of multimedia technology: "Apple has talked extensively about the future of 'multimedia' technology, in which movies, video and graphics stored on CD-ROMs – a version of compact disks – as well as electronic books and other information and entertainment software would be accessible from what is termed a 'nomadic computer'. But integrating the necessary video and communications technologies will require skills in manufacturing and miniaturization that Apple does not possess. ... "We can't compete on the hardware," Michael Spindler, Apple's president, said today in Tokyo. .. "We have to look at the core competencies of different companies. And what we are good at is creating much simplified user interfaces'"(Sanger, 1991).

Conversely, the competence base shrinks through the outflow created when employees die, quit, or are laid off, when the hiring periods of consultants and temporarily hired personnel expire, and when competence-based interorganizational cooperation ceases. Hence, the net effect depends on the influx of new competences, the outflow of existing ones, corrected for changes of the base that stem from competences added or disappearing through internal learning and delearning in the firm.

Competence Transfer

In addition to recruitment of new employees, temporary hiring of competence, and interorganizational cooperation, internal competence development is the main vehicle for organizations to maintain and augment their competence base. The major part of such transfer is made up by exchange of knowledge and skills between employees, which is the most comprehensive type of learning in worklife. Competence transfer embraces two main types of inflow. First, individuals who work for a while in the firm without being employed by it, may pass on competences to its employees. Second, competences can be built through interaction between employees and individuals located outside the boundaries of the organization. Recently, a body of research has emerged that focuses on transfer of competences across organizations (e.g.

Zimmerman, 1982).

Internal competence flows in the form of transfers can be classified according to whether they run between an employee and a work task, between an employee and another employee, or between teams and employees and vice versa. There are also competence flows stretching across organizational units and separate firms (Epple, Argote, and Devadas, 1991). However, since these have to be channelled through employees or teams, they will not be treated as independent flows but viewed as subsumed under the other categories.

Everyone who performs a task does this by applying previously held knowledge and skills that are expected to lead to task accomplishment. Tasks are constituted by some kind of object that is to be influenced, modified, or shaped by the employee (for example, physical material, knowledge, information, customers, clients). Furthermore, in many jobs, some sort of technology or 'tools' in the form of physical equipment, routines, or procedures is necessary in addition to the competence possessed by the person executing the task. Hence, the transfer of competences to tasks can occur directly, as when an employee advises a customer, or indirectly when an employee manipulates an object by applying competence plus technology suitable for such manipulation. In this context, it has to be pointed out that competences and technology are necessary but not sufficient preconditions for successful task performance. The individual must also possess at least the minimum of work motivation which is required to accomplish the task efficiently.

The interpersonal transfer of knowledge and skills occurs in a variety of different ways. In the human resource development and industrial relations literatures, informal on-the-job learning is commonly reckoned to be the most comprehensive type of transfer between employees. Here, learning-by-observing and learning-by-doing dominate, and the advantage emphasized is that the learning is directly connected to the job and the work situation. Thus, the vast bulk of this learning takes place through everyday interaction in the workplace, mentoring, and coaching. Innovation processes in firms provide an illuminating illustration of such learning. New insights and new knowledge are created during intensive processes which are often based on interactive learning between the employees involved (cf. Quinn, 1985).

Yet, this novel knowledge may be difficult or impossible to transfer to others than the few involved: "New experiences are accumulated at a fast pace; the learning curve is steep. The knowledge that resides in the participants in the innovation effort is not yet codified or codifiable for transfer to others. Efforts are very vulnerable to turnover because of the loss of this knowledge and experience. There need to be close linkages and fast communication between all those involved, at every point in time, or the knowledge erodes" (Kanter, 1988: 171).

In addition to the informal, often interactive learning, more formalized modes of transfer are important, such as work-method instruction by peers or superordinates. Besides the exchange between colleagues in the firm, many employees also acquire new competences or strengthen existing ones through interaction with occupational or professional colleagues in external contexts. Examples are professional meetings and conferences, informal contact with colleagues in other organizations, and training provided by external agencies.

Another type of competence transfer takes place between work teams and employees, either individually or in groups. Analytically, oral exchanges can be profitably categorized under interpersonal transfer. However, when the competences of a team are, so to speak, materialized in the form of written material that reflects knowledge and skills, employees may to some degree acquire these by studying the material. In some organizations, project teams before dissolving routinely have to summarize their experiences in order that other teams and individual employees may learn from these experiences, i.e. acquire some of the competences that were developed in the project team. This type of learning is virtually ignored in the human resource development literature and it certainly deserves greater attention.

Finally, learning can occur across organizations, as is often the case in strategic alliances and joint ventures (Lorange and Roos, 1992). In the previous section, competence mobility between cooperating firms in the form of cross-organizational deployment was discussed. Here, the preoccupation is with competence that accumulates from learning across employees and teams in the different cooperating firms. One outcome of interorganizational cooperation which is very difficult or impossible to measure, and hence often remains neglected, is precisely an increments to the firm's internal competence base. If such an increase has occurred, a non-material investment with substantial value for future operations has been made that, if estimated, could significantly alter the explicit economic outcomes of the cooperation. It is therefore reasonable to expect an increasing amount of research on this kind of learning investment in the near future.

An Integrated Framework

Thus far, the notions of competence base, configuration, and flow have been discussed separately. In this section, the purpose is to integrate the three and discuss possible interrelations. An analytical framework depicting the firm as a competence network is shown in Figure 5.4.

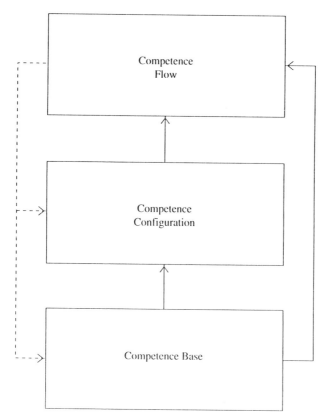

Figure 5.4. An Integrated Framework

The order of the elements of the framework demonstrates a conception that, first, the competence base is considered and thereafter its configuration and the competence flow in the firm. The arrows indicate that the nature of the competence base influences both the way in which it is configurated and the nature of the competence mobility and transfer. For instance, latent competences are of course not configurated because they are unknown, and due to its very nature, tacit competence is far more difficult to transfer between employees than competence that can be easily articulated. Moreover, the feedback arrows imply that the competence flow directly affects the base by determining its composition and size. Furthermore, the configuration of knowledge and skill resources is assumed to have a strong impact on competence flow. This is especially the case with regard to competence transfer between employees, teams, and organizational units, since the configuration largely determines the actual interfaces between these entities.

After having outlined the basic structure of competence networks in organizations, the crucial question about what is gained by applying this new analytical perspective must be raised, that is, what does it offer that the traditional ways of viewing human resources in firms do not?

First, there is a fundamental shift in focus from individual employees as the basic units of analysis to single competences carried by employees and teams. This is already reflected to some degree in practice, illustrated by organizational forms, such as project and matrix structures, that are based upon 'splitting' employees among different assignments based on the competences they possess.

Second, the comprehensive perspective provided by the integration of the competence base, competence configuration, and competence flow opens the way for more holistic managerial approaches to the governing of knowledge and skill resources in firms. For example, competence problems which according to conventional wisdom would be solved by recruiting new personnel, may be solved in alternative ways by analyzing and implementing adjustments in the competence base, configuration, or flow.

Third, a major advantage of the new perspective is that it facilitates a much greater cognitive flexibility in regard to the deployment of human capital. Thinking in terms of the subindividual entities of competences, instead of largely indivisible individuals, creates a much wider array of configurational possibilities and thus offers an extended menu for managerial action. Although this is a more complex approach, it provides a potential to tap more efficiently the competence base by exploring novel combinations and configurations of competences that cannot be uncovered if the focus is solely on the collection of individuals employed.

Fourth, the framework offers a fruitful path for approaching learning in organizations. Whereas the traditional human resource development perspective has been preoccupied with formal employee learning in the form of training, the network perspective allows for far more subtle and precise analyses and planning of competence transfers between employees that occur informally during working hours – without excluding the transfers that occur through training. In relation to research, the framework presented here can be applied to lay bare the webs of partly isolated and partly interwoven knowledge and skill resources in all kinds of organizations. There is, in particular, a need for empirical research on how firms build their competence bases, how they configurate them, and how the bases are utilized. Besides, investigating competence flow both within and between organizations stands out as an important research challenge.

Practitioners may find the framework useful for the planning of human capital provision and may also find that it offers a novel approach to analyzing competence deployment in the organization on the basis of which practical tools tailored to the specific context of the firm can be designed. Furthermore, it provides a perspective that can act as a guide to viewing and treating the organization as a total learning system, designing human resource development systems, and facilitating establishment of readiness for change by trimming the elements of the competence network.

Concluding Comment

In reality, there is little doubt that organizational capabilities to generate and maintain competence bases, configurate them, and design competence flows are among the most important determinants of performance and prospects for future success. Yet, these capabilities have not received much systematic attention, despite the fact that they have been indirectly touched upon in parts of the organizational and human resource management literature. More important, the three capabilities have not been seen as integral components of the organization's overall capacity to perform on the basis of individual and collective action.

The analytical framework marks an endeavor to link the three vital capabilities together, and the ambition is to develop further this analytical perspective and apply it in empirical research on firms as competence systems. Such research may provide valuable contributions also to the world of practice where there is a need for analytical tools that enable management to scrutinize and utilize the available human capital more effectively.

PART III

Training and Learning

Chapter 6

Training Determinants

Introduction

As pointed out in Chapter 1, investments in human capital, especially through personnel training, are considered increasingly important for the success of firms and other organizations as well as for the economic development of geographic regions and countries. Concurrently, growing attention is paid to the division of labor between firms and other work organizations on the one side and markets on the other, epitomized by the distinction between "make" and "buy" decisions.

At the same time, it is common knowledge that some companies invest heavily in developing the competences of their employees through training, whereas other companies do not. However, it is not known what the factors determining these differences are. Since there is no empirical support thus far for drawing conclusions, there is a need to start laying out a theoretical foundation by elaborating propositions about causal forces determining the extent of training and investment in training activities in firms. This is the purpose of this chapter. A second objective is to move one step further by asking what factors determine choices firms make between organizational and market-based solutions in regard to training their employees.

Whereas considerable amounts of research have been devoted to studying education and training as determinants of various outcomes (such as personal income, productivity, and status on the individual level and national income on the country level), very little research has been done on the determinants of the training itself. Only scant attention has been paid to training and training programs as dependent rather than independent variables (Scott and Meyer, 1991). Given the increased focus being set on the significance of human capital investment for the success of firms and other organizations, there is hence a strong need to analyze factors that influence both the extent and types of training in work life.

The discussion in this chapter is limited to the volume or extent of employee training as measured by the annual number of training hours per capita in the firm. We are thus not discussing the amount of monetary investment that is channelled into training, albeit this is in reality probably to a substantial degree correlated with the training volume in firms.

Determinants of Training

In the following, possible determinants of the total volume of employee training financed by firms are discussed. A distinction is drawn between environmental and organizational determinants, depending on whether the factors included reside in the firm's external environment or in the internal organization. Propositions are suggested under each of the two main headings.

Environmental Determinants

Heterogeneity and stability are two classical dimensions of the external environment of organizations (e.g., Thompson, 1967), and it is reasonable to suggest that these dimensions have an impact on organizational needs for employee training. Furthermore, as we assume that firms in general endeavor to cover their objective needs for training, these dimensions are also held to affect the volume of training actually pursued in firms. In heterogeneous environments, employees, and particularly those dealing with external actors, will have to develop broader knowledge bases in order to cope with the external variety the organization is being exposed to. Hence, heterogeneity is asserted to contribute to increasing the amount of training. It may be objected that much of the learning needed to cope with a heterogeneous environment can be achieved through informal learning-by-doing, and in practice this type of learning is probably very frequent. However, it is reasonable to believe that environmental heterogeneity also triggers needs to carry out formal training both for newcomers and current employees, which is intended to mediate knowledge about institutional and political factors connected to different elements in the external environment in order to enable employees to develop behavioral patterns that can match the idiosyncracies of these elements when interacting with them.

The stability of the environment is also essential in this context, as the firm's need to acquire and process knowledge normally clearly increases with decreasing stability. Stated differently, the amount of knowledge required through a given period of time can be viewed as a function of the rate of change in the environment, and this is assumed to influence firms' training volume.

Proposition 1: The more complex the environment of the firm, the larger its training activity.

Proposition 2: The more unstable the environment of the firm, the larger its training activity.

Although analytically valuable, it can be useful to break the comprehensive concept of "environment" down into specified elements. Two crucial elements are the product markets the firm operates within and the labor markets it depends upon for the recruitment of manpower.

Since competition that puts strong demands on product quality requires a knowledgeable and skillful work force, it can be assumed that such competition forces firms to make sustained efforts in training their employees. Similarly, if the competition is characterized by a pressure to innovate through continuous product development, the competences of employees will in general have to be updated very frequently. Furthermore, it is asserted that when there are heavy elements of personal service attached to the marketing of the products, firms are required to train many of their employees intensively in handling customers and their varying needs on the basis of both thorough product knowledge and, not the least, skills in mastering interpersonal relations. Hence, it is assumed that the presence of service elements contributes to heightened training activity.

With regard to the labor market, there seems to be a tendency that the competition for highly qualified employees in many businesses is stiffening. As a consequence, many firms view their efforts in developing human competence also as a way of increasing their attractiveness to potential entrants from the external labor market. Several studies have demonstrated that highly qualified individuals put great emphasis on the prospects of personal and professional development when choosing employer (e.g., Devanna, 1983; Northrup and Malin, 1986:76) and there is no reason to expect that this propensity will diminish in the near future.

Proposition 3: The more the competition in the firm's product markets is based upon product quality, the larger its training activity.

Proposition 4: The more the competition in the firm's product markets is based upon product innovation, the larger its training activity.

Proposition 5: The more the product markets in which the firm operates are characterized by competition on the basis of service elements, the larger its training activity.

Proposition 6: The tougher the competition on the demand side of the labor markets the firm recruits from, the larger its training activity.

Regardless of the nature of the competition in product markets, the speed of technological development within the industry is held to stimulate firms' employee training. In the same way as instability in the environment in general is supposed to increase the amount of training, swift technological changes make it necessary to update existing competences and generate new ones suitable for handling novel technology.

Proposition 7: The more rapid the pace of technological change in the industry the firm operates within, the larger its training activity.

Organizational Determinants

Ceteris paribus, the economic situation of the firm is likely to influence its spendings on human resource development and thereby also its training activity. Moreover, there is reason to surmise that this effect is substantial since spendings on training are not bound for a long time in the same way as are outlays on physical investments, but can be expanded and contracted based on the financial solidity and cash flow in different periods.

Proposition 8: The more profitable the firm, the larger its training activity.

Proposition 9: The larger the cash reserves of the firm, the larger its training activity.

The relationship between organizational design and training needs and amounts is a very complicated one. However, it seems that a rather clear picture may be suggested in respect to the centralization/decentralization dichotomy, along the following lines: If an organization is very centralized when it comes to decision-making, the competences needed for such decision-making can be restricted to relatively few persons. However, if that organization is decentralized, the number of decision-makers will be increased (often substantially) and so will the requirement for competences necessary for making decisions. Then, a need for additional training related to management and decision-making is generated (cf. Scott and Meyer, 1991:311), and to the degree that firms behave rationally in terms of aligning their organizational structure with their employees' competence, they will seek to cover these needs. Put differently, distributed responsibility for decision-making demands both more knowledge and more diffused knowledge than does concentrated responsibility for decision-making.

Proposition 10: The more decentralized the decision-making in the firm, the larger its training activity.

So far, the discussion has focused on factors that are expected to have an impact on the objective needs for employee training in firms and thereby also on the actual amount of training. However, there also exists an important class of assumed determinants that do not necessarily have the property of contributing to creating *organizational needs* for human resource development, but that may influence training via predominantly *individual needs* or *group needs* among employees. In some cases, these needs may coincide with organizational needs, but often they do not. A distinction can be drawn between individual and group needs based on role assignments on the one hand and pressure to fulfill personal competence desires for on the other. In both cases, the behavior in relation to training and other types of human resource development is guided by self-interest seeking. However, in the first case this self-interest seeking follows from the work assignment itself (i.e., making a career by performing the job well) or from the institutional location within the organization, whereas in the second case it follows from a desire to invest in one's own career, regardless of employer. Examples of the former are human resource management and development professionals whose careers are often directly linked to their degree of success in generating competences in the organization. Examples of the latter are general managers who want to make the firm to invest in their firm nonspecific competences which they later can utilize regardless of who the employer is.

One of the duties of human resource development personnel is precisely to facilitate and carry out training for employees. Hence, the actual amount of training may be regarded as a success criterion for this type of personnel, and to the degree that this is the case, they will have an interest in expanding training budgets and activities. Since quality measures are intricate to obtain, one easily resorts to quantitative measures as a foundation for legitimizing this type of work.

Proposition 11: In firms having a Human Resource Development Department, the training activity is larger than in firms without such a department.

The demographic structure of the firm may have a profound impact on the amount of training that is being arranged. Especially important aspects of firm demography in this context are the composition of the work force with regard to age and education, as well as the proportions of professionals and managers in the organization.

First, there is reason to believe that the higher the proportion of employees over fifty years of age, the lower the training activity in the firm. The rationale for this proposition is the fact that, according to several studies in different countries, participation in adult education and personnel training is considerably lower for age groups above this age than for younger groups of people (cf. Cross, 1982).

Second, as research has shown that participation in training increases with level of formal education (for overview, see Cross, 1982 and Nordhaug, 1991a), a similar proposition can be launched with regard to the aggregate level of education in the firm, for example indicated by the average years of higher education taken by employees.

Third, following the same logic, it can be expected that professionals and managers in general demand more training than people from other occupational groups, such as unskilled, low-skilled, and skilled workers, and personnel in non-managerial functions. One of the reasons is that much of the training taken by these individuals is clearly firm nonspecific and thus represents a private future career investment financed by the current employer, notwithstanding the fact that general competences can be carried across employers. This probably applies particularly to middle-level managers who still have opportunities for upward mobility, whereas this is often not the case for top managers who, in addition, normally do not have much time for attending training. Hence, it is proposed that the density of middle-level managers in the organization tends to expand its training activity.

Proposition 12: The higher the proportion of employees above fifty years of age in the firm, the smaller its training activity.

Proposition 13: The higher the aggregate level of formal education in the firm, the larger its training activity.

Proposition 14: The higher the proportion of professionals in the firm, the larger its training activity.

Proposition 15: The higher the proportion of middle-level managers relative to the total employment in the firm, the larger its training activity.

In addition to the structural and demographic determinants suggested above, aspects of the organizational culture of firms have to be taken into consideration. Probably most important among these is the firm's tradition when it regards learning and training. It seems likely that firms with strong traditions in this field will tend to continue having more training than firms with weaker traditions.

Proposition 16: The stronger the firm's tradition for emphasizing learning among employees, the larger its training activity.

Another cultural aspect concerns the prevalent leadership style, and in particular the degree to which this is participative in the sense of encouraging codetermination in decision-making processes. As it is reasonable that broad employee participation in such processes requires a certain level of competence among the personnel to be successful, and that such competence to some degree can be built through training, it is anticipated that participative leadership styles contribute to increasing the amount of training activities in the firm.

Proposition 17: The more participative the leadership style among managers in the firm, the larger its training activity.

Values held by managers and other personnel are at the core of firms' organizational cultures. In this context, values regarding learning and innovation are especially relevant. As noted by Scott and Meyer (1991:298), institutional processes operate to diffuse beliefs in the desirability of training so that, increasingly, over time, the value of training in modern organizations is taken for granted: "Rules and practices supporting training have become value-laden and widely accepted. More specific lines of argument are ensconced as ideologies in modern organizational belief and practice. As such belief diffuse, training spreads throughout organizations over and above the impact of specific causal factors characteristic of particular organizational settings".

Proposition 18: The higher the value attached to innovation in the firm, the larger its training activity

The nature of the compensation and incentive system may often serve to hamper or promote employee training. A special and clear case is constituted by competence-based incentive systems, where individual compensation is determined completely or partially by the "competence credits" each employee holds. An example is Norwegian banks, where a large number employees, while staying within the same job, have increased their salaries after having completed higher levels of formal education offered by the Norwegian Banking Academy. Then, there will easily be a strong pressure from employees toward obtaining more formal training, a demand for training that in fact is normally one of the main goals behind implementing this kind of the incentive system.

Proposition 19: In firms practicing competence-based incentives systems, the training activity is larger than in firms which do not practice such systems.

Finally, aspects of the status of competences in the firm may have a considerable effect on how much training it carries out. Essential in this context is the longevity of the knowledge and skills carried by employees.

Naturally, it can be assumed that the shorter the expected life-cycle of these, the higher the amount of training needed to build new competences that can substitute the ones that become obsolete.

Proposition 20: The shorter the life-cycle of employee competences in the firm, the larger its training activity.

Internal and External Training

An important question relates to how employee training is organized, i.e. what does the specific division of labor within the world of training look like and, moreover, what are the determinants of firms' choices between pursuing in-house training or providing training through markets. The purpose of this section is to contrast in-house training with training offered by external educational providers. Economic and political factors which are held to influence choices organizations make between the two main ways of developing competence through training will be discussed. Moreover, propositions about the relations between assumed determinants and the external/internal training ratio (later called the E/I-ratio), i.e. the relative volume of the two types, are elaborated. Before that, we shall provide a background for the proceeding discussion by delineating aspects of the respective idiosyncracies of internal and external training and related dissimilarities that are relevant in the context of this section.

The research literature contains different definitions of internal and external training. Some authors have emphasized the question of who the participants in the training are. Given that only employees from the same organization enroll in a course program, the personnel training has been regarded as internal. If the participants come from different companies, courses are conceived of as external. Others have defined internal training as educational activities arranged by the firm itself and external training as activities that are arranged for the firm by others (Gooderham, 1985:4).

In the subsequent discussion, the term internal training (being synonymous with in-house training) is understood as educational activities that are planned and arranged predominantly by personnel employed in the firm and that only attract participants who are employed in the firm. External training activities, on the other hand, are arranged and carried out by others, for example consultants and training firms, business associations, and educational institutions.

The main difference between internal and external training relates to their respective degrees of market exposure. In-house educational activities are results chiefly of processes within single organizations. External training manifests itself primarily as a consequence of adjustments between supply and demand in the market for employee training, often through negotiations about price and content. These adjustments are preceded or accompanied by internal organizational processes both within the buying and selling organizations.

Thus, there are different processes through which the two types of personnel training are generated. In reality, however, the borderlines may be diffuse. One may, for example, talk about internal course markets when training departments function as autonomous profit centers in the firm.

Conditions that are expected to affect choices organizations make between internal and external personnel training will now be discussed. The presentation includes economic and political determinants of such choices.

However, before proceeding with the discussion of determinants of firms' choices between internal and external training, there is a need to clarify the concept of E/I-ratio, as previously introduced, by operationalizing it.

There are several possible ways of approaching this. The amounts of training in the fraction may be thought of in terms of number of employees participating, number of courses, number of hours annually, and the direct and indirect costs associated with the two types of training. We shall use the product of the number of employees participating and the number of hours spent by each of them in training. Hence, we obtain a measure of the total number of employee-hours spent. This is held to be a good indicator of costs as well, since the indirect costs of compensation paid to employees during training in most firms is the major single element in the total training costs.

Determinants of Training Choice

We shall start by discussing the influence of economic factors on firms' choices between internal and external training. Intuitively, one might assume that firms choose to organize training in ways that seek to minimize costs. However, this is too simple an explanation, although attempts at minimizing costs in reality probably occur very frequently. Viewing personnel training as a process through which competence is being built, it is nevertheless too narrow to concentrate solely on the amount of resource input. Equally important is the output that is achieved and, most essential, the relationship between resources used and resources generated. In practice, however, the main problem remains that of quantifying economic effects of training activities. Applications of cost-benefit analyses have been relatively rare (for an overview, see Blomberg, 1989; cf. also Cascio, 1987; Spencer, 1986). Nonetheless, we will assume that estimates of the cost-effectiveness of alternative educational and training projects are frequently being made, even though these are not necessarily based on quantitative information. When asked what they emphasize most heavily when choosing between dissimilar projects, HRD- and HRM-managers often respond by pointing to price and quality. The former directly influences the company's cost side, while the rather vague notion of quality is most commonly understood as an ex ante estimate of the expected benefits from training activities. If explicit quantitative assessments of anticipated cost-effectiveness are not carried out, we will assume that at least ex ante judgments of a less formalized nature are made. Concentrating solely on costs, and given that the firm has developed its own internal training system, it would seem favorable to have a low E/I-ratio. Two advantages of internal courses are frequently emphasized by practitioners. First, they are regarded as being considerably less expensive than external training. The course itself usually becomes less costly, and travelling and accommodation costs are not incurred. Second, internal courses can often be timed more flexibly than external courses in relation to fluctuations in actual work loads. Periods with low utilization of production capacity can be utilized to train employees without reducing the productivity. Moreover, firms that have made investments in training-staff and facilities are faced with an imperative toward utilizing these investments by maintaining a high proportion of internal training relative to external training. Considerable parts of such investments, particularly in the human resource development staff, are completely or partially irreversible, at least in the short run.[1]

Proposition 21: The more the firm has invested in training staff and educational facilities relative to its total training costs, the lower its E/I-ratio.

The size of the firm will, in most cases, determine whether it is economically most rational to carry out in-house training or buy training from external providers. Extensive internal training requires human resource development professionals, as the firm must then possess a certain administrative and pedagogic capacity within its boundaries. Establishing such incumbencies will usually not be rational for firms that are small or have modest needs for competence development amongst its labor force.

Proposition 22: The larger the size of the firm, the lower its E/I-ratio.

The presence and strength of internal labor markets in firms, are economic variables that will frequently influence the training policy. Such internal markets are characterized by a need for long-term retainment of employees due to the considerable sunk cost investments that have been made in order to recruit and train them. There is, thus, a stronger need to socialize employees and to create sustained commitment than is the case in firms without internal labor markets. With regard to training, this can normally only be done through internal training activities arranged by other employees who know the culture, values, and norms of the firm and who are hence capable of transmitting these to newcomers and other employees. It is, therefore, reasonable to assume a positive relationship between internal labor markets in firms and the proportion of internal training and, moreover, that this relationship is stronger the more developed is the internal labor market in terms of promotions from within and reliance upon socialization as a control mechanism.

Proposition 23: Firms without an internal labor market have a higher E/I-ratio than firms with an internal labor market.

Proposition 24: The more developed the internal labor market in firms with such markets, the lower their E/I-ratio.

Furthermore, an important economic determinant pertains to the type of employee competences that the firm wants to develop. In this context, the distinction between firm-specific and general or firm-nonspecific competences, as originally developed in human capital theory (Becker, 1975), is particularly relevant. Whereas the former can be used in one firm only, the latter comprises knowledge and skills that can be utilized in several firms.

With regard to generation of firm-specific competences through training, firms, of course, have no choice between internally or externally provided courses. They must be developed in-house, although it is theoretically possible to imagine borderline cases, such as externally provided courses that are intended to uncover implicit elements in the organizational culture in order to make employees more conscious about their own organization. We can thus conclude that when work organizations want to generate firm-specific competences, internal training arrangements must normally be set up.

If, on the other hand, the organization wants to increase its supplies of firm-nonspecific competences, it is reasonable to assume that in most cases training services will commonly be obtained from external providers. It is only in relation to generation of this type of competences that cooperation with schools and universities as well as with other external providers is relevant. Let us give two illustrations of this:

In at least two cases the nature of the firm's strategy will easily affect its combination of external and internal personnel training. First, if the strategy implies entry into new industries where the firm has not operated before, and this reorientation is to be implemented without changing the current labor force, there will be a need for obtaining new industry-specific, firm-nonspecific competences. As these cannot be generated by the firm itself, they will have to be provided by external training agencies capable of transmitting relevant industry-specific knowledge and skills. Second, when firms decide to go international by establishing subsidiaries in foreign countries headed by home-country nationals, there is a need to provide these managers with firm-nonspecific knowledge about the specifics of the countries in question. This usually has to be obtained through external providers of such training. However, after a period of time, much of this training can be carried out internally.

Proposition 25: The more the firm wants to develop firm-specific relative to firm-nonspecific competences among its employees, the lower its E/I-ratio.

In general, due to their size and substantial number of educated personnel possessing firm-nonspecific competences, some firms have the capacity to arrange in-house training that transmits such competences also. For example, apprenticeship arrangements are usually set up partly in order to transfer general competences. Nevertheless, we expect that this is the exception rather than the rule.

The last proposition could also be substantiated on the grounds of transaction cost theory as developed within the New Institutional Economics. Here, transactions rather than individuals or firms, are the basic unit of analysis. All costs that are not directly appropriable to the production of goods and services are defined as transaction costs. The main assumption is that companies acting under bounded, intentional rationality seek to organize their activities in ways so that transaction costs are minimized (Williamson, 1981; 1985).

In this perspective, the extent to which specific activities are organized through markets or internally in the organization depends on the capacity of each arrangement to minimize transaction costs. For the individual firm this pertains to the need to create "efficient boundaries" between the organization and its environment (Ouchi, 1980; Williamson, 1985). Efficient boundaries are formed by exploring which tasks are best solved in the organization ("make") and which are best solved through markets ("buy"). When the required firm specificity of assets or services is high, it will generally be most efficient to provide or develop assets within the organization (Williamson, 1981).

In addition to economic factors, internal political conditions in firms are likely to affect the selection of educational activities and distributions of human resource development among groups of employees as well as across different organizational subunits. Political factors may, hence, pose a strong influence on the choice between internal and external training. Following the classical definition of politics – "who gets what, when, and how?" (Lasswell, 1936) – the question of who receives which training, when, and how is largely a matter of internal power relations.

The actual position and status of human resource management and development departments within the firm may have a great impact on the amount, distribution, and organization of competence development. This position varies strongly across firms. Nevertheless, a general impression is that the status of human resource development units in firms is still relatively low in many countries: "Training departments do not appear to be held in universal high regard, and the level of importance ascribed to training does not carry through to attention to the requests of training directors" (Olson, 1986:33).

At the same time, we would expect that training-professionals, like other professional groups, make deliberate attempts to improve their position and enhance their status by gaining increased influence and acquiring more resources. Such behavior is likely to affect the actual mix of internal and external training. In close cooperation with line managers, human resource managers are in most companies responsible for the planning and execution of both types of training. Moreover, it is worth noting that pursual of internal training often represents the ultimate legitimization of the company's investments in training staff and other human resource development professionals as well as related educational facilities. Usually, this personnel have extensive tasks with regard to planning, organizing, arranging, and teaching courses and training programs carried out by the company itself. Put differently, the purpose of having a training staff is partly to reduce the costs of developing competence and partly to benefit from other advantages of internal training compared to externally provided courses.

Once a training staff is employed, we will expect that it works toward increasing the extent and prestige of the firm's human resource development functions. Thus, an important political determinant of choices between making or buying training is the training staff's capability to legitimize their activities and gain increased power and influence. Because effects of the activities are often very complicated or impossible to estimate, training personnel will probably be inclined to assess their own degree of success in terms of the amount of *input* into training, such as total spendings, number of courses, number of participants, or number of training hours. We will further assume that this especially applies to internal training due to the fact that it is more strongly controlled by the firm's human resource development staff than is external training. There is reason to believe that, all other things being equal, the existence of positions related to training tends to increase the total amount of training and, not least, the proportion of internal training – and the more so the larger the number of such positions.

Proposition 26: The stronger the internal status and power position of human resource management and development staff in the firm, the lower its E/I-ratio.

The tendency to increase the proportion of internal courses may be counteracted by internal pressure groups that have a special interest in pursuing human resource development activities through external training. Among these, professionals and managers are the most important.

In general, professionals are assumed to feel a considerable identification and loyalty with their professional network, often at the expense of their commitment to the organization that employs them (Blau and Scott, 1963: 60-74; Scott, 1987). They frequently adhere to norms and rules which are specific to the profession or semi-profession. A widespread norm is that promotion of individual professional development within the particular boundaries of the profession is necessary and desirable for its members. Even though this will often conflict with the firm's real needs for competence development, strong professional groups may require and succeed in getting expensive external training of this nature. Among other things, this can be due to internal knowledge monopolies implying exclusive rights to define individual needs for professional development regardless of organizational needs (cf. Nordhaug, 1991b).

Proposition 27: The larger the proportion of professionals in the firm's labor force, the higher its E/I-ratio.

From the point of view of line- and staff-managers, individually oriented programs in management training and development provided by external agencies are often perceived as far more prestigious and personally rewarding than similar internal programs. For this reason alone, many managers will be interested in participating at the firm's expense. In addition, and far more important, such programs most often mediate general knowledge and skills as opposed to firm specific competences. Consequently, from the individual managers' point of view, completion of such programs may constitute a substantial gratis investment in his/her personal career prospects, independent of who the future employer will be.

Proposition 28: The larger the proportion of managers in the firm's labor force, the larger its E/I-ratio.

However, it is not only the mere number of managers that is relevant but also their actual preferences with regard to pursuing external or internal management training. In general, it is reasonable to assume that particularly higher-level managers are interested in external training, because this is often their only possible way of obtaining added opportunities of upward mobility. Whereas lower-level managers can often advance their career by augmenting their firm-specific competence, especially if they work within internal labor markets, higher-level managers often have much of their future career potential outside the current organization of employment, i.e. in external labor markets for managers.

Proposition 29: The larger the proportion of higher-level managers relative to the total number of managers in the firm, the higher its E/I-ratio.

It should be pointed out that, although there are obvious gains for the participating managers, external management training is not necessarily without benefits for the firm. Nevertheless, what the firm invests in human capital can later, at least partially, be lost when managers change employer.

In summary, the choices between arranging training in-house or buying it from external providers are held to be affected by political pressure exerted by various internal interest groups.

Concluding Comment

In reality, some of the determinants of training and the mix of internal and external training proposed in this chapter, are likely to be interrelated, and their relative strength may vary considerably from firm to firm. It is, furthermore, reasonable to assert that all the suggested determinants are simultaneously active in any sizable work organization. In other words, we are talking about a complex web of determinants of decisions about firms' provision of the two principal forms of personnel training. The interesting question is, then, under what conditions different combinations of determinants are present and to what degree. This remains open to empirical research. Moreover, an important challenge is to specify different types of determinants that are active, and to what degree, for dissimilar types of training, for example according to whether the target groups are top executives, managers, skilled personnel or unskilled employees.

There is a need both to undertake case-studies of antecedents of decisions related to training and to conduct survey research. The former is necessary in order to generate added knowledge about the groups of determinants delineated in this paper and, eventually, to uncover other groups of determinants as well. When such knowledge has been obtained, survey research on samples of firms can be pursued that may allow for an assessment of the absolute and relative impact of different groups of determinants and that may produce results which are generalizable across firms.

Given the increasing weight on competence development both on the levels of nations and work organizations, more research is needed to produce knowledge about organizational behavior as to the choice between internal administrative solutions and external market solutions in regard to employee training and other competence development. Empirical testing of the propositions suggested in this article, will be a step in that direction. In addition, there is a need to study and compare the effects of the two main types of training in order to indicate their relative efficiency as to the creation of individual and organizational competences.

Note

[1]   Given that the firm exceeds a certain size in terms of employment, turning from using the market to pursuing the training within the organization does not create serious problems, although investments are usually required. On the other hand, once investments in training staff and facilities have been made, it is far more unlikely that companies will return to using the market if competence needs shift from being firm-specific to firm-nonspecific. We will therefore assume that there is mainly a unidirectional relationship in this context, i.e. from market to organization. Expressed differently, it can be assumed that internalization of training appears more frequently than externalization, i.e. sizeable firms more frequently turn from buying external training to carrying out internal training than vice versa.

Chapter 7

Individual Training Rewards

Introduction[1]

Personnel training is a cornerstone in the human resource development systems of most organizations. The extent to which training actually contributes to generating individual rewards has, however, been virtually absent on the research agenda. Nevertheless, this is an important question. As many organizations are confronted with rapid changes in both their external and internal environment, personnel training becomes increasingly vital for developing and maintaining adaptability to changing conditions. If employees who participate in training experience their participation as rewarding, we will assume that they are more inclined to continue participating than if rewards are not perceived. In that way, participation in training may be self-reinforcing.

The point of departure in this chapter is hence an assumption that competence development in worklife may have a substantial rewarding potential and thereby be an implicit part of reward systems in work organizations. We shall uncover experienced rewards from going through training for a sample of former participants. A study of individual outcomes from personnel training is presented and these outcomes are then related to reward systems in work organizations. Focus is set on positive outcomes or benefits as perceived by participants in personnel training.

Separate analyses of the subsamples of male and female participants will also be presented. Furthermore, organizational implications are outlined and discussed.

Background

The structuring of substantial parts of the human resource management and development literature is a reflection of how the field is conceptualized in practical life. Thus, most textbooks distinguish between *activities*, or *functions* such as human resource planning, recruitment and selection, compensation and benefits, job analysis, career planning, performance appraisal, and labor relations.[2] Such classifications may serve practical purposes as well as the need for simplification in introductory courses, and thus far they constitute the traditional foundation of the field of human resource management. However, one of the most serious shortcomings of the practically oriented conceptualizations is that important *interactions* between various parts of the field are ignored. One easily gets the impression that as long as the many different and seemingly separable activities are pursued efficiently, then the organization's overall human resource management systems will by necessity also operate successfully. Thus, possible synergies as well as trade-offs between different activities or subfields are neglected.

In line with this thinking, we shall call attention to and explore aspects of the intersection between personnel training and related individual rewards in the form of training benefits.

Traditionally, training has been treated as a transmitter primarily of work-related competences (see, e.g. Walker, 1981:265). However, what are considered competences from an organizational point of view are likely to be conceived of as rewards from an individual standpoint, because most employees are held to value increases of personal knowledge, skills, and abilities. Hence, what on the organizational level is regarded as intended effects of training, on the level of individuals is largely assumed to have desirable personal benefits as their counterpart. Moreover, employees' expectations as to what benefits they will gain from participating are assumed to influence considerably their readiness to participate in courses. Stated differently, one of the questions we ask concerns the degree to which participation in personnel training may reinforce itself. Such reinforcement will be crucial particularly in organizations which are exposed to swift internal and external change and therefore need to institutionalize recurrent training.

Empirical Analysis

Our data have been gathered through a survey conducted by the Central Bureau of Statistics in Norway. The collection of data was based on a questionnaire about participation in adult education and personnel training.

It is important to point out that the survey was not especially designed for the purpose of the present study. Nevertheless, these data have been utilized because they represent the best available material and because they provide a basis for pursuing an exploratory study.

Data and Method

The total sample consisted of 4,338 respondents and was selected so as to be representative of the adult Norwegian population. During a year 810 persons (both employed and unemployed) had participated in some kind of adult education, whereas 379 employees had participated in personnel training. Respondents who had participated in both training and other types of adult education were excluded from the sample because it is impossible to distinguish between effects from different types of adult education in the data. We were thus left with a subsample of 299 respondents who had participated in firm-level training.

In the survey, respondents were asked whether their participation in personnel training had contributed to creating selected outcomes or not. We are thus working with dichotomous self-report data and the respondents were asked to indicate if participation in their latest course had led to the following consequences: Change of job, assignment of more interesting work tasks, job promotion, increased autonomy in the job, improved ability to participate in voluntary organizations, new assignments in voluntary organi-zations, increased in learning more in general, increased interest in the subjects of the course, increased readiness to participate in training, self-actualization, increased self-confidence, and new friends among the participants.

There are also other limitations in the data. The fact that only two response alternatives were present implies that the variance of the variables becomes restricted compared to the use of an ordinal scale of measurement had been used. Furthermore, self-report data of the present type may suffer from several shortcomings that may lead to measurement errors. First, the respondents' memory about which outcomes they really have perceived may be inaccurate. Second, the fact that participants invest time and effort in training may make them more inclined to report positive effects than non-effects, i.e. an ex post rationalization concerning outcomes. Third, to the degree that participants had high expectations about outcomes before the training, they may have tended to adjust the perceived outcomes in accordance with their initial expectations in order to avoid cognitive dissonance.

Moreover, it is important to note that the analysis of individual outcomes remains within an explorative phase. Consequently, the danger of selection bias as to the set of outcome variables in relation to a theoretical universe of variables should be kept in mind. For example, economic and many types of work-related outcomes were not included in the questionnaire. It should thus be kept in mind that our set of outcome variables is limited and will need to be supplemented in future research.

We shall use factor analysis in the exploration of underlying dimensions of training benefits. This method has been chosen because we want to see if positive relationships between subsets of outcome variables in the survey can be explained by the existence of a small number of hypothetical variables (cf. Kim and Mueller 1978a:9). Both exploratory and confirmatory factor analysis may be applied for this purpose. Confirmatory factor analysis requires that one has some a priori notions about possible underlying dimensions or factors in the data. However, as the amount of research in this field is small and as the data are secondary, exploratory factor analysis is considered the most appropriate method in our context. We do not have any reasons to assume how many underlying dimensions there are for the data. Therefore, exploratory factor analysis is applied in order to ascertain the minimum of hypothetical factors that can account for the observed covariation between the outcome variables.

Reported Benefits

We shall first present the participants' reports of selected types of benefits from their training. The percentages of participants who reported to have experienced selected benefits are presented in Table 7.1.

Table 7.1. Reported Benefits from Training.

Type of Benefit	Percentage	(n)
Job change	5	(279)
More interesting work tasks	28	(277)
Promotion	12	(274)
More autonomous work	18	(275)
Improved ability to participate in non-work organizations	12	(275)
New assignments in non-work organizations	2	(273)
Increased interest in learning more in general	51	(273)
Increased interest in the subjects of the course	72	(283)
Increased desire to participate in training	57	(276)
Self-actualization	65	(283)
Increased selv-confidence	42	(274)
New friends amongst the participants	40	(277)

n = 263

Benefits related to interest in continued training and learning, as well as self-actualization, are the most frequently reported. It is, perhaps, especially interesting to observe the degree to which participation creates motivation to continue participating in training. This result supports Bergsten's (1977:127) finding that persons who had previously participated in adult education were also more inclined to do so in the future than persons who had never participated.

Almost two thirds of the respondents reported that they had experienced self-actualization as a result of their latest course. This result is consistent with findings within leisure-related adult education and general upper secondary education for adults respectively (Nordhaug, 1985).

Numerous research reports have concluded that education contributes to creating increased self-confidence (see, e.g., Hernes and Knudsen, 1976, for a Norwegian overview). Most of this research has, however, concentrated on effects of relatively large amounts of education, i.e. formal education being pursued full-time and spanning years. The result in Table 7.1 indicates that even small amounts of education or training contribute to enhancing the self-confidence of many participants. This effect was experienced by 42 per cent of the respondents. In an identical survey, which was pursued in 1978, the corresponding rate was 41 per cent (Nordhaug, 1982). Furthermore, it is interesting to note that a North American study of anticipated benefits from participation in adult education reported that 41 per cent of the respondents expected to increase their self-confidence by attending courses (Tough, Abbey, and Orton, 1979).

A previous study showed that ".. participation in adult education strongly increases with increased self-confidence..", when self-confidence was defined as the feeling of being able to influence what happens to oneself (Knudsen and Skaalvik, 1979:54). It was found that those who are recruited to courses on the whole have considerably higher self-confidence than non-participants. We have indicated that training leads to additional self-confidence for many participants, which suggest that it contributes to widening inequalities in the amount of self-confidence between employees who participate in training and employees who do not.

From the results, it can furthermore be concluded that personnel training is to some extent a channel of occupational and social mobility. One eighth of the participants (12 per cent) reported promotion as a consequence, one fourth (28 per cent) more interesting work tasks, and 18 per cent reported that they had obtained greater autonomy in their work situation as a consequence of their latest course. These percentages are not high when taking into account the nature of the survey, and they should therefore be carefully interpreted. Nevertheless, the findings *indicate* that previous participation in personnel training in some companies is probably being used as a screening device when various rewards are distributed. To the degree that internal labor markets will expand in the future, this screening function is likely to become increasingly important.

Previous research has shown that leisure-related adult education transmits to participants certain political outcomes (Nordhaug, 1982). The results here indicate that this is to a modest degree the case with personnel training as well. We found that 12 per cent felt they had improved their ability to participate in non-work organizations as a consequence of the training. We have not investigated aspects of the training which contribute to this creation of political outcome. It seems reasonable to assume, however, that it may be partly a result of the social training and the transmission of knowledge and self-confidence through the learning process.

Correlations

We shall examine bivariate correlations between the different kinds of individual benefits in order to obtain an impression of the degree to which they are interrelated. We may thereby get a preliminary indication of potential groupings of variables that may be connected to unobserved underlying dimensions. The product moment correlation matrix (Pearson's r) is shown in Table 7.2. As there was no reason to assume a priori negative correlations between the types of benefits, a one-tailed t-test was applied to test the statistical significance of coefficients.

Job change is generally weakly correlated with the other variables, although five of the correlations are statistically significant. Promotion is substantially correlated with more interesting work tasks (.47) and more autonomous work (.47). There is also a considerable intercorrelation between these two variables. A coefficient of .52 indicates that getting a more autonomous work situation contributes to creating a more

Table 7.2. *Correlation Matrix*
  *Means, Standard Deviations, and Intercorrelations for All Variables**

Variables	Means	SD	1	2	3	4	5	6	7	8	9	10	11	12
1. Job change	0.05	0.14		.25[a]	.15[a]	.18[a]	.01	.02	.02	-.05	.11[a]	.15[a]	-.03	.08
2. Promotion	0.12	0.33			.47[a]	.47[a]	.15[a]	.21[a]	.13[a]	.07	.18[a]	.12[a]	.02	.14[a]
3. More interesting work tasks	0.28	0.45				.52[a]	.12[a]	.14[a]	.15[a]	.20[a]	.20[a]	.12[a]	.02	.21[a]
4. More autonomous work	0.18	0.39					.14[a]	.25[a]	.12[a]	.07	.32[1]	.17[a]	.19[a]	.23[a]
5. Increased readiness to participate in training	0.57	0.50						.50[a]	.31[a]	.32[a]	.26[a]	.21[a]	.08	.16[a]
6. Increased interest in learning more in general	0.51	0.49							.40[a]	.31[a]	.26[a]	.22[a]	.05	.16[a]
7. Increased interest in the subjects	0.72	0.45								.32[a]	.28[a]	.15[a]	-.07	.19[a]
8. Self-actualization	0.65	0.48									.45[a]	.22[a]	.06	.27[a]
9. Increased self-confidence	0.42	0.49										.27[a]	.08	.31[a]
10. Improved ability to participate in organization	0.12	0.31											.19[a]	.25[a]
11. New assignments in non-work organizations	0.02	0.11												.09
12. New friends among the participants	0.40	0.49												

[a] Statistically significant at $p < .05$, one-tailed t-test.

interesting job or vice versa. It is, furthermore, modestly related to an increase in self-confidence, as the intercorrelation here was shown to be .32. It seems as if we may here have a benefit dimension that is related to work and career.

Outcomes related to interest in further training and learning are positively intercorrelated, and to a varying degree, with coefficients ranging from .31 to .50. This makes it possible that we will find an underlying benefit dimension related to further learning.

As could have been expected, self-actualization is most strongly correlated with self-confidence (.45). The variable is positively correlated with the three types of learning-related outcome, whereas correlations with career-related and work-related consequences are substantially weaker.

Increased self-confidence showed positive correlations with the other benefit variables. Moreover, all the correlations but one (with new assignments in non-work organizations) are statistically significant. The presence of an underlying psychological outcome dimension is thus suggested.

The social effect of having acquired new friends is positively related to the other variables and significantly correlated with the majority of them.

Only a few of the correlations were negative, and none of these was statistically significant. This leads us to the conclusion that benefits from personnel training, as they have been measured in this analysis and to the extent that they are related, seem to reinforce rather than compensate each other. Put differently, participants who experience one type of benefit, tend to experience associated benefits as well. The picture thus seems to be characterized by cumulation or independence rather than compensation. Moreover, in the subsequent factor analysis we will expect to find an underlying dimension related to interest in learning, a dimension related to work and career, and a psychological outcome dimension.

Factor Analysis

In Table 7.2 positive and varying correlations between the different outcome variables were demonstrated. The goal is now to explore potential interpretable underlying dimensions in the data, i.e. to trace potential clustering of benefit variables.

Because the data are dichotomous, it is important to check the distributions of variables to determine whether the proportions of cases for any one scale value has not become too large. If the frequency distributions are very skewed, the range of the correlation coefficients will be restricted. As a consequence of this, new assignments in non-work organizations and job change were excluded from the analysis due to their asymmetrical distribution (the limit for exclusion was set to 10/90; cf. Rummel, 1979:225). However, some variables are still included that have a relatively skewed distribution which may lead to an underestimation of their covariation with the remaining variables.

The results of the analysis are reported in Table 7.3 in which are shown the factor loadings in the pattern matrix, communalities, eigenvalues, and accumulated explained variance.

We have used the criterion of unit eigenvalue to determine the number of factors resulting from the analysis (Kaiser, 1960; for a discussion of this and other criteria, see Kim and Mueller, 1978b: 41-45).

The analysis produced three substantively meaningful factors with eigenvalues exceeding 1.00. Factor loadings exceeding .50 are placed in parentheses. Desire to participate more in training, desire to learn more in general, and increased interest in the subjects of the course have high loadings on the first factor. The outcome dimension is related to *learning motivation* and we will name it correspondingly.

The factor represents about one third of the common variance of all the variables and 55 per cent of the variance that is explained by the three factors together.

Variables related to career and work, load strongly on the second factor. Promotion, more interesting work assignments, and more autonomous work have almost equally high loadings, and the factor will be named *career-related outcome*. It adds 15 percentage points to the explained common variance of the variables and represents 26 per cent of the variance that is explained by the three factors.

All variables that had a low loading on the first two factors loaded fairly strongly on the third factor, i.e. self-actualization, increased self-confidence, new friends, and improved ability to participate in non-work organizations. The factor thus reflects a combination of psychological, political, and social outcomes, and will be called *psycho-social outcome*. Whereas the first factor, learning motivation, reproduces more than three times the variance of at least one of the variables, the third factor reproduces approximately the variance of at least one of the variables (eigenvalue 1.07). It adds 11 percentage points to the accumulated explained variance and represents about one-fifth (19 per cent) of the variance reflected by all the factors.

In toto, the three factors represent 58 per cent of the common variance of the variables.

The communalities show the porportion of variance each variable has in common with the other variables in the analysis. Consequently, a low communality indicates the part of the variable's variance that is represented in the factor solution. Except

Table 7.3. *Factor Loadings, Communalities, Eigenvalues, and Accumulated Explained Variance, Rotated Solution for Entire Sample.*

Variables/Factors	F1	F2	F3	Communalities
Promotion	.11	(.81)	-.12	.66
More interesting working tasks	-.02	(.78)	.09	.64
More autonomous work	-.01	(.80)	.11	.69
Increased readiness to participate in training	(.80)	-.01	.00	.63
Increased interest in learning more in generel	(.84)	.12	-.08	.71
Increased interst in the subjects of the course	(.62)	-.01	.15	.46
Self-actualization	.30	-.14	(.62)	.56
Increased self-confidence	.09	.09	(.69)	.56
New friends	-.17	.09	(.75)	.54
Improved ability to participate in non-work organizations	.04	.00	(.58)	.35
Eigenvalues	3.20	1.52	1.07	–
Accumulated explained variance	.32	.47	.58	–

n = 263

for one variable, improved ability to participate in non-work organizations, communalities were relatively high.

Oblique rotation was employed in the analysis, thereby allowing the factors to be intercorrelated. Compared to orthogonal rotation, it gives a more realistic empirical representation of the data. Oblique rotation may, however, raise problems if the inter-correlations turn out to be very high, in that the dimensions measured may be difficult to distinguish from each other. In our case the correlation (Pearson's r) between F1 and F2 was .

18, between F1 and F3 .25, and the correlation between F2 and F3 was .35. These intercorrelations are not regarded as substantial. It must be noted, however, that the three factors cannot be interpreted as being completely independent of each other.

A reliability test was carried out in order to check the internal consistency of the factors, and values for overall scale reliability (Cronbach's alpha) for the three factors were .67, .74, and .63 respectively.

An interesting question concerns whether there are dissimilar benefit dimensions for male and female employees who have participated in training. If we find different dimensions for the genders, these dissimilarities would need to be examined and hypotheses about possible factors behind the differences could be elaborated.

Separate analyses were therefore carried out for male and female participants. The results of the factor analysis for the male subsample are given in Table 7.4.

The rotated solution resulted in three distinct factors. These are identical with the factors that were found in the analysis of the entire sample, i.e. psycho-social outcome, career-related outcome, and learning motivation. Of the three factors, psycho-social outcome is the strongest. It accounts for the greatest proportion – about one-third – of the total explained variance. Furthermore, it represents 56 per cent of the variance accounted for by the three factors together, whereas career-related outcome and the outcome of learning motivation represent 26 and 18 per cent, respectively. There is a weak tendency that self-actualization, increased self-confidence, getting new friends, and improved ability to participate in non-work organizations are accompanied by promotion, more interesting work tasks, more autonomous work, and increased interest in the subjects of the course.

Table 7.4. *Factor Loadings, Communalities, Eigenvalues, and Accumulated Explained Variance, Rotated Solution for Male Subsample.*

Variables/Factors	F1	F2	F3	Communalities
Promotion	-.24	(.82)	.15	.69
More interesting working tasks	.24	(.69)	.05	.56
More autonomous work	.22	(.79)	.03	.74
Increased readiness to participate in training	.00	-.03	(.81)	.66
Increased interest in learning more in generel	-.10	.21	(.82)	.71
Increased interst in the subjects of the course	.21	-.05	(.57)	.45
Self-actualization	(.56)	-.19	.29	.50
Increased self-confidence	(.72)	.17	-.04	.57
New friends	(.65)	.10	-.02	.44
Improved ability to participate in non-work organizations	(.62)	-.03	.05	.50
Eigenvalues	3.16	1.50	1.08	–
Accumulated explained variance	.32	.47	.57	–

n = 173

A similar, although weaker, tendency is present if we look at the loadings of the variables on the second factor. Promotion, more interesting work tasks, and more autonomous work are to a small degree accompanied by increased interest in learning more in general. Finally, we note a modest tendency toward increased readiness to participate in training, increased interest in learning more in general, and increased interest in the subjects of the course are followed by perceived self-actualization.

Totally, the factors account for 57 per cent of the variance. Intercorrelations between the factors were moderate. The bivariate correlation between F1 and F2 was .17, between F1 and F3 -.34, and between F2 and F3 -.16. We may conclude that the factor learning motivation is negatively correlated with the other two underlying dimensions that were found.

Reliability tests of the factor showed alpha values of .61 (F1), .79 (F2), and .64 (F3).

Corresponding results for the subsample of female participants are presented in Table 7.5.

Once again, three dimensions were produced. Their pattern is similar to the factor pattern that was found for the entire sample, except for the order of the factors. In the female subsample, the outcome of learning motivation is the strongest factor, career-related outcome the second strongest, and psycho-social outcome the third strongest factor. This is identical with the pattern for the entire sample.

Table 7.5 demonstrates a weak tendency toward, for the first factor, increased readiness to participate in training, increased interest in learning more in general, and increased interests in the subjects of the course are accompanied by self-actualization, and increased self-confidence. No such tendencies are present for the second and third factors.

The total explained variance (62 per cent) is slightly higher than for the entire sample and the subsample of male participants. The first factor accounts for 53 per cent of this, the second factor for 29 per cent, and the third factor for 18 per cent. In general, communalities are relatively high. An exception is the variable improved ability to participate in non-work organizations (28 per cent).

The correlation between F1 and F2 was .14, between F1 and F3 .29, and between F2 and F3 .28. There is thus little doubt that the

Table 7.5. Factor Loadings, Communalities, Eigenvalues, and Accumulated Explained Variance, Rotated Solution for Female Subsample.

Variables/Factors	F1	F2	F3	Communalities
Promotion	.08	(.78)	.10	.70
More interesting working tasks	.04	(.90)	-.06	.80
More autonomous work	-.06	(.80)	-.01	.62
Increased readiness to participate in training	(.74)	.03	.02	.56
Increased interest in learning more in generel	(.85)	-.06	.04	.73
Increased interst in the subjects of the course	(.71)	.10	-.01	.54
Self-actualization	.36	-.04	(.65)	.67
Increased self-confidence	.27	-.01	(.68)	.63
New friends	-.29	.06	(.83)	.66
Improved ability to participate in non-work organizations	.04	.04	(.50)	.28
Eigenvalues	3.30	1.75	1.14	–
Accumulated explained variance	.33	.51	.62	–

n = 90

factors reflect dimensions that are largely independent of each other. Cronbach's alpha was computed to .71 (F1), .79 (F2), and .66 (F3).

In summary, the analyses produced clear factor patterns with both low factor complexity and low variable complexity. Moreover, the factors could be assigned substantively meaningful names.

Learning motivation was the strongest underlying outcome dimension for women. This implies that outcome of learning motivation is the benefit dimension that most distinctly distinguishes the individual female participants in personnel training concerning their benefits from the training. Independent of this, career-related outcome and then psycho-social outcome also separate these participants.

With regard to the male subsample, psycho-social outcome was the strongest dimension, followed by career outcome and learning motivation. In the male subsample, there was a weak tendency toward cumulation of benefits along all the underlying dimensions, whereas such a tendency for female participants was only present in respect to learning motivation.

Organizational Implications

The empirical analysis showed that for the sample under study, three distinct benefit dimensions were present at the individual level. From the perspective of work organizations (including firms and public enterprises), the reported benefits which have been traced in this paper are intermediate outcomes. The crucial condition for achieving effects on the company level lies in the degree of transferability of these outcomes to the job situation and the wider organizational context. We shall now focus on possible organizational implications by discussing how the reported individual outcomes may be converted into vital resources and effects on the organizational level.

Learning Motivation

It was found that for a majority of participants in the sample, motivation for further learning was experienced as an outcome from training. This may indicate that personnel training does not, as the conventional wisdom in many organizations would imply, predominantly transmit knowledge and skills of immediate relevance to work operations. Outcomes in the form of attitudes toward training and learning in general also seem to play a central role. Generation of individual learning motivation is a prerequisite for self-perpetuating learning in the workplace. Furthermore, learning motivation within employees is crucial for the establishment of efficient learning environments in organizations. We believe that learning environments will act as important determinants of organizational adaptability to altering conditions. For most organizations, strengthened adaptability will influence positively on prospects of continued survival.

Career Outcome

In our context, career outcomes relate both to transition between job positions and to work-related development within the current job. On the organizational level, career benefits involve essential functions by calling attention to the fact that previous participation in training may be part of the information basis when selection decisions are made. Among other things, it can be interpreted as an indicator of employees' degree of trainability (cf. Thurow, 1979). Consequently, training may serve as one of the screening devices applied within internal labor markets.

The fact that training contributes to internal career mobility may also have important signal effects. Employees already inside the organizations may interpret substantial spendings on training as part of an effort to facilitate potential career moves. This will approximate a Hawthorne-effect if employees get a feeling that the management pays serious attention to their future professional and personal development.[3] Moreover, it may make the organization attractive to potential future employees, who will often be inclined to evaluate the quality of possible employers on the basis of expected opportunities for career development (cf. Northrup and Malin, 1986:76).

Career outcome in our analysis also embraces factors related to the current job. Factors such as how interesting and autonomous the work is perceived, are likely to have direct relevance to the level of job satisfaction that is experienced by employees, thus influencing the opportunities of making a meaningful occupational career also within the current position. Furthermore, organizational encouragement of career development may contribute in several ways to creating organizational adaptability. First, employees become used to planning their own future career, whether it be vertical or horizontal moves to other positions or simply development within their current job. This is assumed to generate increased individual flexibility, which is likely to reduce potential resistance against organizational changes. Second, career mobility creates multicompetences in the organization because employees acquire varied experience by moving across different jobs. This may make the organization less vulnerable to unexpected turnover in vital positions (cf. Lawler and Ledford, 1986).

Training can also contribute to creating employee benefits that were not included in the above analysis. Personal income may, for example, increase in several alternative ways as a consequence of training. A higher "certification" through course certificates and credits may, for example, be converted into change to better paid jobs. This may occur through a change of employer, internal promotion, enhanced compensation within the current job, or improved opportunities for getting extra income. The way in which such changes take place heavily depends on the degree of firm-specificity inherent in the competencies that are transmitted to employees (cf. Williamson, 1985). The higher the human asset specificity, the more able firms will be to retain their work-force because it becomes less rational for competitors in the labor market to offer their employees jobs at comparable levels of compensation.

Psycho-Social Outcome

Psycho-social development of employees may facilitate important processes in organizations. In many contexts, *self-confidence* represents a vital part of the "human infrastructure" in that it hampers or promotes the use of other individual capabilities which are valuable in organizations. Underutilization of employee competences may, in many instances, be due to lack of self-confidence (cf. Bakke, 1959:143-144).

A likely effect of employees making new acquaintances during internal courses is that the social integration amongst groups of employees is strengthened. As a result of this, informal communication networks within the organization are extended. When this is the case, the training can contribute to generating within individuals and groups an increased tolerance across formal boundaries as well as a greater overall perspective of the organization's operations and policies. This effect has been emphasized in the training programs of Japanese companies and has by some authors been interpreted as one of the keys to the success of many of these companies (see, e.g., Saha, 1987:16).

Development of political resources among employees may also have organizational implications. Recent research in organization theory has assigned great significance to political processes in companies (Pfeffer, 1981; Kilmann, Saxton, Serpa et al., 1985; Yates, 1985). Some authors maintain that the individual abilities to participate in these processes are very unequally distributed among organization members and that political competence ought to be more evenly disseminated in order to increase the efficiency of "political markets" (cf. Pfeffer and Salancik, 1977). Although our data are too limited to analyze this in depth, we have indicated that personnel training contributes to creating some amount of political competence in the labor force.

Organizational Ambiguity

The analysis has indicated that personnel training may lead to a variety of individual benefits or rewards in work organizations. From the organizations' point of view, the perceived training benefits represent competence resources which may be utilized when work tasks are to be performed. From the individual point of view, we have argued that the benefits are congruent with different types of rewards which contribute to cause or supplement rewards inherent in the formal reward system. This intersection is believed to have substantial implications for how training is planned, designed, pursued, and evaluated.

We have shown that training to a considerable extent is perceived as rewarding by participants. Consequently, it is reasonable to assert that employees also have expectations as to the personal returns they will receive from participating. Intuitively, it will be rational for firms to endeavor to meet these expectations of rewards, as that may increase the probability of retaining employees that expose a high readiness for competence development. However, if on the other hand, expectations are met which stem solely from individual opportunism[4], the organization may experience negative effects. One example is when employees engage in training programs which are financed by the firm and that transmit general competences, and the employees intend to use these competences to make a profitable shift of employer when the program is completed. For many firms, this type of competence-drain or brain-drain constitutes an expensive problem (cf. Rowan and Barr, 1986:98). They incur training costs which are later utilized by other, perhaps competing, firms (see Chapter 8 for a further discussion of the organizational competence-drain problem).

Hence, the fact that training is an implicit part of reward systems confronts organizations with substantial ambiguity. Whereas individual monetary compensation and fringe benefits require that employees remain in the company, rewards which take the form of personal and professional development are inseparably tied to individuals and can be carried over to other employers.

Concluding Comment

The findings reported in this chapter are limited in several ways. First, they are based on an exploratory analysis of a limited data set on training outcomes. The research needs to be supplemented by studies in which a wider range of possible training outcomes is examined for different types of training. There is also a need on this basis to further classify and examine outcomes on the level of employees and analyze possible determinants of such outcomes. Second, our analysis has been confined to the level of individuals. Research on organizational effects of training is at least equally important to conduct in the future, and we shall look into this in the next chapter. The relationship between training and other means of human resource development as to the creation of organizational effects also raises essential research questions.

It can be predicted that a substantial proportion of the labor force must be prepared to change work and/or occupation several times during their working lives. Thus, it not unlikely that individual careers will be determined to an increasing degree by the individuals' ability to readjust and to acquire new knowledge quickly and more or less permanently. In that case, training and education are assumed to play an increasingly important role in the distribution of careers and career-related rewards. Such prospects indicate that the need for research on the mobility effects of individual competence development is rising.

Notes

[1] The first version of the chapter was published in *Human Relations*, volume 42.

[2] See, e.g., Walker, 1981; Foulkes and Livernash, 1982; Flippo, 1984; Mathis and Jackson, 1985; DeCenzo and Robbins, 1988; Scarpello and Ledvinka, 1988.

[3] The so called Hawthorne-effect was derived from studies of labor productivity in the Western Electric company in the U.S.A. in the 1920s. Among the experiments carried out was one of increasing the intensity of the light for one work group. However, the productivity increased both in the experiment groups and in the control groups. The conclusion was drawn that the increases in productivity were caused by the attention the workers were given through the experiments (Roethlisberger and Dickson, 1939; Landsberger, 1958; Mouzelis, 1973).

[4] The concept of opportunism is here used synonymously with Williamson's (1983:9) definition: "... a lack of candor or honesty in transactions, to include self-interest seeking with guile." Opportunistic behavior may express itself through strategic manipulation of information or misrepresentation of intentions (Williamson, 1983:26).

Chapter 8

Training and the Organization

Introduction[1]

The issue in this chapter, is the relationship between personnel training and the fundamental organizational challenges of human capital provision and transformation. Effects of training that are held to be particularly important in this respect are identified and discussed. These comprise occupational qualification, screening capacity, labor market reputation, enhancement of decision-making capacity, development of learning environments, organizational brain drain, socialization, legitimization, social integration, organizational adaptability, competence mismatch, and generation of internal vulnerability. Research findings that have relevance to such effects are presented and needs for future empirical research pointed out.

Background

Organizations face two basic problems in their management of human capital. The first problem concerns the provision of human capital in the form of employee competences, whereas the second problem concerns the transformation of the acquired human capital into work performance. In the following, the purpose is to discuss possible contributions of training and development to solving these fundamental problems. The intention is to discuss related effects that training and development may have on the organizational level of analysis. In particular, the intention is to assess the empirical research in this field and indicate needs and directions for future research.

The amount of time and money that is spent on human resource development in companies and public organizations is today substantial and, moreover, seems to be increasing in many countries. Hence, thorough analyses of the results of these spendings are accentuated. Traditionally, the effects of training and other human resource development activities have, in some firms, been evaluated on the individual level of analysis. This is, however, insufficient given the intentions of training and development which, in most cases, are directed at desirable *organizational* effects. Although many companies explicitly state that the development of human resources is among their goals, this is primarily an intermediate goal which is intended to contribute to the ultimate objective of survival or economic success. Analyses and advice regarding individual effects of training and development also dominate in the research literature. Very little work has been done on the organizational effects. The following discussion does not pretend to provide an exhausting examination of such effects, but intends to shed light on vital aspects in relation to the basic problems of provision and transformation of human capital.

Provision of Human Capital

We shall first discuss how training and development may contribute to human capital provision in organizations. More accurately, our topic concerns the capacity of training with regard to acquisition, advancement, and retainment of human competence. The discussion considers five possible effects of training and development which are believed to be particularly important in this respect: occupational qualification, screening capacity, labor market reputation, decision-making capacity, development of learning environments, and 'brain-drain'.

Qualification

Transmission of knowledge and skills that are directly significant for employees' work performance is the most recognized function of employee training and development. Traditionally, this is viewed predominantly as a matter of instilling competences suitable for solving operative work tasks. The purpose is to increase labor productivity by continually adjusting the qualifications of the workforce to fit new technology and new tasks. It may partly be a matter of training people to master new jobs and partly of updating knowledge related to new technology. Such learning becomes especially important during processes of restructuring and strategic reorientation in which companies alter major parts of their activity and policy. Simultaneous changes both in the system of knowledge and in the learning environment will often be necessary in such processes.

Most firms seem to be less preoccupied with the parallel need to develop employee competences that are less technical or task-specific, in the sense that they can be applied to a broad range of tasks. These have been called meta-competences, and examples are communication skills, ability to cooperate with colleagues, problem solving skills, analytical capacities, and ability to cope with change (cf. Chapter 3). Transmission of such competences is commonplace within executive training and management development. However, there is a growing need to provide development of meta-competences among ordinary employees and middle managers as well due to the increasing rate of change in many firms' external environments and derived needs to alter the organization. Consequently, there is reason to believe that companies will be more willing to supply non-executives with some of the elements that are inherent in much of the management training.

In turn, the individual competences acquired represent an essential input into the work-groups that most employees function within. The fact that one may talk about work-groups which are more or less resourceful reflects a conception of aggregate individual competence at the group level. Likewise, from an organizational viewpoint, the stock of individual competences in the firm may be seen as an aggregate intangible asset, a potential that can be utilized to improve organizational performance.

Screening Capacity

In the sociology of education, the school system's role as an agent of certification has been in focus. Education's function as a screening device in the labor market, as well as a source of social status, has been emphasized. However, the certification may also serve other purposes. It may work as a standardized way of signalizing certain minimum qualifications. If one knows, for instance, that a person has a craft certificate or a specific university degree, it may generally be possible to estimate his/her fundamental qualifications. That saves the companies from testing the knowledge and skills the person possesses. Certification may, in other words, be used both as a time and money-saving screening device, or as a "filter" (Arrow, 1973:194). Expressed differently, the transaction costs of recruitment and promotion of employees are reduced. It can be expected that this also relates to parts of the personal training.

Participation in and individual outcomes from personnel training may be used as criteria for selection and promotion, thus improving the internal screening capacity of firms. First, participation has a subjective aspect, as the employee by pursuing training demonstrates motivation and interest in professional development and improvement of job performance. Second, the degree of participation is easily observable and may thereby serve as a supplement to other objective selection or screening criteria. In companies where personnel training is highly developed, it will often be taken for granted that employees participate, and the possibilities of promotion may partly depend on individual readiness to pursue training. Third, individual outcomes from training in the form of increased or altered competences may be subject to tests or other evaluations. In this way, objective measures of competence-level and, eventually, future trainability may be obtained (cf. Thurow, 1979).

The employees' capacity and readiness to keep on learning will probably be crucial for organizational survival, particularly when looking at enterprises confronted with rapid changes in markets or technology. That is why it is considered likely that participation in and desirable outcomes from training will be more frequently rewarded. In two similar nationwide studies with representative samples of the work-force, it was reported that about one tenth of the participants in employee training (11.6 per cent in 1977/78 and 11.3 per cent in 1982/83) reported a perception that participation in personnel training had contributed to their promotion (Nordhaug, 1985:65; Nordhaug, 1989).

It has thus been indicated that training's function as a screening device is not without importance. In addition, it can be noted that empirical evidence from the U.S. shows that a majority of those respondents who themselves wanted upward social mobility in the labor market, looked at education and training as the best way of attaining this (Cross, 1982:16). However, empirical research on this issue is needed before the significance of training participation and outcomes as screening criteria can be established.

Labor Market Reputation

The organization's reputation amongst existing and potential customers or clients can be regarded as one of its most essential assets (Itami, 1987). In the same way, its labour market position will be crucial in relation to the problems of acquiring and retaining the competence needed.

The perceived status of an organization's stock of competence and its efforts at developing it, will often be interpreted both by current and prospective employees as an indicator of the priority management sets on personnel training. Studies have indicated that university graduates assign high ranks to the perceived opportunities for personal and professional development among factors they regarded as important for the choice of first job after graduation (see, e.g., Granovetter, 1974). According to Northrup and Malin (1986:62), many companies have found that engineers and scientists seeking employment search for information about how the company may contribute to their future growth and development. At the same time we know that the proportion of employees with high education is growing, and we also know that the demand for and actual participation in training expands with increasing education (cf. Knudsen and Skaalvik, 1979; Berntsen, 1984). Consequently, there is reason to expect that companies' and other work organizations' stock of competence bases, as well as the resources they spend on training, will be increasingly significant for their ability to compete with other companies in tight labor markets.

Decision-Making Capacity

Decentralization of organization structures is currently very common both within private business and the public sector. In general, a condition for such processes to succeeed is that the capacity of decision-making on lower levels in the organization is actually being developed. Training and development are central measures to achieve this. This is true of both task-oriented training as well as training which aims at disseminating information about interrelations between local decisions and the strategic goals of the organization. A special problem associated with this is so-called suboptimalization. If the organization is to avoid departments or other subdivisions pursuing their own goals in ways that harm the company's overall objectives, a certain minimum of dispersed knowledge is needed as to which courses of action are desirable from the top management's point of view. Especially in companies shifting from a centralized to a more decentralized structure, training that transfers knowledge of superordinate goals and strategies will often be a crucial part of the change process.

Successful decentralization of decisions, which is often intended to increase the overall capacity of decision-making, requires that the relevant competence is present on lower levels in the organization. Training is a central means to attain this, and especially training that disseminates information about relations between local decisions and strategic goals. Consequently, courses directed at increasing the decision-making capacity are often designed to convey knowledge about economic prospects, markets, technology, and organizational structure, which can stimulate employee involvement and participation.

Analytically, it is useful to distinguish between three types of competence transferred through employee training: operational, administrative, and institutional. This distinction has previously been used to categorize different levels in organizations (see for instance Parsons, 1960; Thompson 1967; Scott, 1981:97). One of the objectives has been to indicate how adaptations and decisions vary according to organizational level. It is fruitful to extend this categorization to human competence, because different kinds of decisions will often require different competence bases.

The content of most of the training pursued is designed primarily to fit the specific character of jobs. This often implies that workers, supervisors, and lower white-collar employees are mainly given operatively oriented training. Middle and top level managers generally acquire knowledge related to administrative or tactical decisions (for example negotiations, personnel policy, interpersonal relations, and budget control). Top managers are expected to participate more frequently in courses and seminars that emphasize development of corporate strategy, or that focus on innovations within administrative sciences (in addition to personality-oriented activities). Thus, for the latter type of training it is, generally, to a greater extent a matter of institutionally or strategically oriented knowledge.

In this perspective, a course of action used by some firms has been to stimulate and facilitate participation and involvement on lower levels in the organization by providing employees on these levels with training that includes elements of the business strategy and environment (see, e.g., Carlzon, 1987).

We may thus anticipate that due to the need to enhance the decision-making capacity through decentralization, it seems likely that companies to an increasing extent will arrange employee training that seeks to disseminate knowledge of overall goals and strategies to middle- and lower-level employees.

Learning Environment

As a result of rapid and frequent changes in technology and the environment that most organizations face today, a labor force that is highly motivated to continuous learning will probably be one of the most crucial competitive advantages in the future (Hall, 1989). Even though knowledge of a tactical and strategic character is important, however, it will often be necessary to start with task-oriented training to be able to proceed to a higher level. Experience from employee training is likely to arouse the interest in informal learning in the companies. Thus, the impact of training on the learning environment may be measured by the degree to which it motivates individuals to pursue further formal and informal training which is relevant to the companies.

In Chapter 7, learning motivation, defined as a drive toward further personal and professional development through educational activities, was found to be a significant type of individual training outcome. On the group and organization level, we may speak of aggregate learning motivation in the work force as an important intangible asset. A labor force that is highly motivated for continuous learning is likely to be among the most substantial competitive advantages in the future.

Aggregate learning motivation may be transformed into second-order effects through its contribution to development of learning environments. The latter is widely defined as the totality of factors in the organization that facilitate or hamper continuous employee learning. It can thus be considered a type of infrastructure for work-related learning. It follows that the extent to which a learning environment is valuable depends on the actual mix of conditions that promote and hamper continuous learning. Further, its value depends on how strongly the organization needs an efficient learning environment. It can, for example, be assumed that the needs of organizations that are exposed to a relatively stable and homogeneous external environment are smaller compared to organizations operating in a rapidly changing and heterogeneous external environment. Likewise, the pace of relevant technological development affects the need for continuous learning in the firm's labor force.

In addition to outcomes from training, effects of informal learning are essential for the development of learning environments. Moreover, there is reason to assume a close relationship involving spill-over effects between the two types of work-related learning. Confidence in informal learning probably motivates participation in formal training, and it is reasonable to assume that experience from employee training stimulates informal learning within companies. Thus, training's impact on learning environments may be indicated through the degree to which it motivates individuals to pursue further formal and informal training which is relevant to their work. Research findings on the individual level of analysis have shown that a majority of participants in employee training (57 per cent) reported that they had been stimulated to further training through having attended their latest course (Nordhaug, 1989). This can be interpreted as a factor that contributes to strengthening learning environments.

Competence Drain

Several examples can be found of companies that have benefited from training costs previously incurred by other organizations. We will assume that employee transfers are especially common when training costs are high. In the computer business, for example, some companies probably find it tempting to offer highly skilled specialists better remuneration than competitors do. In that way, they may attract competent individuals and incur lower costs of training. Within other industries, some companies are also likely to be free-riders, letting other firms pay the costs of training. 'Brain-drain' or 'competence-drain' in organizations is assumed to be closely related to the types of knowledge and skills that are transferred through training and development. General (in the sense of firm nonspecific) knowledge, that can be converted through external labour markets, makes this educationally induced turnover possible. However, firm specific knowledge can, by definition, be realized only within one single internal labour market. In other words, the effect of training can be regarded as potentially more dysfunctional the more general the knowledge transferred is. As transmission of general knowledge makes the workforce more mobile in the external labour market, the result may be that smaller companies to a greater extent than big companies educate employees out of their own organization. Because considerable parts of the total training and development have to be bought externally and provide employees with predominantly general knowledge, it may therefore act like a drainpipe for learning motivated and talented employees; and particularly so in smaller firms. However, this remains an empirical question.

Transformation of Human Capital

In this section, we shall discuss ways in which training and development may produce effects that facilitate or hamper the transformation of human capital into work performance. A distinction is drawn between the organizational effects of socialization, legitimization, social integration, organizational adaptability, competence mismatch, and generation of internal vulnerability, and these are discussed separately.

Socialization

Employers will usually be unable to specify in detail what an employee is expected to do during working hours, i.e. the labor contract is incomplete (Blau and Scott, 1970:140; Braverman, 1974; Williamson, 1985:262). It thus has to be supplemented with a psychological contract which is often implicit and serves to ensure that human capital is, to some degree, transformed into work performance.

In addition to developing purely task-oriented competences, training and development also transmit values, attitudes, and norms. The clearest examples can be found in introduction courses for new employees. Through these courses, the management in most cases wants to present and promote the firm's philosophy, goals, and strategies. The purpose is to make new employees identify with the organized philosophy and goals as early as possible. This process consists both of learning and 'delearning'. In order to make individuals internalize local norms, it will often be necessary to change or eliminate previous values and attitudes. An important and interesting empirical research task is to analyse to what extent training activities actually support this kind of socialization within companies.

Organizational socialization can be defined as the process by which a person learns the values, norms, and required behaviors which permit him or her to participate as a member of the organization (Van Maanen, 1976:67). Hence, it is a form of social control that contributes to making employees' behaviours more predictable and thereby reduces uncertainty in the organization. Socialization may be more or less intentional and more or less efficient. The object is usually to gain support and enthusiasm for the goals and policy of the company, i.e. to generate a certain level of internal homogeneity and consensus. To the degree that managers actually succeed in doing this, they have established a type of social control which normally can be held to be more efficient than other forms of control, because the need for direct supervision and evaluation of the employees' job performance is reduced.

Legitimization

In any organization there must be a certain amount of legitimacy related to goals, strategies, compensation systems, and decisions if it is to function efficiently. Some of this may be created through training. Elements of legitimization are expected to be found especially in the value-oriented parts of training and development. In addition to the fact that the very content of various types of training and development may prepare for acceptance of goals, strategies and decisions, participation in such training and development may, as mentioned before, act as a selection criterion for promotion or distribution of rewards. It gives an apparently objective and fair standard for the evaluation of individuals' motivation and effort: "A belief in the merit-based and non-political aspect of careers is important in order to maintain the legitimacy of the organization's internal labor market and to help assuage the feelings of those who earn less than others in the organization" (Pfeffer, 1981:246-7).

In this picture, training and development may contribute to legitimize inequalities in compensation and career development. If the ideology implies that everyone has the opportunity to pursue training and thereby get promoted, potential dissatisfaction caused by a differentiated compensation system is likely to be reduced.

Furthermore, training is a potential means for legitimization of decisions. After mergers, it seems to be customary to set up special courses designed to provide an ex post legitimization of the decision to merge and to promote tolerance for the culture of the other party in the merger. The same applies to joint ventures between two or more companies.

Social Integration

Training and development may also contribute to strengthening the social integration in organizations. Courses that include employees from different parts of the company are probably particularly important. Employees are then given the opportunity to exchange experience from their respective fields of activity, which in turn may lead to an increased understanding of problems and working methods in other parts of the company. They may thus obtain a broader and more holistic perspective of the organization. Moreover, intra-firm social networks are extended. As a consequence, informal communication across formal unit boundaries is likely to become more frequent. This may, in turn, reduce the information load on formal communication channels. In a recent study, it was demonstrated that a substantial proportion (40 per cent) of the participants in Norwegian personnel training had gained new friends through their participation in training (Nordhaug, 1989). Although a seemingly trivial finding, this is likely to result in a certain extension of interpersonal networks in the organization. Courses or programs that include employees from different parts of the company are of particular interest in this context, even though development of external networks through courses involving employees from other companies may also be important. In internally organized training, employees are offered the opportunity to exchange experience from their respective work fields and subunits, which, in turn, may increase the mutual understanding of problems and working methods within other parts of the company, i.e. develop what we may call the amount of "intraorganizational empathy". Usually it is this effect that is sought after in job rotation programs and trainee programs involving movements across different subunits in an organization (cf. Saha, 1988). To the extent that social and professional networks between colleagues are expanded through training, this represents an added resource from an organizational point of view. We may use the concept of *social capital* to characterize the aggregate of social networks (Coleman, 1988). These represent a sort of intangible capital in the same manner as does human capital.

The increments in intraorganizational social capital the firm is assumed to gain from personnel training can, in turn, be converted into second-order effects. First, extended social networks are expected to contribute to increased social integration. Second, extended social networks may have the effect that informal communication across formal subunits becomes more frequent. This may lead to a reduction of the load on formal communication channels and thereby contribute to making the flow of information more efficient (cf. Galbraith, 1977; Itami, 1987:21).

Organizational Adaptability

The demand for continuous adaptation in organizations is multifaceted. New technology must be identified and implemented, and new products have to be developed. Companies need to adjust to changes in the constituencies they serve. Organizational structures have to be modified in order to cope with altered external and internal conditions. The capacity for these and other types of *readjustments*, if present, constitutes an increasingly vital intangible asset.

Consequently, competence related to mastering organizational change and a turbulent external environment is crucial for the survival of many companies. Developing this competence is partly a matter of training people to master new jobs and partly a question of updating the knowledge and skills required to master new technology. Furthermore, generation of change-relevant individual competences, such as the capacity to cope with uncertainty and adjust to new situations, is paramount (cf. Carnevale, 1991). This kind of competence development becomes especially important during processes of restructuring and reorientation during which companies alter major parts of their activity and policy. Simultaneous changes both in the system of knowledge and in the learning environment will often be a key ingredient in such processes.

Competence Mismatch

Training and development are dysfunctional if they do not lead to, at least, a minimum of correspondence between achievement of qualifications and the company's need for qualifications that fit current work tasks. Mismatch may take two forms: misplaced training and overeducation. The former concerns the content of the training, whereas overeducation refers to the quantity of training relative to job requirements.

Misplaced training is often caused by insufficient analysis of organizational needs for human competences. Other things being equal, it can be assumed that the extent of misplacement is generally smaller when training is arranged in-house by internal staff, because it is more likely to be accurately tailored for the specific situation of the company than externally provided training. One reason is that the staff have their careers closely tied to the organizationally perceived success of training. When courses are bought externally, the possibilities of courses being adjusted to the needs of the company are usually smaller. Standard courses offered through the market are naturally characterized by their firm nonspecific contents.

Overeducation, i.e. the extent to which employees acquire education that results in their being overqualified for the jobs they actually get, has been studied chiefly on the macro-level and the individual level (Berg, 1970; Freeman, 1976; Collins, 1979a; Burris, 1983). Although this problem has traditionally been studied on the basis of employees' initial education, there is no reason to assume that the problem does not concern training and development as well. In some companies, training employees is to a considerable degree a matter of organizational prestige. Besides, the growing professionalization of personnel and training administration may in some cases generate training for its own sake. Training-administrators will often be inclined to measure their rate of success in quantitative terms, such as number of partici- pants, number of courses, and the size and growth of the training budget. Consequently, there is a risk of an increasing degree of overeducation, which may be suboptimal.

Internal Vulnerability

The internal division of labor is a central dimension in organization theory. Generally, it is assumed that the greater the interdependence among different subunits in the organization, the more vulnerable it is to potential hostile individual and group behavior. Highly developed division of labor may also make supplementing the work force more complicated. If personnel has to be strongly specialized to meet the specific job requirements of the company, it may be more difficult to substitute labor. In addition, employees then have a substantial power base vis-à-vis the management.

Both within the sociology of industrial relations and the socio- logy of professions, one has studied the power of groups that possess exclusive knowledge of vital interest to the organization (Crozier, 1964; Hinings et al., 1974; Hernes, 1975:114-121; Clegg,

1979). If personnel training is used in such a way that it serves to create, support or strengthen *competence monopolies*, it may be dysfunctional in relation to efficiency goals. The result is a concentration of power which makes the organization vulnerable and often difficult to alter according to changing external conditions. Viewed against this background, a possible strategy will be to disseminate or decentralize important knowledge as much as possible. Consequently, the power tied to knowledge will also be dispersed (cf. Pfeffer, 1981b).

The way in which training strategies are designed may thus have considerable impact on the degree of specialization. To put it simply, management may pursue one of three principles: Further the existing specialization, reduce it, or keep status quo. Only one of these principles, "despecialization", will contribute to reducing interdependences and thus vulnerability. The increased effort in many companies to systematically create multiskills within employees is illustrative of such a strategy. Moreover, some companies have also created incentive systems that reward individual acquisition of multiskills (cf. Lawler and Ledford, 1985).

Empirical Research

Thus far, we have outlined possible effects of personnel training as to the two fundamental problems of human capital provision and transformation. We shall now turn to empirical aspects by reviewing research with regard to the outlined effects. Moreover, needs and directions for future empirical research will be addressed.

Human Capital Provision

Most of the empirical research that has been reported on training effects has concentrated on issues related to their capacity to provide or develop human resources. These are the most direct effects of personnel training and, therefore, often the most easily observable ones. The vast bulk of research has focused on effects in the form of development of knowledge and skills in relation to occupational qualification, and evaluation studies have dominated the scene (see Goldstein, 1980 for an overview).

Effects of training in the form of certification and selection have not been much studied, but some evidence exists. In two Norwegian survey-studies, more than one tenth of the participants in employee training reported that their participation had contributed to their promotion (Nordhaug, 1989; see also Chapter 7). Hence, it has been shown empirically that the training's function as a channel of mobility and selection criterion is not without importance. In addition, it should be mentioned that empirical evidence from the U.S. has demonstrated that a majority of those who themselves wanted upward social mobility in the labor market considered education and training to be the most efficient means of attaining this (Cross, 1982:16).

The relationship between training and development of learning environments within organizations has not been paid any considerable attention in empirical research. However, research findings on the individual level of analysis have indicated that a majority of the participants in training are being stimulated by their participation to pursue further training. For example, research on credit-giving adult education has shown that participation in less demanding courses in one's spare time is often a stepping stone to more demanding training or education (Gooderham, 1984). Empirical evidence from England has suggested a similar tendency concerning personnel training. Killeen and Bird (1981) indicated that participants in technically oriented courses, apart from emphasizing the directly work-related outcomes, emphasized even more strongly benefits in the form of increased understanding and widened intellectual horizons. Furthermore, it appeared that most of the participants wanted to pursue more training. This result is similar to that of the empirical study reported in Chapter 7 in which more than one half of the participants reported that their motivation for further education had increased as a result of their latest course.

Even though there is no direct evidence with regard to training's contributions to creating learning environments on the organizational level of analysis, the referred findings might be interpreted as pointing in this direction. However, the lack of strong evidence marks the need for empirical analyses of the relationship between training and learning environments carried out on the organizational level of analysis. A reasonable proposition would be that organizations which spend large amounts of resources on training also tend to be the ones that have developed stimulating learning environments. Establishing a causal link between training efforts and such environments is, however, difficult as there is probably a highly reciprocal relationship between the two.

Human Capital Transformation

As mentioned earlier, studies that have explicitly addressed the issue of personnel training's facilitation of human capital transformation are virtually non-existent. However, research that may give us indirect indications of this has been reported.

Concerning social integration as an organizational effect of training, one survey study showed that a considerable proportion (40%) of participants in personnel training reported that they had gained new friends through their participation in courses (Nordhaug, 1991). Although this result does not allow for conclusions on the organizational level, a hypothesis implying that training contributes to social integration, is suggested.

The phenomenon of mismatch between individual qualifications and job requirements in the form of overeducation has been extensively studied within the field of sociology of education. Berg's study (1970) of the relationship between education and individual productivity in the U.S. reported that individual productivity did not rise in proportion with the amount of previous education. Moreover, he concluded that overeducation caused reduced job satisfaction within jobs requiring low qualifications (Berg, 1970:105, see also Quinn and de Mandilowich, 1975). Burris (1983) also reported a negative correlation between overeducation and job satisfaction. We would expect a similar relationship to be present also with regard to "overtraining" in firms. Empirical research has furthermore indicated that various occupational groups or professions tend to defend their positions against competing or potentially competing groups, as far as status and income are concerned, by acquiring additional education and training (e.g., Collins, 1979b). The conceptualization of education or training as a positional good is descriptive of this logic (see, e.g., Ultee, 1980). With increasing numbers of individuals who obtain education, its value is being deflated, given that the upward social mobility in society does not increase at a corresponding rate. Consequently, occupational groups react by acquiring more education as a defensive way of protecting their "market share" (Collins,1979a; Thurow,1979:333). There is no reason to assume that such mechanisms may not be present on the organizational level as well, thus contributing to overeducation or "overtraining". Investigating this is an important task for future empirical research. As has been shown, research on overeducation has been restricted to initial education, whereas personnel training and other types of adult education have not been systematically analyzed in this respect. A reasonable conjecture is that the results will not be very different for initial and recurrent education. Empirical research is, however, needed to substantiate this.

Without having empirical evidence at hand, we would anticipate that much of the personnel training that is executed contributes to increased specialization and thereby internal interdependence in organizations. The reason is that there generally seems to be a strong emphasis on technical, in the sense of task-specific, training that serves to further existing work specialization (see Chapter 3).

The degree to which training contributes to socialization of employees is not known and would probably be impossible to estimate due to the fact that socialization processes are very complex. Moreover, most of the socialization that takes place is neither planned by the organization nor recognized by the employees. As noted by Caplow (1964:173) organizations that conduct training programs tend to conceive of them as imparting technical skills, but analysis of any particular training program invariably shows it to be implicitly concerned with the communication of values, the development of an ambiance, the rejection of prior affiliations, and the development of "an appropriate self-image". Although it is very difficult to grasp socialization effects of many types of training, one may gain valuable insights by first concentrating on the study of training programs that explicitly aim at creating such effects. Consequently, it is reasonable to start with empirical studies of introduction courses for new employees and "internal marketing campaigns" as part of organization development. We also know that many large companies arrange most of the training themselves in order to better control the socialization of their employees (Lusterman,

1977). Some have concentrated increasingly on in-house training and have developed corporate training centers or "corporate colleges" (Normann, 1983; 60-61; Eurich, 1985), which may be efficient socialization tools. An important research task is to study the amount of internalization of training and the rationale behind it as well as the socialization effects that are generated.

Concluding Comment

Traditionally, training has been viewed largely as a separate subfunction grouped under the heading of human resource development. However, it is important to stress that it is also a central part of human resource management, since provision and transformation of human capital are the core functions of any firms' human resource management. Furthermore, it is essential that personnel training and other types of competence development be viewed as an integral part of ongoing organization development in companies. The conventional wisdom, implying that training is predominantly a distinct and, thus, easily separable activity, can be favorably replaced by a more holistic view, encompassing the whole functioning of the organization. The human resource development literature has been characterized by a substantial measure of what we may call *training myopia*, implying that focus has been limited primarily to operative, directly job-related and task specific effects of training programmes. If this bias is not corrected, the consequence can easily be that the potential of personnel training is underestimated and, in turn, that available human resources are underutilized.

The aim of this chapter was to demonstrate that training may have a wide variety of important organizational effects in addition to technically preparing employees for work tasks. The discussion of possible effects of training grouped under human capital provision and transformation did not pretend to be exhaustive. We have, however, endeavored to present effects that are held to be particularly important for organizational performance. Moreover, we have attempted to avoid the traditional bias of examining only positive effects by including possible dysfunctional effects also.

There is a strong need for empirical research in this field, including studies that are generalizable across firms. However, the field remains within a typically explorative phase, thus accentuating a need for in-depth case studies. This will enable researchers to uncover *possible* organizational effects of training. Such research will, in turn, constitute a basis for asking the question about which training effects are *probable* in organizations and pursue generalizable survey studies to approach this. Furthermore, as personnel training embraces a variety of activities with differing characteristics, it will be necessary to examine effects of dissimilar types of training in order to assess their relative contribution to organizational goals.

The main single challenge for future research is to link the levels of organization and individuals. Important questions are how and under what conditions individual effects of training may be converted into organizational effects and what measures organizations can take to facilitate an efficient transformation process.

Note

[1]   An earlier version of the chapter was published in *Human Resource Management Journal*, Volume 1 (2).

Chapter 9

Learning Barriers in Firms

Introduction

In this chapter, the intention is to outline and discuss significant barriers to employee learning in the form of individual acquisition, exchange, and application of work-related competences. The focus hence is on transfer and utilization of knowledge and skills as delineated in Chapter 5, together with individual competence development.

In the comprehensive training literature, great emphasis has been put on the importance of evaluating education and training activities. This literature has, especially on the practical level, been preoccupied with needs analyses and technical aspects of work-related instruction and to a considerable degree been anchored in psychological approaches (see, for example, Nordhaug, 1985; Goldstein, 1986; Laird, 1986). Inhibitors of learning other than those being present in the learning situation, have received relatively scant attention. Research on organizational learning has been more preoccupied with certain types of learning barriers. This has particularly been so with respect to the structural level where the concentration has largely been on cognitive organizational systems of beliefs and values as well as related cognitive barriers. One illustration is the concept of 'defensive mechanism' as presented by Argyris (1990). A third body of literature relevant to our context, contains those parts of the literature on innovation in organizations that have identified and analyzed factors inhibiting innovation and internal diffusion of innovation in firms (see Kanter, 1988 for an overview). Many of the perspectives offered here are relevant in the context of this chapter, and parts of the organizational innovation literature will, therefore, be drawn upon.

Traditionally, the literature on training issues has strongly emphasized the significance of evaluating learning activities in order to assess their efficiency. However, this perspective is restricted to formal learning in work life, whereas most of the learning takes place informally on the job. Although not unimportant, evaluation furthermore implies a very limited perspective in that it is only easily definable units of training which are considered, frequently viewed in isolation from the organization where the results should ideally be transformed into improved work performance.

The alternative which is advocated in this chapter, is to take the organization as the point of departure and endeavor to uncover and analyze factors that serve to hamper or promote learning among employees. Then a much broader perspective is obtained, and at the same time the analysis may facilitate corrective action in order to remove learning barriers embedded in the organization and the interaction between individuals. The information gained from evaluating single educational units often has no value beyond establishing the efficiency of those single units and providing feedback that may be used to improve each unit, if it is to be repeated at all.

A broad spectrum of barriers to employee learning exist in firms. This was, among others, noted by Hall and Fukami (1979:144) who identified five general factors affecting such learning: The entry process and early socialization, the job itself, the boss and the work group, organizational structure, and personnel policies. Moreover, they noted that the vast bulk of the research had focused on entry and socialization, the job itself, and the role of superordinates and work groups. We shall not structure the presentation on the basis of these factors but rather systematize the discussion of learning barriers encountered by individual employees by distinguishing between barriers that are present on different levels in the organization. In the following, barriers on the micro and macro levels are discussed separately.

Micro Level Barriers

Barriers on the micro level comprise intrapersonal and interpersonal factors. Intrapersonal competence barriers include all types of psychological factors that either prevent individuals from entering learning activities or from completing activities they have engaged in. Much of the learning that takes place in work life occurs through individual interaction with colleagues and superordinates as well as interactions within work teams. Then, in order to make learning efficient, the interrelations between employees are crucial. Furthermore, these relations are essential when it comes to application of new knowledge and skills.

Since a discussion of individual psychological inhibitors of learning in firms is clearly not within the scope of this book, in the following focus is set on barriers related to current competence, practice opportunities, individual opportunism, the relationships between employees and superordinates, and the functioning of groups.

Current Competence

The competences carried by individuals may in several respects act like strait-jackets which inhibit acquisition of new competences, as indicated in the formulation "to put one's mind in blinkers". This has been described through the emphasis many authors have put on the need for delearning as a prerequisite for new learning.

Existing competence can inhibit the acquisition of new knowledge and skills in different ways. First, it may be detrimental to the new competences, implying that the individual must throw away old wisdom and replace it. This is often a psychologically painful process that hinders learning. Second, an individual-level analogy can be drawn to the observation made by Levitt and March (1988:322) that a "competence trap" can occur when favourable performance with an inferior procedure leads an organization to accumulate more experience with it, thus keeping experience with a superior procedure inadequate to make it rewarding to use (cf. also Huber, 1991; Cohen and Levinthal, 1990). Employees who feel they are performing pretty well as it is, will often not admit any need to accumulate new knowledge and skills, which they may simply consider less productive or just not required to improve job performance. Third, demonstration of high competence levels through skillful action may in certain instances actually produce actual incompetence. The reason is that skilled performance occurs more or less automatically and is completely taken for granted.

Thus, it is largely based upon an unawareness which, paradoxically, inhibits learning. In the terms of Chris Argyris (1990:21-22), we could lose our skills if we were required to pay attention to our actions. This reasoning has much in common with Ponalyi's (1964) analysis of tacit knowledge which was discussed in Chapter 3 and Chapter 4. Fourth, existing competences may be wrapped up in cognitive maps that emphasize certain theories of practice. This may pertain to how a problem is to be analyzed or how a solution is to be implemented – and can be exemplified by the knowledge professionals receive through their education. Substantial parts of that knowledge can be viewed as a body of cognitive maps and repertoires of how certain problems are to be approached. New knowledge incompatible with this knowledge may then not be accepted at all or only hesitantly so. Formulated sharply, all types of professional training inculcate some amount of myopic mental vision in the people being educated. When bodies of knowledge about how problems are to be analyzed and solved are passed on to learners, there will always be other bodies of relevant knowledge and skills that are not passed on due to time limits or beliefs that some types of knowledge are superior compared to alternative knowledge within the same field of work. Much of the underlying rationale for conflicts and continuous rivalry between adjacent professions is buried in this territory.

Similarly, managers may individually or within teams develop compact perceptual filters which are dysfunctional by preventing strategically vital information from passing through and thus from being taken into consideration (Starbuck and Miliken, 1988; Ireland, Hitt, Bettis and DePorras, 1987; Schwenk, 1984; Dearborn and Simon, 1958).

Practice Opportunities

Competences share one property with muscles – they are strengthened and maintained when activated, and shrink when not in use for an extended period of time. In the same manner as feedback is necessary to create added motivation for learning, having the opportunity to practice what is learned is necessary to retain and develop knowledge and skills. Hence, lack of opportunities to apply competences may lead to negative learning, that is, loss of knowledge and skills. Likewise, if there are no opportunities to utilize the competences acquired, individuals will easily be disencouraged to pursue new learning projects. Effective learning requires demonstration of new behaviors, and some authors have emphasized that such behaviors must be *overlearned* through practice so that smooth performance can be maintained under stress and other difficult conditions (Hall and Fukami, 1979:140).

Opportunities to practice are, not least, important for team learning in order to develop collective competences. However, such practice if often missing in reality. As pointed out by Senge (1990), the almost total absence of meaningful practice or rehearsal is probably the predominant factor that keeps most management teams from being effective learning units: "Imagine trying to build a great theater ensemble or a great symphony orchestra without rehearsal. Imagine a championship sports team without practice. In fact, the process whereby such teams learn *is* through continual movement between practice and performance, practice, performance, practice again, perform again" (Senge, 1990:238). In addition to lack of opportunities to practice their own competences, individual learners may be inhibited by not having the opportunity to *observe* skillful employees practicing their skills. Brown and Duguid (1990:16) provide an illustration of this, noting that learners pick up valuable "know how" – not just information but also manner and technique – from being on the periphery of competent practitioners going about their business.

Opportunism

Employees may be motivated for work-related learning but still be unwilling to pursue learning projects due to tactical considerations. To the degree that such avoidance is in conflict with the needs of the organization, it can be subsumed under the label individual opportunism. This concept is here used synonymously with Williamson's (1983:9) definition of opportunism as a lack of candor or honesty in transactions, including self-interest seeking with guile, which is frequently expressed through strategic manipulation of information or deliberate misrepresentation of intentions. One widespread form of opportunism is when employees fear that their position or their privileges might be put in jeopardy if they acquire a new set of competences that make them more mobile inside the firm – thus concluding that they will be better off avoiding participation in the training or informal learning activities in question. A related type, which is more purely opportunistic, occurs when employees who secretly plan to leave the firm seek employee-financed competence development that conveys firm nonspecific knowledge and skills – and avoid acquisition of firm specific competences. What they actually do is to act as free-riders by luring firms to finance their private human capital in order to strengthen their own chances of succeeding in external labor markets.

Firms can meet this type of opportunism by applying a variety of measures. One is to design reward systems that encourage development of new skills, such as competence-based pay (Lawler and Ledford, 1986; Tosi and Tosi, 1986). Another is to make clear that employees who are unwilling to acquire new knowledge and skills are the first at risk of losing their jobs if lay-offs or downsizing become necessary. A third is to make individual competence development a prerequisite for advancement within the organization, hence indirectly punishing those unwilling to pursue such development.

Relationships between Employees

Transfer of competence between employees is reckoned to be among the most important forms of learning in work organizations. However, the frequency and amount of such transfer strongly depends on the actual relationship between colleagues who interact during working hours. In this context, there is a wide array of potential barriers, some of which are based on tactical considerations tied to giving away knowledge and skills to others and some of which are based on the "personality chemistry" amongst employees.

The role of managers is crucial in regard to competence development among employees. Basically, it is their responsibility to assess needs for such development, to inform employees about training and other learning opportunities, to report competence needs to the human resource management or development department, and to encourage subordinates to pursue training. When managers fail in doing this – regardless of whether this is due to communication problems, fear of getting too competent subordinates, or general managerial incompetence – very serious competence barriers are present. These can be removed either by replacing managers, training them to internalize an awareness of the significance of competence development, designing managerial incentive systems that encourage appropriate managerial action in this field, or through combinations of these options.

An additional managerial responsibility is to provide feedback to subordinates who have acquired new competences and who successfully go on to convert these into work performance. After noting that learning which is rewarded (positively reinforced) tends to be repeated, remembered, and utilized in other situations, Hall and Fukami (1979: 140) maintain that probably the most potent source of positive reinforcement for new learning would be the immediate superior and the work group. That requires a good working relationship between them.

Concerning utilization of acquired competences, factors such as colleagues' feeling of job ownership and related protection of job territory, and conservatism among superordinates, represent important inhibitors. As pointed out in Chapter 2, employees who try to expand their job territory after having gained new skills and knowledge may meet with strong resistance from other employees who feel that their own territory is thereby threatened (cf. Dylander and Olesen, 1976). Such reactions are likely particularly when there are no strong traditions of cooperativeness in the firm and when it is bureaucratically organized in a way that promotes boundary-oriented thinking..

Group Functioning

To an increasing degree, employees work together in teams which are regulated by various types of informal group norms. Some norms may be productive in relation to individual competence acquisition, transfer, and application, and some norms may be counterproductive. Among the latter are norms that often emerge in teams or larger groups of subordinates who are relatively isolated from the managerial ranks of the organization – norms that imply a more or less permanent state of suspiciousness and distrust.

If such subcultures are allowed to develop and bloom, the result is often a collective unwillingness to acquire new competences, since human resource development activities are interpreted as just another managerial idea that has to be fought. This type of behavior was described by Lysgaard (1960) in his classical study of the informal collectivities of subordinate workers in a Norwegian manufacturing plant. He uncovered a mentality that distinguished sharply between "we" (the subordinates) and "they" (the managers), laying bare largely antagonistic cultures in the organization. In such contexts, there will often be implicit rules among subordinates regulating the amount of effort that should be spent working for the firm, implying negative sanctions of those who break the rules by working too much or too efficiently. Then, it is reasonable to assume that also the amount of knowledge and skill acquisition is similarly regulated and accompanied by sanctions to ensure that nobody exceeds the limits set by the collectivity.

In work teams there are often dysfunctional ways of operating that put a brake both on performance and interpersonal exchange of competences. The phenomenon of 'groupthink' is probably the most well-known example of such dysfunctional processes in teams (Janis, 1982). This is descriptive of a development toward homogeneous thinking in a group, often characterized by partial isolation from the environment and cultivation of self-confirming attitudes and beliefs. The group then becomes less critical to its performance and own way of functioning – and less open to new learning. Knowledge that may direct attention to critical aspects of the group and its processes is filtered away by more or less automatically being regarded as distorted or false. This tendency to develop a sense of joint exclusiveness and self-righteousness is a risk any work team is exposed to, and this may emerge unless group members are aware of the danger and other parts of the organization stay in close touch with the team.

The groupthink syndrom may also extend beyond processes in formal work teams and exist as a general phenomenon in firms and other organizations. Kanter (1988) maintains that such a situation may easily emerge especially in large, bureaucratic organizations, hence hampering learning and innovation. She observes that once people enter a field, they spend most of their time with other people just like themselves who share their beliefs and assumptions, and she furthermore makes a special, illustrative case of higher-level managers: "At the top, leaders are increasingly insulated from jarring experiences or unpleasant occurrences that cause them to confront their assumptions about the world, and they spend an increasing portion of their time with people exactly like themselves. And if corporate culture encourages an orthodoxy of beliefs and a nonconfrontational stance, then idea generation is further discouraged" (Kanter, 1988:176; Senge, 1990).

If the level of conflict in a team exceeds a certain level, learning will be hampered. In groups characterized by a dominance of discussion as opposed to dialogue, this will often be the case. Discussions inherently involve individuals' fighting for different viewpoints with the ultimate goal of winning whereas dialogues per definition imply that individual views are exchanged – and, in addition, revised or even abandoned in order to reach collectively better analyses or solutions (Senge, 1990). A similar point has been made within the innovation literature, emphasizing interactive learning as a precondition for high performance (Quinn, 1985).

It has, moreover, been indicated that the structure of groups may inhibit exchange of knowledge and skills between the members. According to Kanter (1988: 194), the need for interactive learning in teams makes them particularly vulnerable to member turnover, since a certain level of continuity is necessary to produce innovation. Every loss-and-replacement can jeopardize the success of the innovation process in three different ways. First, employees who leave the team carry competences that are not yet routinized or systematized as a part of the team, and consequently they remove these competences when leaving. Second, new persons replacing those who leave require attention and training from the remaining team members and, thus, an extra effort must be made that absorb energies which could otherwise have been more productively utilized. Third, newcomers also often want to build their own power base within the team and may want to change the course of action, failing to consider the competences and insights that have been accumulated in the team over an extended period of time.

The composition of the team or project group is crucial to its subsequent performance and learning. First, a dysfunctional "personality chemistry" generating destructive conflicts obviously represents a strong barrier to learning within the team. Second, if the competence variance in the team is restricted, there simply may not be very many competences to exchange between members. This is often the case in those executive teams where the members have been selected because their educational and professional background is equal or similar to that of the other top executives. In such a situation, the members easily confirm each others' analyses and judgments and create a micro milieu which is either immune to or even not exposed to differing viewpoints and arguments. An additional effect may be groupthink effects as described above. Consequently, a certain minimum amount of heterogeneity in the competence mix of the team can serve to counteract such ramifications. Likewise, it is important that teams and team members individually have contacts with people outside the group. Studies have demonstrated that teams showing high performance are characterized by communicating more with fellow employees outside the group than teams with low performance (see, for example, Allen, 1984). Similarly, Pelz and Andrews (1966) in their studies of research scientists in organizations reported that the most productive and creative scientists were those with more contacts outside their fields – those who spent more time with others not sharing their values or beliefs. In a comment, Kanter (1988:176) notes that at the same time the dangers of closing off were also clear: "It took only 3 years for a heterogeneous group of interdisciplinary scientists who worked together every day to become homogeneous in perspective and approach to problems. Sociologists have used the terms 'occupational psychosis' and 'trained incapacity' to describe the tendency for those who concentrate on only one area and interact only with those who are similar in outlook to become less able over time to learn new things".

Finally, the group's joint ability to create interactive learning must be stressed. While in some teams, members view the group as a collection of largely independent individuals, in other teams, they look at the group as a composite of different competences that can and should be diffused between them in order to expand the team's collective capabilities. An illuminating example is provided by de Geus (1988:74): "Human beings aren't the only ones whose learning ability is directly related to their ability to convey information. As a species, birds have great potential to learn, but there are important differences among them. Titmice, for example, move in flocks and mix freely, while robins live in well-defined parts of the garden and for the most part communicate antagonistically across the borders of their territories. Virtually all the titmice in the U.K. quickly learned how to pierce the seals of milk bottles left at doorsteps. But robins as a group will never learn to do this (though individual birds may) because their capacity for institutional learning is low; one bird's knowledge does not spread. The same phenomenon occurs in management teams that work by mandate. The best learning takes place in teams that accept that the whole is larger than the sum of the parts, that there is a good that transcends the individual".

Macro Level Barriers

So far, focus has been set on competence inhibitors which can be found on the level of individuals, interpersonal relations, and groups. In addition, there are structural factors in organizations that may have similar effects, although the underlying mechanisms are different. It is, however, important to note that there is also a crucial relationship between the macro level and micro level in this respect. Organizational structures may represent barriers to acquisition, exchange, and utilization of competences – but at the same time the effects of these structures will have to be mediated at the micro level, that is through individual or group behavior, in order to influence learning processes.

In the following, six different competence barriers on the macro level are discussed. These include the work system, organizational design, the incentives system, organizational culture, human resource development (HRD) priority, and time perspective.

Work System

The way work is organized is among the most important determinants of competence development in firms. Central aspects of the work system include how jobs are designed and the extent to which they are being developed, the degree to which rigid boundaries between jobs have been drawn, the amount of bureaucratic control routines and decision making, the mobility across jobs and organizational units, and the extent to which development of multiskills is encouraged in the firm.

Although the significance of job design and development has for a long time been emphasized in the organizational literature, in many work organizations little systematic work is done in this area. A consequence is that human resources are not being efficiently utilized and, moreover, that employee learning is inhibited. This is especially the case in organizations where rigid boundaries are drawn between jobs, frequently on the basis of job analysis characterized by cumbersome bureaucratic procedures. A widespread sense of job-ownership and related protection of job territory then easily penetrates the work system and creates an environment that may easily becomes hostile toward interpersonal exchange of knowledge and skills – and even more so toward application of new competences that might question the present division of work into jobs and accentuate alternative divisions.

A major choice that has to be made, explicitly or implicitly, is that between designing narrow versus broad jobs. Narrow jobs are very specialized and founded on a belief that when human beings limit themselves to repeatedly solving a small range of tasks, they can be brought to the peak of their potential performance. Since they then master simple, repetitive tasks, employees hence do not need to pursue further learning unless their jobs disappear or are changed by implementation of new technology. This is the logic underlying the Taylorist principles of work organization and which was earlier described in detail by Karl Marx (1970/1868) in his analysis of the transformation from crafts production to manufacture production.

Albeit being applicable to simple manufacturing contexts, these principles have little or no value in other industries characterized by higher complexity and less divisibility of tasks into small elements. The alternative is to design jobs covering a wider range of tasks which provide the individual with an opportunity to shift between dissimilar tasks and thereby create variation in the daily work. This was early pointed out by Thorsrud and Emery (1970) who formulated a set of "psychological job requirements" that should be met in order to equip employees with human dignity, challenges, responsibilities, and learning opportunities which in turn would help them improve their work performance.

Discussing innovation in organizations, Kanter (1988:179) argues that generation of ideas is facilitated when jobs are defined broadly rather than narrowly, when people have a range of skills to use and tasks to perform to give them a view of the whole organization, and when assignments focus on results to be achieved rather than rules or procedures to be followed. She furthermore maintains that this, in turn, gives people the mandate to solve problems, to respond creatively to new conditions, to note changed requirements around them, or to improve practices, rather than blindly following previously designed procedures. Moreover, in innovation-generating companies a substantial proportion of problem solvers being in a "libero position", that is, floating freely around in the organization, can often be found. Hence, the existence of manpower slack in the organization may contribute to create learning and innovation, since idea generators in exchange for anticipated innovative ideas can be granted degrees of freedom they would otherwise not have enjoyed (cf. Kanter, 1983).

One thing is how jobs are designed, another is the scope of competences organizations aim at developing amongst their employees. When jobs are predominantly narrowly defined and the firm practices a one-to-one relationship between jobs and competences, the knowledge and skills of employees will be very limited in scope (although not necessarily limited in depth). The organization then employs individuals who may function quite productively within their strictly confined jobs, but who possess virtually no potential for mastering shift of job or changes in the work system and the organization at large. Hence, work systems characterized by rigid and heavily compartmentalized job design and absence of job development generate employees who may be high-performing here and now, but who may be degraded to low-performing personnel in the future because no flexibility is built into their individual stock of competence. This is the reason that many firms deliberately develop multiskilled employees who may take over each others' jobs when needed and who develop a much broader perspective of the organization and the tasks of the firm. As pointed out later in this chapter, some firms have also found it useful to design compensation and incentive systems that place a wage premium on possessing a variety of different competences – and which are thus implicitly rewarding individual readiness to step in for others or to change jobs if necessary. Such flexibility is also deemed to be positive in regard to innovation in organizations: "Furthermore, when broader definitions of jobs permit task domains to overlap rather than divide cleanly, people are encouraged to gain the perspective of others with whom they must now interact and therefore to take more responsibility for the total task rather than simply their own small piece of it. This leads to the broader perspectives that help stimulate innovation" (Kanter, 1988:179).

The amount of bureaucratic decision-making is another aspect of the work system that has an impact on the learning in firms. The more decisions are made on the basis of strict rules, routines, and procedures, the less learning and innovation is likely to occur in the work system. Such decision-making easily leads to a reliance upon the past and its solutions rather than on meeting new challenges and situations which require altered work behaviors. Instead of generating the best possible solutions given the concrete work challenges, individuals become preoccupied with finding solutions that fit existing instructions and routines as tightly as possible. A related effect then is that employees concentrate much of their energy on doing things correctly instead of doing them as efficiently as feasible under the circumstances. Hence, risk-aversive behavior is encouraged and rewarded. In such situations there is no wonder that the amount of innovation and learning remains modest, as that is in accordance with the rationality of a bureaucratic system. A general insight is that the more jobs are formalized, with detailed outlines of work tasks and specified duties, the less innovation is normally generated in the organization, whilst low formalization is accompanied by more innovativeness (Hage and Aiken, 1967).

The organization's career system constitutes another important macro level factor in relation to employee learning. This system structures the intrafirm mobility and hence also the individual opportunities of gaining diverse competences through work. In this perspective, there is a great difference between career planning systems based on separate, monolithic promotion ladders and those based on transfer of personnel across different ladders. In the former case, employee learning is limited to acquisition of competences that are specific for the one ladder on which their career is located. As a consequence, there will often be little cross-functional learning. In the latter case, such cross-learning is achieved and equips employees with broader, more firm-wide mental maps as well as increased tolerance to the situation and problems of other units and individuals in the organization.

The technology which is applied in work affects the acquisition, exchange, and utilization of competences in several different manners. First, similar to jobs, technology may be narrow or broad with regard to the demands it puts on the qualifications of users. Thus, when there is a shift from a technology which is relatively simple to operate to a more complex technology, employees must concurrently change their knowledge and skills in order to be able to master the new equipment. This is the main effect technology has on individual acquisition of competence. Second, in the same way as does the job design characterizing the work system, the technology determines the opportunities for employees to interact while performing work tasks. One extreme is the assembly line which ties the individual to one specific location and hinders interaction which might have involved exchange of competence and hence have created learning. Third, technology is a major determinant of employees' opportunities to utilize their existing skills and knowledge. If the technology is too simple to make it feasible for personnel to apply all the potentially productive competences they possess, there is a "waste-of-talent" effect implying that parts of the available competence base of the firm are drained away. This issue is acquainted with the organizational problem of overeducation or overqualification which was among the topics addressed in Chapter 8.

Incentives System

The ultimate goal of incentives systems is to influence human behavior in such a direction that prefixed objectives on the organizational level can be attained, regardless of whether these are profitability, growth, consolidation, or just survival. Incentives systems thus contribute to determining the rationality of different individual behavioral patterns. However, it is intricate to design such systems, not least because they always produce some unintended consequences that may at worst shatter the individual rationality context that was sought after.

Traditionally, one has in the literature on compensation and incentives been preoccupied with the relationship between pecuniary and psychological rewards on the one hand and work performance on the other. However, there is good reason to include effects that incentives have on the mobility, exchange, and utilization of competences in organizations. Even though work performance and organizational performance are ultimate standards of success, those performances are both inextricably tied to the knowledge and skills possessed by individual employees. Moreover, as will be shown, there are trade-offs between incentives that primarily promote job performance directly and incentives that stimulate competence development.

Career or promotion planning in organizations is a crucial part of their incentive system, since advancement is tied to receiving greater pecuniary rewards as well as status and prestige. The way in which this planning is carried out also influences the conditions for acquisition, transfer, and application of competences. Individual competence development will be most strongly stimulated by a career system that puts the main emphasis on employees' skills and knowledge when promotion decisions are made. If the system is based on past performance, individuals will easily be tempted to postpone educational and training activities because it is rational to work as hard as one can in the short run to achieve the best possible long term career results. Consequently, a conflict between short term and long term performance is accentuated. Employees who work hard and do not take the time to update themselves will at some point of time find that they have exhausted their competence wells without paying any attention to filling them up with new competences. In regard to individual acquisition of knowledge and skills, seniority-based career systems are probably the least efficient ones, as all that matters is the number of years a person has been working for the firm. In principle, length of service is used as a proxy or equivalent for the amount of firm specific experience. However, under such a system there is no particular incentive for employees to expand their own competence foundation, as this does not affect promotion decisions whatsoever.

On the other hand, application of the seniority principle is likely to have a positive influence on the amount of competence transfer between colleagues. Since it is predetermined who will be promoted the next time there is a vacancy, nobody will have a career-related interest in withholding skills and knowledge from other employees in the firm. This is very different under a promotion system based on prior performance. Then, individuals who want upward mobility in the organization will be interested in keeping their competences to themselves, since transferring them to others may qualify these people so that their performances might exceed one's own. Few persons would want to strengthen their rivals while fighting against them over a scarce good.

On the other hand, performance based promotion will normally ensure a better utilization of competences than career systems based on competences or on length of service in the organization. As long as results are all that ultimately count, all those interested in advancing will try to apply their skills and knowledge so as to create high performance. Competence-based promotion can easily lead individuals to channelling their energies toward piling up knowledge or skills rather than to using them to the benefit of the firm. Thus, at worst, investment in competence development may be perverted into investment in private future potentials financed by the firm rather than investment in productive human resources (cf. the previous discussion of individual opportunism). Finally, when a seniority principle is ruling there is no special incentive to utilize one's competences as efficiently as possible, since superior performance does not pay off careerwise anyway.

In addition to the career system, the compensation system plays a central part concerning acquisition, exchange, and application of individually held competences. Whereas career planning and promotion principles are to a large degree geared toward the long term operation of the firm, salaries and wages are set or negotiated in order to secure short term efficiency in current jobs. In addition, many compensation systems are deliberately designed to encourage the highest possible short term performance. Examples are piecerate payment, individual bonus systems for salespeople, and executive incentive arrangements which generate bonuses on the basis of economic results during periods of three, four, or six months. There is no reason to believe that such systems stimulate individual learning or transfer of competence to colleagues. On the contrary, there is an inherent danger that employees working under a strong short term pressure concentrate almost solely on utilizing the skills and knowledge they already possess and do not want to "waste time" building new competences. This trade-off is logically parallel to that between exploitation and exploration of knowledge as discussed in the literature on organizational learning (March, 1991).

During the last decade, an increasing number of organizations have implemented compensation arrangements using the amount of competence possessed by employees as a main criterion (Henderson, 1989). These arrangements are often used to supplement other pay arrangements based on criteria such as performance or seniority. Viewed against the above discussion of reward systems encouraging short term results, an interesting option is to incorporate competence-based elements in such systems to counteract the incentive to work so hard that longer term needs of updating and developing individual competences are ignored. Furthermore, pay systems building on employees' knowledge and skills can be used to efficiently broaden the competence mix and the organizational perspective of personnel (cf. Tosi and Tosi, 1986).

Finally, turning to incentives directly related to the learning process, all learners are dependent on some sort of feedback or information about results in order to be able to assess their own learning. Likewise, it has been demonstrated that feedback received during the learning process increases the amount of learning. Moreover, the sooner the feedback, the greater its effect. Lack of feedback hence constitutes an important barrier to individual acquisition of knowledge and skills. According to Hall and Fukami (1979:140), feedback aids learning by clarifyings expectations and learning goals, helping to direct and shape effort by correcting mistakes, helping to define and evaluate performance, and serving as an intrinsic reward for good performance. In general, the sooner the feedback and rewards appear after the learning response, the larger their impact.

The importance of positive feedback in relation to learning has also been pointed out in the literature on innovation in organizations. Ability to create novel ideas and innovations is thus a necessary – yet clearly not sufficient – prerequisite for innovation to take place. Employees must also feel that their efforts in this direction are appreciated and that there is enough tolerance for possible failures. An atmosphere where serious endeavors are encouraged and appreciated, also when they do not turn out successfully, is therefore assumed to promote learning and innovation.

HRD Priority

Firms differ greatly in regard to the priority set on human resource development, but today there is a growing tendency to assign this field a higher priority than before. One of the reasons is that the competition for highly qualified personnel has grown fiercer in many industries and geographic regions and will continue to do so in the decades to come. It is reasonable to suggest that firms assigning a high priority to competence development will succeed better than other firms in creating good learning environments and competence flows which add to the total competence base. Empirically, the priority actually assigned to this field can be indicated by three major factors: First, the monetary and time resources devoted to creation of learning in the firm is a valid indicator. The second indicator is the institutional role and status of human resource development work, for example, illustrated by the position of the head of human resources in the executive hierarchy and the extent to which line managers pay attention to personnel issues. Third, the priority is reflected by the attention directed to competence issues by the top management. The actions of executives, and particularly the top manager's behavior and allocation of time on various tasks and groups,normally get considerable symbolic value attached to them by the other members in the organization. At the same time, it is fair to assume that employees put the emphasis on what executives do and less on what they say. This is why managerial lip service to human resource development efforts often fails completely. It is rarely sufficient to limit oneself to repeating statements pronouncing the employees as the most valuable assets of the firm.

Organizational Culture

An important element in any organizational culture is a normative structure that defines rules of legitimate conduct and behavior and contains general values which individuals can use as a support when making decisions about how to act under varying circumstances. In our context, this normative structure is important, and, in particular, the parts of it containing values and norms attached to individual acquisition, transfer, and utilization of work-related competences. In short, the symbols and values related to learning processes and results are paramount by contributing to establishing the rationality for individuals to pursue training and other competence development activities. If a basic assumption in the culture is that the organization should follow a traditional strategy, there is probably a lot less encouragement to develop new competences than if it is assumed that the important thing is to facilitate and promote frequent changes in the strategy. It has been noted elsewhere that this distinction is crucial with regard to innovation, and it is reasonable to extend it to learning in general.

At the same time as the culture structures learning in organizations, it is itself a repository of past learning and a means through which this learning as well as new knowledge are communicated between individual employees.

There is, hence, a dialectic or interactive relationship between culture on the macro level and human action on the micro level in that culture partly determines individual behavior and is in part concurrently constituted and altered through human behavior. Language plays a crucial role in this relationship, and especially language which is specific to the firm, i.e. deviating from the language or code of other firms. For example, a reasonable hypothesis would be that there are substantial dissimilarities in the languages of firms which are strongly oriented toward creating learning and innovation and firms that are not. A language in which the frequencies of using terms like 'challenges', 'competence', 'novel ideas', 'creativity', and 'personal growth' are high is more likely to reflect an innovation-centered organization than a language where such terms are rarely applied. Recently, many firms have used language more explicitly by formulating 'authorized' slogans pinpointing the need for continuous learning in the organization. Illustrations are slogans such as 'Don't ask me – try it out', 'It's better to ask for forgiveness than permission', 'Trying and failing are a virtue'. The degree to which these slogans are actually followed up by action in the organization and by the management probably varies considerably among firms. Yet they mirror the fact that language is a crucial element in the organizational culture in relation to learning. It acts as a means of focusing on what is regarded as important, and an analysis of intrafirm language and code may therefore serve to uncover attentional biases in organizations. This has been discussed by Normann (1985:229) who contends that "too many organizations – perhaps as an inheritance of the golden days of conglomeratism of the late 1960s – are dominated by a poor figure-oriented language, focusing on budgets, profit-and-loss performance, and procedures but not on the substance of the business".

Normann (1985:231) furthermore interprets the growing interest in the concept of culture as an increasing interest in organizational learning – in understanding and making conscious and effective as much as possible all the learning that has taken place in an organization: "To be aware of culture is to increase the likelihood of learning. Only when the basic assumptions, beliefs, and success formulas are made conscious and visible do they become testable and open to reinforcement or modification". This reasoning is acquainted with the logic of so-called defensive mechanisms in organizations, which are reflected in strong unwillingness to discuss the hidden, basic assumptions and beliefs embedded in the organizational culture (Argyris, 1990). In other words, there are certain taboos as to what issues can be raised and discussed. Nondiscussibility often applies to cognitive maps that form the very foundation of the analysis of the firm's situation and the goals and strategy which have been formulated, i.e. maps providing the basic meaning of the firm and being attached to it. Much of the resistance and hesitance toward setting these maps on the agenda probably rests in a fear that this constructed 'the-meaning-of-it-all' may crumble and leave individuals drifting around without an anchor. This is related to what we may call the 'believe-in-what-you're-doing' syndrom which frequently generates a dysfunctionally strong commitment to the chosen course of action or the way of doing the job (cf. Staw, 1980) and which forms a mental barricade that more or less automatically serves to reject undesirable information, however critical and accurate it may be. When such mental barricades are accompanied by a culturally enveloped inclination to attribute problems to external forces, there are serious problems in the organizational culture that may lead to disastrous consequences (cf. Starbuck and Hedberg, 1977). Ironically, this may often be the case in cultures which are commonly characterized as strong in the sense that there is a high commitment to the firm and its strategy and very homogeneous values and beliefs among the organizational members. Then, the groupthink phenomenon has spread to penetrate the whole organization, and the result may at worst be a firm burdened by compact self-righteousness and collective complacency. It is even more ironical that success easily breeds such sentiments. There is a saying that it takes a strong back for a human being to carry previous success. Using this as an analogy to organizations, previous and contemporaneous success also incorporate serious future risks in the form of emerging myopia and complacency. This has been repeatedly emphasized by Hedberg: "Organizations cannot afford to scan their environments, continuously searching for conditions that require actions. They search intermittently, they rely on attention-directing standard operating procedures, and they question these procedures only when problems begin to mount. Although affluence sometimes initiates searches for opportunities, it is usually the case that scarcity, conflict, and substandard performances lead to actions, whereas wealth, harmony, and goal accomplishment breed complacency and reinforce current behaviors. Learning is typically triggered by problems" (Hedberg, 1981:16).

Previous success has a tendency to reinforce the theories of action applied in firms (cf. Cyert and March, 1963). Then, and also when success has been achieved despite, and not because, of this theory (for example, due to unaccounted external factors), the organization is likely to continue relying upon an action theory which would, in fact, need to be altered (Argyris and Schön, 1978; Starbuck and Hedberg, 1977). Hedberg makes the important point that necessary unlearning is in this type of context made particularly difficult and that there are times when organizations should treat their memories as enemies (cf. also March and Olsen, 1976). He furthermore points out that unlearning represents particular problems for organizations that shift from stable, benevolent environments into unstable, hostile ones (Hedberg, 1981:18; cf. also Hedberg et al., 1976).

Organizational Structure

Organizational structure carries important consequences for much of the activity in firms. The formal organization chart is every-where supplemented by an informal structure which deviates from the official structure but which still strongly influences the configuration of competences through the organizational location of individuals and teams. It has been common to speak of division of labor in organizations, partly mirrored by their structure. It is equally relevant to talk about the division of competence, since the structure reflects where the various employees and competences are placed. Thus, the structure will determine what job moves and career paths are available for employee development and, in turn, affect individual competence development. In this perspective, changes in organizational design have consequences also for employee learning.

One of the most central dimensions of organizational structure is the degree to which it is centralized. There is widespread consensus in the organizational literature that, in general, high centralization is not particularly favorable for employee learning. It has, for example, been observed that whereas modest, incremental changes are more likely in centralized organizations, decentralized structures contribute to creating more revolutionary changes or innovations (Cohn and Turyn, 1984; Kanter, 1988). The rationale for the wave of decentralization that has swept over Western countries in the course of the last decade has partly been a need to move decision-making authority down to the lowest possible level of competence suitable to make the decisions in question – and especially to levels where incumbents are in frequent contact with the external environment (for example, customers). The main goal has often been to make firms more market-oriented and more sensitive to the preferences of customers. In earlier literature on organizational design, emphasis was put on the need to relieve the burdens on information channels associated with centralized structures. Decentralization was hence viewed as a method of reducing the communication overload on higher levels of the hierarchies (Galbraith, 1977). Later, the link between decentralized structure and learning has been emphasized (Hedberg, 1981:14).

Another important aspect of organizational structure which is highly relevant to learning is the extent to which it allows for contact and interaction across jobs, professions, teams, and subunits. This particularly concerns the transfer of competences between colleagues. If the structure is rigid, various departments are segmented and largely confined to themselves, and most of the communication follows formal channels, exchange of ideas and skills across formal boundaries is made difficult. If, in addition, the structure is 'materialized' through physical division of buildings and offices, cross-unit and cross-functional learning is likely to be even more strongly inhibited.

Lateral connections and liaison-type assignments are among the means that have been used by many firms to counteract the negative ramifications of such organizational structures. Yet other firms have chosen a looser organization by applying principles of project work and matrix structures where personnel from different units are blended together to solve specific tasks in cooperation. Expressed in the terms of this book, such solutions represent looser and more diversified configurations and reconfigurations of the available competences. The objective of establishing cross-unit work teams is precisely to mix *dissimilar* skills and knowledge in order to make the team as competent as possible. At the same time, the combination of employees carrying different competences in itself contributes to enhancing the cross-unit learning in the organization. It is no coincidence that matrix structures were developed in large projects in the aerospace industry to support technological innovation – and that they are found mostly in swiftly changing organizations geared toward innovation (cf. Kanter, 1983).

Organizational design also involves making choices as to the number of subunits and the size of each of these. Concerning learning and innovation, small units are considered to be more favorable than large units (Quinn, 1985). However, there is a downward limit to size. If units are too small, they cannot encompass all the functions and specialties needed to generate the professional and creative cross-fertilization that promotes learning.

Organizations embrace boundary-spanning roles and positions in relation to the external environment, and some subunits are more boundary-spanning than others. The information about competitive factors and trends that is received in these positions and units is often vital to other parts of the firm, and the extent to which it is disseminated in the organization is of great importance. Stated differently, we may ask how well prepared the firm is to collect and process all the external information received by single employees. Personnel with one foot in the organization and one on the outside are crucial in the sense that they influence or even determine which information flow about external factors and events is to be reported to their own organization. If it is rational for employees in such positions to filter out 'undesirable' information, for example, in fear that the messenger of bad news is the first one to be killed, the firm will not be able to learn enough about its environment. Hence, there is reason to look for learning barriers located in the interface between people in boundary-spanning positions and the organization.

Time Perspective

In the discussion of incentives systems, the time focus was emphasized. However, the time perspective is significant also in other organizational contexts relevant to employee learning. An important issue concerns the degree to which spendings on development of competence are regarded and treated as long term investments. In most firms there seems to be a tendency toward viewing these spendings as pure costs, thus applying a short term perspective. This is, among other things, due to the fact that, contrary to many other expenses, outlays on human resource development are not frozen by previous decisions. Once made, investments in physical capital incur interest payments and depreciation costs which are not optional to the firm, at least not in the short run. During financial crises firms normally search for areas where expenses can be cut as soon as possible, and competence development is an area that readily lends itself to being shaved by the budgetary knives. Investments in human capital are frequently considered as residual budget elements which can be expanded or contracted as the economic conditions change. However, the paradox is that the firms being forced to cut these expenses quite often are those that need to develop their human resources the most. In that way, short term adjustment to difficult economic circumstances may damage the firm's long term potential since necessary human resource investments are either not made at all or postponed. Another reason behind the treatment of such expenses as residual factors lies in the fact that competence resources are invisible and largely non-quantifiable. There is substantial uncertainty attached to the expected and actual return on such investments compared to investments in tangible production equipment, and this contributes to strengthening what we may call the cost-focus syndrom in the field of human resources. This syndrom accentuates the need to investigate firms' investment behavior in relation to competences as compared to other resources that are mobilized. Whereas the cost-focus syndrom primarily affects the level of spendings on competence development, the static fit syndrom influences the composition of such spendings. When maximum short term static fit or congruency between work tasks and employee competences is sought after, the capacity to alter the work system and the organization in response to changed external conditions in the future is harmed. If one is simply not thinking ahead of the current competitive situation and this situation changes quickly, the firm may have great difficulties in adjusting because of the strong fit created which has now suddenly been turned into rigidity. This points back to the discussion of task nonspecific competences in Chapter 3 and their significance for organizational flexibility. There, it was argued that firms concentrate heavily on generating competences tailored exclusively to short term promotion of static fit between tasks and human resources.

Concluding Comment

Diminishing and ultimately eliminating crucial barriers against individual acquisition, transfer, and utilization of competences represents a paramount challenge in most work organizations today. This is particularly so for firms which operate under strong competitive pressure and face rapidly changing environments. De Geus (1988:74) contends that "...the only competitive advantage the company of the future will have is its managers' ability to learn faster than their competitors. So the companies that succeed will be those that continually nudge their managers towards revising their view of the world". This represents a focus specifically on managerial learning. However, it seems more fruitful to consider *the joint capacity to learn* in organizations as being the single most important competitive factor and thus a critical condition for continued survival in the decades to come. If that is correct, increased attention will have to be paid to the creation of productive learning environments inside firms. Naturally, this cannot be achieved through conducting assessments of educational needs and evaluation of single training ventures. However, a great deal can be achieved by focusing on learning barriers and measures to reduce them. It can therefore be expected that an increasing number of firms and other work organizations will carry out analyses of factors which inhibit learning among employees and teams. Some firms may already possess valuable information collected in connection with surveys of elements in their organizational culture. Such surveys have been quite popular for some years. However, a reasonable prediction is that they will gradually be substituted by studies of learning conditions which go more directly to the heart of the important matter in firms, that is to lay and maintain the foundation for efficient organizational performance both in the short and the long run. In such studies, detecting learning inhibitors is commonly the end goal, but it is also important to uncover factors which serve to facilitate and create learning so that these can be maintained and nurtured.

PART IV

Future Directions

Chapter 10

Determinants of Human Resource Management

Introduction

The purpose of this chapter is to propose elements in a descriptive economic theory of human resource management in firms. A conception that the substance of human resource management is contingent on the character of such resources and their productive outcome serves as the point of departure. The theory formulation builds on an economically based classification of internal governance structures in firms, defined by their combinations of human asset specificity (firm specificity) and measurability of individual labor productivity (Williamson, 1981, 1985). In addition, it is argued that the measurability of team productivity is necessary to include when the full impact of governance structures is to be addressed. Propositions about how firms, when seeking economic rationality, will manage their human capital under different conditions are presented and discussed. Human resource management is viewed as including planning, recruitment, development, compensation, and control of employees.

Background

The question of how firms manage their human resources has not been systematically dealt with in neoclassical economics, with the exception of those theoretical and empirical parts of the human capital approach that have been preoccupied with the education and training of employees and compensation (e.g., Schultz, 1961, 1981; Becker, 1964; Mincer, 1962, 1974; Blaug, 1976; Freeman, 1977;

Wachter and Wright, 1990). However, the institutionally oriented literature on the functioning of labor markets contains many studies of human resource management practices with regard to the interests of firms and employees concerning the application of principles of promotion and job security in internal labor markets (Doeringer and Piore, 1971; Colbjørnsen 1986; Doeringer, 1986; England and Farkas, 1986; Jacoby, 1990). Yet, many firms have developed an internal labor market, and in those that have, this market does not always cover all employees in the organization. Dissimilar basic human resource management practices are hence applied for different groups of employees also *within* firms. Consequently, there is a need to ask under which conditions it is likely that firms apply differentiated human resource management practices that are deliberately designed to treat employees unequally on economic grounds. In order to address this question, it is necessary to trace characteristics of human resources and their outcome that contribute to determining the likeliness of various forms of human resource management, that is dimensions specifying under which conditions such forms are likely to vary.

Specificity and Measurability

Firms have two fundamental needs that are assumed to determine their management of human resources: The need to match these resources with tasks in order to achieve work performance – and the need to measure or estimate the productivity of human resources in use in order to be able to determine the compensation of employees in a reasonable way.

Fitting individuals and job tasks is largely a question of the type of competence involved. In this context, human capital theory offers the distinction between firm specific and general or firm nonspecific competences (Becker, 1964). Whereas general skills and knowledge can be sold in external labor markets, firm specific competences are valuable in one firm only. Furthermore, once generated, the marginal cost of utilizing firm specific competence is considered to be small relative to the cost of forming it through training and development (cf. Aoki, 1986:25). Consequently, both the firm and the employees possessing the specific knowledge and skills will normally be interested in and benefit from an enduring contractual employment relationship.

The need to measure productivity is related to the need to reward employees in an economically reasonable way. Substantial uncertainty is involved because, basically, companies obtain "crude labor" – not work performance. Hence, it is not productivity but potential performance that is bought in the first place. In other words, it is not primarily work results that are obtained but the employee's mere presence or time, and the transformation of human time and competences into work performance still remains. The concept of "incomplete labor contract" has been used to characterize this way of reasoning (Coase, 1937; Blau and Scott, 1962; Braverman, 1974; Williamson, 1985). Because within the contractual relationship between firm and employees it is difficult or impossible to specify in exhaustive detail what the employees shall do and how they are to perform their duties, the management faces a governance problem concerning how to utilize available human competence efficiently. Expressed differently, the legal employment contract has to be supplemented by organizational and personnel-related measures and implicit contracts that ensure cooperation from employees (Okun, 1980). However, the difficulties are not confined to extracting the best possible work performance from the competence available. The problem lies equally as much in evaluating or metering the performances, since individual productivity is often impossible or very difficult to isolate from the productivity of other employees working in the same team and, moreover, because the collective performance of each team may be difficult to separate from that of other teams.

Internal Governance Structures

By combining the dimensions of firm specificity and measurability, four distinct internal governance structures for human resources are obtained (Williamson, 1985:247). As will be demonstrated later, these are assumed to have clear implications for the management of human resources, and therefore a brief overview is given to illuminate the basis of the subsequent discussion.

If the human competence applied is general and its output easily measurable, there is an internal spot-market where transactions between employer and employee occur frequently. The employer can evaluate individual productivity and the worker has a general or uniform competence which can be sold to several companies. Therefore, none of the parties has any particular interest in extending the mutual relationship. Workers are highly mobile across employers without risking reductions in their productivity, and employers can substitute labor without having to train new workers. Consequently, it is not necessary to maintain employment relations over longer periods of time. The internal spot-market is thus in a sense closer to hiring competence temporarily through external transactions than to labor organization characterized by employment contracts of extended duration. Temporary use of ad hoc workers in shops, potato-pickers, workers loading and unloading ships, and fruit-pickers can serve as examples.

In primitive teams, no idiosyncratic competences are required, and individual performances are very difficult to separate and identify. However, collective performance may under certain conditions be measured. As noted by Alchian and Demsetz (1972:779), companies emerge when work tasks are technically inseparable from each other; "The output is yielded by a team, by definition, and it is not a *sum* of separable outputs of each of its members". This fundamental separability problem in turn generates a metering problem. Illustrations of primitive teams comprise simple assembly line production, autonomous work groups with general competence, and work groups that carry out collective assignments through internal specialization (for example construction workers, movers, and roofers).

An obligational market is described by employment relations where the competence is firm specific and the individual productivity is easy to evaluate. Since the individual competence in this context is tied to the firm, it does not have any value in external labor markets, and employees will therefore normally find long-term employment contracts rational. This is also the case for employers who have made sunk cost investments in firmspecific skills. Hence, both parties have an interest in maintaining the mutual relationship over an extended period of time. At the same time, performances are easily measurable, and rewards can be allocated on the basis of individual productivity. Jobs demanding knowledge and skills related to application of technology (equipment, routines, and procedures) that is unique to the firm and are composed of easily separable tasks, can illustrate obligational markets. Relational teams are characterized by a combination of firm specific human competence and low measurability of individual performances. In the same way as in obligational markets, both employers and employees have an interest in maintaining the contractual relationship, because competences are highly firm specific. Concurrently, the individual productivity is difficult or impossible to meter, as the collective performance of the team cannot easily be subdivided into individual contributions. Williamson (1981, 1985) argues that this type of team corresponds to Ouchi's (1980) "clan organization", which is characterized by tight relations between employees and indirect governance through the use of values, norms, and symbols in order to create identification and commitment.

By focusing solely on the measurability of *individual* productivity, Williamson stays within the limits of the discussion previously presented by Alchian and Demsetz (1972). An important point, however, is that although individual productivity frequently cannot be measured, it may in some cases still be possible to obtain reasonably accurate estimates of the collective performance of work teams, thereby making productivity measures feasible also for primitive teams and relational teams in some cases. Then, the firm is provided with an opportunity to reward the employees involved on the basis of their collective performance. In the proceeding discussion, the measurability of team productivity in these two governance structures is therefore included as a supplementary dimension.

Propositions

Propositions about how different combinations of the human resources' degree of specificity and the measurability of their individual, and, possibly, collective productivity affect human resource management will now be formulated. It is asserted that the four internal governance structures place dissimilar demands on firm's planning, recruitment, development, compensation, and control of their human resources. Furthermore, these demands are assumed to influence the design and contents of each of these elements.

Planning, Recruitment, and Development

Since they are all part of the broader phenomenon of human resource acquisition, and thus strongly interrelated, planning, recruitment, and development are discussed together. In internal spot-markets, human resource planning is expected to occur in an ad hoc fashion. It is, furthermore, characterized by a short-term orientation, since transactions between the parties take place frequently and there is no rationale for setting up contractual arrangements. At the same time, it is expected that recruitment of employees also occurs ad hoc and that there is little or no need to pursue human resource development in the form of training, mentoring, or job rotation.

In primitive teams, human resource planning is not expected to occur very systematically and is, moreover, anticipated to be pursued on a short-term basis given that labor is easily substitutable. Assuming there is no scarcity of relevant labor in external labor markets, it would not be rational to use substantial amounts of resources to plan and obtain competence through recruitment and human resource development. However, because of the lower probability of being caught shirking due to the low measurability of individual productivity, it becomes reasonable to search for employees in possession of cooperative skills who are, in addition, not inclined to shirk. More resources are, therefore, expected to be used on selection and recruitment than in internal spot-markets.

In obligational markets, personnel planning is more systematic and long-term oriented. Because of the high firm specificity of competences and due to the fact that the short-term substitutability of labor is consequently low, the firm is more vulnerable to changes in the labor force. It is thus likely to plan the future supply of human resources thoroughly on the basis of information about factors such as the demographic structure of the work force, turnover, absenteeism, the composition of the internal labor market, and trends in external labor markets. Besides, substantial resources have to be used on facilitation of learning and training in order to maintain and develop firm specific skills and knowledge.

In the case of relational teams, both personnel planning and recruitment are systematic and long-term oriented, as employees possess firm specific competences that are both time-consuming and costly to develop. This implies that human resource forecasting, personnel inventory systems, career planning, and surveillance of external labor markets are relevant elements in the planning processes. The need to develop firm specific competences further implies that it is rational to screen potential employees on the basis of their estimated trainability. Whereas in internal spot-markets and primitive teams individuals are usually equipped with the necessary general qualifications when they enter the transactional relationship, in obligational markets and relational teams further training and other forms of learning are indispensable parts of the human resource management system. Moreover, since the measurability of individual performances is low, and because there is a long-term employment relationship, it becomes rational to search for employees possessing ability and willingness to cooperate with others in a team. The selection process thus becomes highly important.

This leads to the following propositions:

Proposition 1: In internal spot-markets and primitive teams, human resource planning tends to be unsystematic and short-term oriented.

Proposition 2: In obligational markets and relational teams, human resource planning tends to be systematic and long-term oriented.

Proposition 3: In internal spot-markets and primitive teams, recruitment and selection tends not to be assigned high priority and not to be thoroughly pursued.

Proposition 4: In obligational markets and relational teams, recruitment and selection tend to be assigned high priority and to be thoroughly pursued.

Proposition 5: In internal spot-markets and primitive teams, few, if any, human resource development activities are carried out.

Proposition 6: In obligational markets and relational teams, comprehensive human resource development are carried out.

Compensation and Rewards

When individual performance can easily be measured and the competence is firm nonspecific, the reward or compensation system is expected to be limited to wages based on assessment of individual productivity. There is no need to offer additional rewards in order to make the firm attractive to employees, because the relationship is of a short duration anyway.

In primitive teams, it is more intricate to find rational the criteria for compensation, since individual productivities cannot be measured. Use of seniority principles as criteria for distributing rewards will in this situation be irrelevant. Experience accumulated by working in the firm has little value inasmuch as the competence required is general. However, if the performance of the team can be estimated, a possible solution to the reward problem is to give all employees in identical or similar jobs the same wages, based upon the collective performances they have contributed to generating. From the management's side it is then assumed that individual productivities are approximately equal for all employees involved in such group. This type of equal compensation may, however, lead to an increase in costs created by individual shirking or free-riding caused by the fact that the compensation received by each employee is not influenced directly by the work performance of that single employee. The team's performance is dependent upon the performance of all employees and, concurrently, not on the performance of any particular employee. On the other hand, rewards based on collective performance will, as a rule, promote within the group a mutual control with individual work efforts and contributions, because everyone's compensation depends upon the level of collective performance. However, if team performance cannot be estimated with reasonable accuracy, it can in this context be expected that, in the absence of other objective criteria, rewards are distributed on the basis of seniority in the firm.

In obligational markets and relational teams, wages are likely to be supplemented with other extrinsic rewards, such as different types of perquisites and fringe benefits. Incentives in the form of favorable pension schemes, gain sharing, profit sharing, and employee stockownership represent other possible extensions of extrinsic reward systems, Such incentives may contribute to generating increased commitment, thus creating a stronger lock-in of employees in the firm. Moreover, within obligational markets and relational teams, firms are expected to attempt to influence employee's intrinsic rewards, because such rewards are also assumed to be important for the prospects of long-term retainment – which is essential due to the sunk cost investments in firm specific competences. Even though intrinsic rewards are beyond the direct control of management, they may be indirectly influenced through measures such as improvement of the work environment, decentralization of decision-making authority, increased employee involvement and participation, and job design. Likewise, when competences are firm specific, firms have an incentive to establish compensation schemes that generate wages which deviate from employees' marginal products. By designing and using deferred compensation systems, that is, wage-for-age schemes, or efficiency wages that are higher than the corresponding wages in the external labor market, they may create a lock-in of employees, thereby strengthening personnel retainment. In principle, this requires that individual productivity can be measured and, consequently, applies solely to obligational markets.

The following propositions are hence derived:

Proposition 7: In internal spot-markets, wages tend to be distributed on the basis of each worker's marginal productivity.

Proposition 8: In obligational markets, wages tend to be distributed on the basis of individual performance but not necessarily on the basis of employees' marginal productivities.

Proposition 9: In primitive teams and relational teams where team performance can be measured, rewards tend to be distributed on the basis of team performance.

Proposition 10: In primitive teams and relational teams where team performance cannot be measured, rewards tend to be distributed on the basis of seniority.

Proposition 11: In internal spot-markets and primitive teams, extrinsic rewards tend to be limited to wages.

Proposition 12: In obligational markets and relational teams, wages tend to be supplemented with other extrinsic rewards.

Proposition 13: In obligational markets and relational teams, indirect influence on employees' intrinsic rewards is sought after.

Proposition 14: In internal spot-markets and primitive teams, indirect influence on employees' intrinsic rewards is not sought after.

Control

In internal spot-markets and obligational markets, it is easy to evaluate individual productivity. Thus, the control of employee performance can be carried out through evaluation of individual work results. Being based upon information about earlier performances, this type of control is past-oriented. However, the degree of firm specificity creates a difference between the two governance structures. In obligational markets, where retainment of labor is important to achieve, the firm will benefit from adding control through socialization, given that employees are inclined to take the risk of changing employer although their competence is chiefly firm specific. In such a situation, socialization intended to generate identification and commitment constitutes a crucial part of the control system.

In the case of relational teams, employers and employees are strongly interrelated. The fact that employee competences are firm specific and the lack of clarity concerning the individual employee's actual performance, create a need for management to integrate the employee beyond what can normally be accomplished by using extrinsic rewards. In addition to the managerial measures mentioned under obligational markets, this need may be covered through development of common values and norms with the aim of inducing a maximum number of employees to perform so as to promote the firm's goals. Socialization aimed at developing commitment through information about the company's goals, strategies, and policies is thus accentuated (Van Maanen, 1976; Van Maanen and Schein, 1979). This is a future-oriented form of control which has frequently been associated with the concept of clan organizations (Ouchi, 1980). It is not based upon what employees have done in the past but rather on what they are influenced and hence expected to do in the future.

Proposition 15: In internal spot-markets, evaluation of information about individual performances is the dominant control mode.

Proposition 16: In primitive teams, a combination of direct surveillance of employees and internal social control in the work group is the dominant control mode.

Proposition 17: In obligational markets, a combination of evaluation of information about individual performances and socialization of employees is the dominant control mode.

Proposition 18: In relational teams, a combination of socialization of employees and internal social control in the work group is the dominant control mode.

Discussion

In reality, parts of the logic outlined in this chapter can be challenged when institutional arrangements and political conditions in firms are taken into account. The importance of such conditions resides in the fact that they may alter the context of rationality by involving potential costs related to conflict between employer and employees. For example, one possible line of criticism is that the influences of unions and labor regulations were not paid attention to. Institutional conditions such as minimum-wage agreements, legal employment protection against arbitrary dismissal, and union-shop arrangements may alter or distort the hypothesized relationships between the four governance structures and human resource management practices, particularly with regard to internal spot-markets and primitive teams. Williamson (1981) makes an effort to circumvent this type of objection by stating that the discussion of internal governance structures refers mainly to staff rather than production-level employees. In spite of this, three of his four illustrating examples are occupations located at the "production level" (manual freight loaders, migrant farm workers, and custodial employees). Furthermore, administrative personnel may also be members of unions or professional organizations with similar functions.

However, despite possible empirically founded criticism, the purpose was not to attempt to grasp the entire institutional complexity encompassing human resource management. On the contrary, the picture has been deliberately simplified in order to focus on fundamental economic dimensions that are assumed to determine how human resources are managed.

As pointed out in the introduction to this chapter, many firms comprise parallel, yet dissimilar, internal governance structures for human resources. In accordance with the propositions suggested, it would then seem rational to pursue different human resource management practices for employees located in each of these structures. This may be the case to the degree that the different governance structures are enclosed in separate administrative units having their own human resource management function. However, if this is not the case, it can be argued that it may be more rational to apply uniform practices throughout the organization, regardless of the human asset specificity and the measurability of work performance. If the firm is to design and pursue different practices tailored to the four types of internal governance structures, transaction costs related to segregating human resource management practices may exceed the cost reductions achieved by applying discriminant practices. Expressed differently, potential gains of standardization are lost, implying that there is an important trade-off in this context which must be taken into account. However, although relevant generalizable empirical evidence is not at hand, it is common knowledge that many firms apply different human resource management practices for dissimilar groups of employees. The extent to which they actually do this on the basis outlined in this chapter or on the basis of other criteria, remains open to empirical research.

A particularly vulnerable part of the reasoning presented in this chapter relates to the assumption that workers with general competences are readily mobile and hence have no interest in entering a long-term employment relationship with the employer. This implies that risk attitudes among buyers and vendors of labor are symmetrical, which is a highly debatable assumption. In his work on the cooperative game theory of the firm, Aoki (1986:17-18) argues that "... because of the limitation of human learning capacity and the present institution of a fixed work day in the business firm, it is neither wise nor possible for suppliers of labour services to diversify their investment in human capital and to hold several jobs simultaneously. As a result, individuals in their capacity as suppliers of labour services are likely to be more risk-aversive than the collectivity of many small shareholders. The asymmetry of risk-attitudes between the employees and the employers is a natural consequence of the ingenious social contrivance of the corporate institution."

If the above argument is extended beyond the present context, some of the workers in internal spot-markets would be interested in obtaining a long-term employment contract with the firm and these markets might then shrink. However, yet other workers are likely to prefer the flexibility of internal spot-markets due to, for example, family obligations, a preference for working only periodically, or an appreciation of the freedom to change employer, workplace, or geographical location swiftly. Thus, although the arguments for asymmetrical risk attitudes may be valid for some employees, the existence of internal spot-markets is not inherently incompatible with such asymmetry.

Concluding Comment

Most of the human resource management literature has focused on applied matters and practical concerns. There is thus a strong need for development and application of basic concepts and theories that can contribute to the academic advancement of the field. In order to supplement the comprehensive psychologically oriented literature it is, moreover, paramount to link the field more closely to organization theory and institutional economics. Application of knowledge from these disciplines may deepen the understanding of human resource management by relating it to basic needs, structures, and processes from which it emerges in organizations.

The concept of internal governance structures establishes a link between institutional economics and the research field of human resource management. It has a clear potential with regard to development of increased insight into economic aspects of organizational behavior as to the handling of human capital in firms. An immediate challenge ahead is to develop operationalizations of the dimensions making up the approach and test the propositions.

Chapter 11

Challenges to Research and Practice

Introduction

In this closing chapter, central challenges to research and practice with regard to competences and learning in organizations are reviewed and discussed. These challenges follow partly from the presentation in this book and partly from major changes that the societies and work life of economically advanced nations are undergoing and that will play an important role in relation to the acquisition, development, and utilization of human capital for productive purposes in work organizations.

Challenges to Research

As has been noted in previous chapters, research on competences and learning in organizations is confronted with many important challenges, and in the following some of the most central challenges are discussed.

The issue of financing competence development contains a conflict potential between employees and employers. According to neoclassical human capital theory, the employer will pay for development of firm specific knowledge and skills, whereas development of general competence will have to be financed by the individual. As the latter is transferable across employers, it will not be rational for the current employer to finance development of human capital that may in itself stimulate competence-drain from the organization unless costly exit-barriers are established. The logic of human capital theory at this point is consistent as long as firms operate within relatively stable environments. However, if they face increasingly swift environmental changes that require both individual and organizational adjustments, the adequacy of the theory is highly questionable. In Chapter 3, it was pointed out that certain meta-competences will be necessary to facilitate adjustment to change. As a result, firms may find it rational to finance, partly or fully, development of such competences, because their availability may be crucial for the prospects of organizational survival. Firms may therefore be ready to tolerate a higher economic risk with regard to investment in competence than postulated in human capital theory, to the extent that they thereby anticipate to reduce an even greater prospective risk related to a lack of needed change capacity.

Moreover, the distinction in human capital theory between general and firm specific skills does not render any opportunity to analyze the evolution, change, and demise of different types of competence. By introducing the dimension of task specificity, and thereby creating added substance to the understanding of competences, this is made possible since the dimension allows for analytical distinctions between different competences as to their development over time. One illustration of this is the complete or partial "metamorphosis" of employee competences into technology either in the form of physical equipment or codified procedures such as computer programs. As noted by Flynn (1988:17), the technology life cycle suggests that the development and introduction of new technologies generate relatively high-skill professional and technical needs: "As a technology matures, some relatively high-skill maintenance and repair tasks also can be expected. Concurrently, increasing levels of standardization and mass-production techniques cause the deskilling of a wide range of tasks. In its extreme form, the deskilling process results in the elimination, rather than just the simplification, of certain tasks". It is reasonable to assume that competences characterized by high task specificity (standard technical competences, technical trade competences, and unique competences) have a higher probability of being "materialized" as the relevant technology matures than competences with a low task specificity. In general, meta-competences cannot be embodied into technology, although efforts at creating "artificial intelligence" and "expert knowledge systems" may be interpreted as steps in such a direction. However, they seem to be the exceptions that contribute to confirming the rule.

Likewise, it is difficult to imagine intraorganizational competences being incorporated into technology to any considerable extent.

An essential challenge to future research concerns the relations between incentive systems in firms and employees' provision of work-related competences, their readiness to transfer these to colleagues, and their readiness to transform the competences into work performance. Fundamentally, this relates to the issue of competence flow in firms as introduced in Chapter 5. Given that employee competences are among the most crucial resources in today's work life, more research on factors that condition their acquisition, development, and utilization of human capital is clearly needed.

One of the most important research challenges related to the study of human capital in firms is to link competences on the levels of employees, teams, and organizations. Since competences on more aggregated levels of analysis cannot be conceived of as the mere sums of competences on less aggregated levels, there is a need to develop theories and models that seek to specify the relationships between the three levels. Even though this is a particularly intricate research problem, it is necessary to approach if deepened understanding of the nature and role of human capital in organizations is to be achieved.

One of the intentions of Chapter 5 was to suggest a way of tracing missing links between individual competences and competences on the organizational level. The question of how firms' collective or, more narrowly, their core competences are generated was not directly addressed. However, core competences can be viewed as being a special case of the problem of establishing a link between organizational and individual competences. The question raised in the literature on distinctive or core competence has not been what the firm is able to do in toto, but what it can do better than other firms in a competitive perspective (Grønhaug and Nordhaug, 1992; Prahalad and Hamel, 1990; Naugle and Davies, 1987). There is thus a need to single out and endeavor to isolate empirically the individual knowledge and skills, group-related competences, and the parts of aggregated competence bases that contribute specifically to the constitution of core competence on the organizational level. Hence, one may be able to derive practical implications, for example, in regard to which individual competences are particularly valuable to a firm and should accordingly be protected more strongly than other competences. Stated differently, in order to fruitfully develop the competence perspective on firms, there is an apparent need to track the analysis of core competences down to the micro level in organizations and, moreover, specify the relationships between the individual level, the team level, and the organizational level. It has been argued in this book that the concept of competence base represents a useful conceptual tool in this respect. However, there is reason to emphasize that core competences, as well as the total organizational competence they are a part of, embrace more than mere aggregates of knowledge, skills, and aptitudes possessed by employees. There are synergies that should be investigated, for example, at the level of work groups. Moreover, the configuration and coordination of individual and group competences are decisive for the extent to which, as well as the way in which, core competences are actually constituted. It is not simply sufficient to possess a number of useful competences, these must also be clustered and interlinked in such a way that there are synergies and integration effects leading to the generation of core competences on the organizational level.

It is essential that future research to an increasing degree pays attention to qualitative aspects of individual competences and organizational competence bases. There is a strong need to pursue further conceptual work in this field and to develop theories linking qualitative dimensions of competence bases with organizational performance variables. Likewise, a cricital research task is to operationalize the descriptors of competence bases in order to make empirical exploration feasible. Finally, there is a need for explorative case studies that can lay bare other dimensions than those delineated and discussed in Chapter 4. This is particularly so because the study of competence in organizations is still in its infancy.

Also, with regard to learning barriers, case studies will at this stage offer the most fruitful approach to empirical investigation. An avenue that could be worthwhile pursuing would compare samples of successful and failing firms in respect to learning conditions and frequency of competence development. Then, one might be able to assess if, and, eventually, to what degree, the learning environment really makes a difference to organizational performance. Furthermore, two interesting questions regard whether or not there are specific clusters of barriers that can be identified and isolated from other clusters – and whether learning barriers are cumulated in some firms while being rare in others. Approaching this issue will require a larger investigation involving use of surveys. Altogether, more empirical research is required to counterbalance and supplement the predominantly abstract theorizing about organizational learning which often lacks the elements of human action and competence.

In general, there is also a strong need to investigate more closely into the forces governing the generation of human resource management and development in organizations. By gaining empirical knowledge in this area, one may also get valuable insight into the investment behavior of firms as to acquiring human capital. To the extent that public authorities in various countries would want to stimulate such investment through tax incentives or other measures, such knowledge is absolutely required if such public policy measures in this field are to create the intended effects. Uncovering determinants of human resource management and investment is, moreover, a necessary step toward establishing theoretical and empirical links between firms' human capital investment and management on the one hand and their internal efficiency and external effectiveness on the other.

Challenges to Practice

Probably most firms focus on provision, development, and utilization of *technical*, in the sense of task specific, competences. This is due to a strong concentration on operatively oriented qualifications according to requirements that are inherent in the current contents of jobs. However, too narrow a focus on this aspect of competence development may have harmful ramifications.

First, many jobs cannot generally be reduced to a bundle of easily separable operational tasks, each demanding just a set of particular task specific competences. They also require vital *overarching competences*, for example, related to communication and cooperation with colleagues, as well as adjustment to working in teams, which makes it crucial to possess competences that exist independently of and are, concurrently, cross-cutting different work tasks. Second, jobs are enclosed in a wider organizational context

that has an impact both upon employees, job content and development, and performance standards – and that therefore require more
from most employees than just doing the job in purely technical
terms. Third, if firms develop only technical competences,
inflexibility may be built into the organization since the need for
generating more change-related competences is then ignored.

Fourth, this focus on task specificity is short term and solely
related to requirements inherent in *present* jobs. This is clearly
paradoxical, since adaptability to requirements in future jobs is also
highly important (cf. Doeringer et al., 1991:186). This view is
supported by a joint study conducted by the U.S. Departments of
Labor, Education, and Commerce (1988) which reported that
employers need "employees with the ability to learn, be flexible,
and respond to change quickly" (see also Hornbeck, 1991).

Several authors have stressed the significance of developing and
blending dissimilar types of competences in every employee, and
in recent contributions there seems to be a trend toward emphasizing meta- competences and intraorganizatonal competences. One
author emphasizes the emergence of altered competence requirements in the "new network economy" and stresses the importance
of blending different types of skill and knowledge: "The substitution of flexible networks for top-down hierarchies means
employees need interpersonal skills to get along with customers
and co-workers, listening and oral communication skills to ensure
effective interaction, negotiation and teamwork skills to be effective
members of working groups, leadership skills to move work teams
forward, and organizational skills to utilize effectively the work
processes, procedures, and culture of the employer institution. More
flexible organizational formats in combination with more powerful
and flexible technologies also grant individual employees greater
autonomy at work. Employees need sufficient self-management,
goal setting, and motivational skills to handle this new autonomy"
(Carnevale, 1991: 157). In a similar vein, Cohen and Levinthal
(1990:135) focus on the need for firms to integrate certain classes
of complex and sophisticated technological knowledge into its
activities. This requires an internal staff of technologists and
scientists who are both competent in their fields *and* who are
concomitantly familiar with the firm's idiosyncratic needs,
organizational procedures, routines, complementary capabilities,
and extramural relationships.

As pointed out, thus far the impression is that firms have been far more willing to spend resources on development of task nonspecific competences in managers than in other groups of employees (cf. Doeringer, 1991). The implicit rationale for this is probably a conception that change-related skills are only needed by those managers whose responsibility it is to initiate and implement organizational changes. However, it will be increasingly important to generate readiness and capacity for mastering such changes on virtually *all* levels in firms that operate in competitive environments. Against this background, it is reasonable to assume that, in the future, investments in development of meta-competences and intraorganizational competences will soar in absolute terms and at the same time increase their proportion of the total investments in human capital as well – also at lower positional levels in work organizations.

In conclusion, there is an obvious risk that firms which concentrate all their effort on highly task specific competences may thereby develop organizational schlerosis and inertia, due to the fact that they, then, emphasize the need for static fit between jobs and job incumbents at the expense of the widespread need for organizational adaptability to changing external and internal conditions (cf. Lengnick-Hall and Lengnick-Hall, 1988, 1990). The typology introduced in Chapter 3 may, consequently, be applied as a tool for in-house analyses and assessments of competence sets that are required in jobs. If firms in obvious need of adaptability realize that almost all their efforts are spent on providing and developing standard technical competences, technical trade competences, and unique competences, they will then get the opportunity to take corrective action in this field.

It can be expected that efforts to detect and activate latent competences in firms will become an increasingly important human resource management activity. The reason is that the supplies of skilled labor in many nations will shrink due to demographic trends involving smaller cohorts of young people entering the labor market. As noted by Pines and Carnevale (1991:244), employers who used to be able to "cream" the most qualified workers from an oversized labor pool increasingly will have to *make* rather than *buy* skilled employees: "These same forces are redefining our notions of the public human resources policies. Public policy makers are now concerned with increasing the size of the labor pool to meet demand, increasing access to the workplace for those at the margins, and increasing productivity to benefit all Americans" (see also Carnevale, Gainer, and Meltzer, 1990; Packer, 1991). Hence, the demographic development will make it rational for firms to pay greater attention not only to competence development and utilization but also to putting a stronger emphasis on retainment of competent employees and, not least, tracing latent competences and potentials for developing new competences among their labor force.

An overall challenge to most firms in the next decades will be to increase the formal and informal learning that takes place in the organization. In many sectors, there will be shortages of qualified labor, implying that competences must increasingly be developed internally or in cooperation with external training providers. In transaction cost economics terms, a shift from "buying" to "making" competent employees can be anticipated (cf. Pines and Carnevale, 1991: 244). Another force pulling in the same direction is the fact that qualified individuals in external labor markets will tend to evaluate critically potential employees on the basis of their reputation and expenditure in regard to competence development and career planning. Thus, many firms must strengthen their training systems both to generate the knowledge and skills needed to operate *and* to be able to attract educationally qualified employees. Although advanced technology in some areas can replace labor, the tendency seems to be a growing preponderance of jobs requiring high qualifications in the economy in general, combined with increasing competence requirements in existing jobs (Johnston and Lawrence, 1988; Kutscher, 1989; Carnevale, 1991:150).

As noted in previous chapters, the amount of team-work is growing in virtually all parts of current work-life. At the same time, in many organizations little effort is spent on qualifying employees for performing productively in groups. The competence development that occurs in this field, seems to be generally limited to executive and managerial levels. It is, of course, highly important that members of management teams acquire skills in coping as team members, not least because the learning that takes place in such teams is crucial to the future performance of the firm.

However, learning in teams is likely to be the dominant type of competence generation and the main context of performance also on lower organizational levels – hence making it paramount that team members on these echelons, too, are equipped with the necessary skills to make efficient learning feasible. In line with the discussion in Chapter 3 and this chapter, there is thus reason to expect that, on the whole, there will be an increase both in technical skills requirements and probably even more in needs for meta-competences related to working in teams and handling interpersonal relations in general. This development demands a shift from the traditional way of thinking with regard to training and learning, namely that skill needs are largely limited to technical aspects of performing the current job tasks as efficiently as possible, to a way of reasoning where task nonspecific competences are regarded as crucial.

A cognitive revolution as to what work-related competences, training, and learning is all about can, therefore, be expected in firms preparing for future business challenges and continued organizational survival.

Bibliography

Akerlof, G. and Yellen, J. (1986). *Efficiency Wage Models of the Labor Market.* Cambridge: Cambridge University Press.

Alchian, A.A. and Demsetz, H. (1972). Production, information, costs and economic organization. *American Economic Review, 62*, 777–795.

Allen, T.J. (1984). *Managing the Flow of Technology: Technology Transfer and the Dissemination of Technological Information within the R&D Organization.* Cambridge, MA: Cambridge University Press.

Angle, H.L., Manz, C.C., and Van de Ven, A.H. (1985). Integrating human resource management and corporate strategy: A preview of the 3M story. *Human Resource Management, 24*, 51–68.

Anderson, C.A. and Bowman, M.J. (1976). Education and economic modernization in historical perspective. In L. Stone (Ed.), *Schooling and Society: Studies in the History of Education.* Baltimore: Johns Hopkins University Press.

Aoki, M. (1986). *The Co-Operative Game Theory of the Firm.* (Paperback edition.) Oxford: Clarendon Press.

Argote, L., Beckman, S.L., and Epple, D. (1990). The persistence and transfer of learning in industrial settings. *Management Science, 36*, 140–154.

Argyris, C. (1990). *Overcoming Organizational Defenses. Facilitating Organizational Learning.* Boston: Allyn and Bacon.

Argyris, C. and Schön, D.A. (1978). *Organizational Learning: A Theory of Action Perspective.* Reading, MA: Addison-Wesley.

Arrow, K. J. (1973). Higher Education as a Filter. *Journal of Public Economics, 2*, 193–216.

Bakke, E.W. (1959). *A Norwegian Contribution to Management Development.* Bergen: Administrative Research Foundation (AFF).

Becker, G.S. (1983)(1964). *Human Capital.* (2nd edition.) Chicago: University of Chicago Press.

Beer, M. et al. (1984). *Managing Human Assets.* New York: Free Press.

Bennett, J.C. and Olney, R.J. (1986). The communication needs of business executives. *Journal of Business Communication, 8*, 5–11.

Berg, I. (1970). *Education and Jobs. The Great Training Robbery.* New York: Praeger.

Blau, P. and Scott, W.R. (1970). *Formal Organizations.* London: Routledge & Kegan Paul.

Bergsten, U. (1977). *Adult Education in Relation to Work and Leisure.*

Stockholm: Almqvist & Wiksell International.

Berlew, D.E. and Hall, D.T. (1980). The socialization of managers: Effects of expectations on performance. *Administrative Science Quarterly, 11,* 207–233.

Berntsen, H. (1984). *Kurs i forbindelse med jobben: Hvem deltar og med hvilket utbytte?* (Work-Related Courses: Who Participates and What are the Outcomes?) Mimeo. Bergen: NAVFs Center for Advanced Training in the Social Sciences, University of Bergen, 1984.

Bigelow, J.D. (Ed.) (1991a). *Managerial Skills.* Newbury Park, CA: Sage.

Bigelow, J.D. (1991b). Afterword. In J.D.Bigelow (ed.), *Managerial Skills.* Newbury Park, CA: Sage.

Blau, P.M. and Scott, W.R. (1963). *Formal organizations.* London: Routledge & Kegan Paul.

Blomberg, R. (1989). Cost-benefit analysis of employee training: A literature review. *Adult Education Quarterly, 39,* 89–98.

Boam, R. and Sparrow, P. (1992). The rise and rationale of competency-based approaches. In R. Boam and P. Sparrow (Eds.), *Designing and Achieving Competency.* London: McGraw-Hill.

Bond, F.A., Hildebrandt, H.W., and Miller, E.L. (1984). *The Newly Promoted Executive: A Study in Corporate Leadership.* Ann Arbor, MC: University of Michigan Graduate School.

Bower, G.H. and Hilgard, E.R. (1981). *Theories of Learning.* Englewood-Cliffs, NJ: Prentice-Hall.

Boyatzis, R.E. (1982). *The Competent Manager: A Model for Effective Performance.* New York: John Wiley.

Braverman, H. (1974). *Labor and Monopoly Capital: The Degradation of Work in the Twentieth Century.* New York: Monthly Review Press.

Brown, J.S. and Duguid, P. (1990). Organizational learning and communities of-practice. *Organization Science, 2,* 40–57.

Burris, V. (1983). The social and political consequences of overeducation. *American Sociological Review, 48,* 454–467.

Cameron, K.S. and Whetten, D.A. (1983). A model for teaching management skills. *Exchange: The Organizational Behavior Teaching Journal, 8,* 21–27.

Caplow, T. (1964). *Principles of Organization.* New York: Harcourt, Brace and World.

Carley, K. (1991). Organizational learning and turnover. *Organization Science, 2,* 20–46.

Carlzon, J. *Riv pyramidene!* (Tear Down the Pyramids.) Oslo: Gyldendal, 1987.

Carnevale, A.P. (1991). *America and the New Economy.* San Francisco: Jossey-Bass.

Carnevale, A.P, Gainer, L.J., and Meltzer, A.S. (1990). *Workplace Basics.* San Francisco: Jossey-Bass.

Cascio, W.F. (1987). *Costing human resources.* (2nd ed.) Boston: Kent.

Chakravarthy, B.S. and Lorange, P. (1992). *Managing the Strategy Process: A Framework for a Multibusiness Firm.* London: Basil Blackwell.

Clegg, S. (1981). Organization and Control, *Administrative Science Quarterly, 26,* 545–562.

Coase, R.H. (1937). The nature of the firm. *Ecoonomica, 4,* 386–405.

Cobb, A.T. (1986). Political diagnosis: Applications in organizational development. *Academy of Management Review, 11,* 482–496.

Cohen, M.D. (1991). Individual learning and organizational routine: Emerging connections. *Organization Science, 2,* 135–139.

Cohen, W.M. and Levinthal, D.A. (1990). Absorptive capacity: A new perspective on learning and innovation. *Administrative Science Quarterly, 35,* 128–152.

Colbjørnsen, T. (1986). *Dividers in the Labor Market.* Oslo: Norwegian University Press & Oxford University Press.

Collin, A. (1989). Managers' competence: Rhetoric, reality and research. *Personnel Review, 18* (6), 20–25.

Collins, R. (1979a). *The Credential Society.* New York: Academic Press.

Collins, R. (1979b). Functional and Conflict Theories of Educational Stratification. In J. Karabel and A. H.Halsey (Eds.), *Power and Ideology in Education.* New York: Oxford University Press.

Cross, K.P. (1982). *Adults as Learners.* San Francisco: Jossey–Bass.

Crozier, M. (1964). *The Bureaucratic Phenomenon.* Chicago: University of Chicago Press.

Cyert,R.M. and March, J.G. (1963). *A Behavioral Theory of the Firm.* Englewood Cliffs, NJ: Prentice-Hall.

Dale, E. (1960). Management must be made accountable. *Harvard Business Review, 38,* 49–59.

Davies, I. (1973). *Competency-Based Learning.* New York: McGraw-Hill.

Dearborn, D.C. and Simon, H.A. (1958). Selective perception: A note on the departmental identification of executives. *Sociometry, 21,* 140–144.

de Geus, A.P. (1988). Planning as learning. *Harvard Business Review,* March-April, 70–74.

DeCenzo, D.A. and Robbins, S.P. (1988). *Personnel/Human Resource Management.* Englewood-Cliffs, NJ: Prentice Hall.

Devanna, M.A. (1983). *Male and Female Wage Gaps: A Look at MBA Careers a Decade Later.* New York: Center for Research in Career Development, Columbia University.

Doeringer, P.B. (1986). Internal labor markets and noncompeting groups. *American Economic Review, 76,* 46–52.

Doeringer, P.B. et al. (1991). *Turbulence in the American Workplace.* New York: Oxford University Press.

Doeringer, P.B. and Piore, M.J. (1971). *Internal Labor Markets and Manpower Analysis.* Lexington, MA: Heath.

Dulewicz, V. (1989). Assessment centres as the route to competence. *Personnel Management, 21,* September, 56–59.

Dyer, L. (1983). Bringing human resources into the strategy formulation process. *Human Resource Management, 22*, 257–271.

Dyer, L. (1984). Linking human resourcs and business strategies. *Human Resource Planning, 7*, 79–84.

Dyer, L. (1985). Strategic human resources management and planning. In K.M. Rowland and G.R. Ferris (Eds.), *Research in Personnel and Human Resources Management* (pp. 1–30). Greenwich, CT: JAI Press.

Dylander, B. and Olesen, K. (1976). *Effekter af medarbejderuddannelsen.* (Effects of Personnel Training.) Copenhagen: Teknologisk Instituts Forlag.

Edström, A. and Galbraith, J. (1977). Transfer of managers as a coordination and control strategy in multinational organizations. *Administrative Science Quarterly, 22*, 248–263.

Edström, A. and Lorange, P. (1984). Matching strategy and human resources in multinational corporations. *Journal of International Business Studies,* Fall, 125–137.

Ellis, H.C. (1965). *The Transfer of Learning.* New York: MacMillan.

Elstad, B. (1992). Læring i lederteam. (Learning in management teams.) Mimeo. Bergen: Norwegian School of Economics and Business Administration.

England, P. and Farkas, G. (1986). *Households, Employment, and Gender.* New York: Aldine.

Epple, D., Argote, L., and Devadas, R. (1991). Organizational learning curves: A method for investigating intra-plant transfer of knowledge acquired through learning by doing. *Organization Science, 2*, 58–70.

Estes, W.K.(1970). *Learning Theory and Mental Development.* New York: Academic Press.

Eurich, N.P. (1985). *Corporate Classrooms – the Learning Business.* Princeton, NJ: The Carnegie Foundation.

Evans, P.A.L. (1975). Oriental conflict in work and the process of managerial career development. INSEAD research paper 166. Fontainebleau: INSEAD.

Evans, P.A.L. (1986). The strategic outcomes of human resource management. *Human Resource Management, 25*, 149–167.

Evans., P.A.L. and Doz, Y. (1990). The dualistic organization. In P.Evans, Y.Doz, and A.Laurent (Eds.), *Human Resource Management in International Firms.* New York: St. Martin's Press.

Evans, P.A.L., Lank, E., and Farquhar, A. (1990). Managing human resources in the international firm: Lessons from practice. In P.Evans, Y.Doz, and A.Laurent (Eds.), *Human Resource Management in International Firms.* New York: St. Martin's Press.

Fagan, E.R. (1984). Competence in educational practice: A rhetorical perspective. In E.C. Short (Ed.), *Competence: Inquiries into its Meaning and Acquisition in Educational Settings.* Lanham: University Press of America.

Feltham, R. (1992). Safeway plc: Use of competencies in recruitment. In R. Boam and P. Sparrow (Eds.), *Designing and Achieving Competency.*

London: McGraw-Hill.

Financial Times (1986). Training. Don't get sacked, get smart. July 24.

Flanders, L.R. (1981). *Report 1 from the Federal Manager's Job and Role Survey.* Washington, D.C.: U.S. Office of Personnel Management.

Flippo, E.B. (1984). *Personnel Management.* New York: McGraw.Hill.

Flynn, P.M. (1988). *Facilitating technological change: The human resource challenge.* Cambridge, MA: Ballinger.

Flynn, P.M. (1991). The life-cycle model for managing technological change. In P.B.Doeringer et al., *Turbulence in the American Workplace.* New York: Oxford University Press.

Ford, J.R. et al. (1986). Changing patterns of labour recruitment. *Personnel Review,* January, 14–18.

Foulkes, F.K. and Livernash, E.R. (1982). *Human Resource Management.* Englewood-Cliffs, NJ: Prentice Hall.

Freeman, R. B. (1976). *The Overeducated American.* New York: Academic Press.

Freeman, R.B. (1977). Investment in human capital and knowledge. In American Assembly, Columbia University (Ed.), *Capital for Productivity and Jobs.* Englewood Cliffs: Prentice-Hall.

Galbraith, J. *Designing Complex Organizations.* Reading, MA: Addison-Wesley, 1973.

Ghiselli, E.E. (1963). Managerial talent. *American Psychologist, 18,* 631–642.

Goldstein, H. (1980). *Training and Education by Industry.* Washington, D.C.: National Institute for Work and Learning.

Goldstein, I.L. (1986). *Training in Organizations.* (2nd ed.) Monterey, CA: Brooks/Cole.

Golen, S. et al., (1989). An empirically tested communication skills core module for MBA interviewees. *Organization Behavior Teaching Review, 13,* 45–58.

Gooderham, P. N. (1984). *Adult Education and Social Mobility.*Trondheim: Norwegian Institute of Adult Education.

Gooderham, P.N. (1985). *Bedriftsintern opplæring.* (In-house employee training). Trondheim. Norwegian Institute of Adult Education.

Gottsleben, V. (1991). Weiterbildung als Gegenstand der Bildungspolitik. In "Mitteilungen aus der Arbeitsmarkt- und Berufsforschung, no. 2/91. Stuttgart, Berlin, Köln, Mainz.

Granovetter, M.S. *Getting a Job: A Study of Contacts and Careers.* Cambridge, MA: Harvard University Press, 1974.

Grønhaug, K. and Nordhaug, O. (1990). Læringsbarrier (Learning barriers). In O.Nordhaug et al., *Læring i organisasjoner* (Learning in Organizations).Oslo: TANO.

Grønhaug, K. and Nordhaug, O. (1992). Strategy and competence in firms. *European Management Journal, 10,* 438–444.

Grønhaug, K. and Nordhaug, O. (1993). Strategy, competence, and market success. *Proceedings American Marketing Association's Winter*

Conference, vol. 8, 111–117.

Hage, J. and Aiken, M. (1967). Program change and organizational properties: A comparative analysis. *American Journal of Sociology, 75,* 553–579.

Hall, D.T. (1984). Human resource development and organizational effectiveness. In C.J. Fombrun, N.M. Tichy, M.A. Devanna et al., *Strategic Human Resource Management.* New York: Wiley.

Hall, D.T. (1986a). Careeer development in organizations: Where do we go from here? In D.T. Hall et al., *Career development in organizations.* San Francisco: Jossey-Bass, 1986.

Hall, D.T. (1986b) Dilemmas in linking succession planning to individual executive learning, *Human Resource Management, 25,* 235–265.

Hall, D.T. and Fukami, C.V. (1979). Organization design and adult learning. *Research in Organizational Behavior. 1,* 125–167.

Hall, J. (1980). *The Competence Process, Managing for Commitment and Creativity.* The Woodlands, TX: Teleometrics International.

Harre, R. (1981). Philosophical aspects of the micro-macro problem. In K. Knorr-Cetina and A.V. Cicourel (Eds.), *Advances in Social Theory: Toward an Integration of Micro- and Macro-Sociologies.* Boston: Routledge & Kegan Paul.

Harris, P.R. (1985). *Management in Transition.* San Francisco: Jossey-Bass.

Hall, R. (1989). The management of intellectual assets: A new corporate perspective. *Journal of General Management, 15,* 53–68.

Hedberg, B.L.T. (1981). How organizations learn and unlearn. *Handbook of Organizational Design, 1,* 3–27.

Hedberg, B.L.T., Nystrom, P.C., and Starbuck, W.H. (1976). Camping on seesaws: Prescriptions for a self-designing organization. *Administrative Science Quarterly, 21* 41–65.

Heisler, W.J., Jones, W.D., and Benham, P.O., jr. (1988). *Managing Human Resource Issues.* San Francisco: Jossey-Bass.

Henderson, R. (1989). *Compensation Management.* Englewood-Cliffs: Prentice Hall.

Hernes, G. (1975). *Makt og avmakt.* (Power and Powerlessness.) Bergen: Norwegian University Press.

Hernes, G. and Knudsen, K. (1976). *Utdanning og ulikhet* (Education and Inequality). Oslo: Norwegian University Press.

Hinings, C.R. et al. (1974). Structural conditions of intraorganizational power. *Administrative Science Quarterly, 19* (1), 22–44.

Hornbeck, D.W. and Salamon, L.M. (Eds.)(1991). *Human Capital and America's Future.* Baltimore: Johns Hopkins University Press.

Hornby, D. and Thomas, R. (1989). Towards a better standard of management. *Personnel Management, 21,* January, 52–55.

Huber, G.P. (1982). Organization information systems: Determinants of their performance and behavior. *Management Science, 28,* 135–155.

Huber, G.P. (1991). Organizational learning: The contributing processes and the literature. *Organization Science*, 2, 88–115.

Huber, G.P. and Daft, R.L. (1987). The information environments of organizations. In F.Jablin, L.Putnam, K.Roberts, and L.Porter (Eds.), *Handbook of Organizational Communication*. Beverly Hills, CA: Sage.

Ireland, R.D., Hitt, M.A., Bettis, R.A., and DePorras, D.A. (1987). Strategy formulation processes: Differences in perceptions of strength and weaknesses indicators and environmental uncertainty by managerial level. *Strategic Management Journal*, 8, 469–485.

Ishida, H. (1986). Transferability of Japanese human resource management abroad. *Human Resource Management*, 25, 103–120.

Itami, H. (1987). *Mobilizing Invisible Assets*. Cambridge, MA: Harvard University Press.

Jacoby, S.M (1990). The New Institutionalism: What can it learn from the Old? In D.J.B Mitchell & M.A. Zaidi (Eds.), *The Economics of Human Resource Management*. Cambridge: Basil Blackwell.

Janis, I.L. (1982). *Groupthink: Psychological Studies of Policy Decisions*. (2nd ed.). Boston: Houghton-Mifflin.

Jarvis, P. (1985). *The Sociology of Adult and Continuing Education*. London: Croom Helm.

Johnston, R. and Lawrence, P. (1988). Beyond vertical integration: The rise of the value-adding partnership. *Harvard Business Review*, 66, 94–101.

Kalleberg, A.L. and Reve, T. (1993). Contracts and commitment: Economic and sociological perspectives on employment relations. *Human Relations* (in press).

Kandola, R. and Pearn, M. (1992). Identifying competencies. In R. Boam and P. Sparrow (Eds.), *Designing and Achieving Competency*. London: McGraw-Hill.

Kanter, R.M. (1983). *The Change Masters*. New York: Simon & Schuster.

Kanter, R.M (1988). When a thousand flowers bloom: Structural, collective, and social conditions for innovation in organization. *Research in Organizational Behavior*, 10, 169–211.

Katz, R.L. (1955). Skills of an effective administrator. *Harvard Business Review*, January February, 33 42.

Katz, R.L. (1974). Skills of an effective administrator. *Harvard Business Review*, 1974, September-October, 90–102.

Killeen, J. and Bird, M. (1981). *Education at Work: A Study of Paid Educational Leave in England and Wales 1976/77*. Leicester: National Institute of Adult Education.

Killman, R.H., Saxton, M.J., Serpa, R., et al. (1985). *Gaining Control of the Corporate Culture*. San Francisco: Jossey-Bass.

Kim, J.O. and Mueller, C.W. (1978a). *Introduction to Factor Analysis*. Quantitative Applications in the Social Sciences. Beverly Hills, CA: Sage.

Kim, J.O. and Mueller, C.W. (1978b). *Factor Analysis. Statistical Methods and Practical Issues*. Quantitative Applications in the Social Sciences. Beverly Hills, CA: Sage.

Klemp, G.O.,jr. (Ed.)(1980). *The Assessment of Occupational Competence.* Washington, D.C.: National Institute of Education.

Knudsen, K. and Skaalvik, E.M. (1979). *Deltakelse i voksenopplæring* (Participation in Adult Education). Trondheim: Norwegian Institute of Adult Education.

Kotter, J.P. (1978). Power, success, and organizational effectiveness. *Organizational Dynamics*, Winter, 27–40.

Kotter, J.P. (1982). *The General Managers.* New York: Free Press.

Kram, K.E. (1986.) Mentoring in the workplace. In D.T. Hall et al., *Career development in organizations.* San Francisco: Jossey-Bass.

Kutschner, R.E. (1989). Projections summary and emerging issues. *Monthly Labor Review, 112*, 66–75.

Kuznets, S. (1966). *Modern Economic Growth.* New Haven: Yale University Press.

Laird, D. (1986). *Approaches to training and development.*(2nd ed.) Reading, MA: Addison-Wesley.

Landsberger, H.A. (1958). *Hawthorne Revisited.* Ithaca, NY: Cornell University Press.

Lasswell, H. (1936). *Politics: Who gets what, when, and how.* New York: McGraw-Hill.

Lawler, E.E. III (1986). *High-Involvement Management.* San Francisco: Jossey-Bass.

Lawler, E.E. III, and Ledford, G.E, Jr. (1986). Skill-based pay: A concept that's catching on. *Personnel*, September, 30–37.

Lazear, E.P. (1981). Agency earnings profiles, productivity, and hours restrictions. *American Economic Review, 71*, 606–620.

Lengnick-Hall, C.A. and Lengnick-Hall, M.L. (1988). Strategic human resources management: A review of the literature and a proposed typology. *Academy of Management Review, 13*, 454–470.

Lengnick-Hall, C.A. and Lengnick-Hall, M.L. (1990). *Interactive Human Resource Management and Strategic Planning.* New York: Quorum Books.

Levitt, B. and March, J.G. (1988). Organizational learning. *Annual Review of Sociology, 14*, 319–340.

Livingston, J.W. (1971). The myth of the well-educated manager. *Harvard Business Review, 49*, 79–89.

Lorange, P. and Roos, J. (1992). *Strategic Alliances: Formation, Implementation and Evolution.* London: Basil Blackwell.

Lusterman, S. M. (1977). Education in Industry. In D. W. Vermilye (Ed.), *Relating Work and Education.* San Francisco: Jossey-Bass.

Luttringer, J.M. (1991). Worker access to vocational training – a legal approach. Paper presented at conference on "Adult Learning and Work: A Focus on Incentives" arranged by OECD and the University of Pennsylvania, Philadelphia, November 4–5, 1991.

Lysgaard, S. (1960). *Arbeiderkollektivet.* (The Workers' Collectivity.) Oslo: Universitetsforlaget.

Main, B.G.M. (1990). The new economics of personnel. *Journal of General Management, 16* (2), 91–103.

Mann, F.C. (1965). Toward an understanding of the leadership role in formal organization. In R.Dubin, G.C.Homans, F.C.Mann, and D.C.Miller (Eds.), *Leadership and Productivity.* San Francisco: Chandler.

Manwaring, T. (1984). The extended internal labour market. *Cambridge Journal of Economics, 8.*

March, J.G. (1991). Exploration and exploitation in organizational learning. *Organization Science, 2,* 71–87.

March, J.G. and Olsen, J.P. (1976). *Ambiguity and Choice in Organizations.* Bergen: Norwegian University Press.

Marshall, A. (1920). *Principles of Economics.* (8th edition) New York: Macmillan.

Marx, K. (1970)(1868). *Kapitalen* (Das Kapital.) Vol. 1. Oslo: Pax.

Mathis, R.L. and Jackson, J.H. (1985). *Personnel/Human Resource Management.* St.Paul, MI: West Publishing Company.

McClelland, D. (1973). Testing for competence rather than for 'intelligence'. *American Psychologist, 28,* 1–14.

McKnight, M.R. (1991). Management skill development. In J.D. Bigelow (Ed.), *Managerial Skills.* Newbury Park, CA: Sage.

Mincer, J.(1962). On-the-job training: Costs, returns, and some implications. *Journal of Political Economy, 70,* 50–79.

Mincer, J. (1974). *Schooling, Experience, and Earnings.* New York: Columbia University Press.

Mintzberg, H. (1975). The manager's job: Folklore and fact. *Harvard Business Review, 53,* 49–71.

Mintzberg, H. (1980) *The nature of managerial work.* Englewood Cliffs, NJ: Prentice-Hall.

Mitchell, D.J.B. and Zaidi, M.A.(Eds.)(1990). *The Economics of Human Resource Management.* Cambridge: Basil Blackwell.

Morgan, G. (1988). *Riding the Waves of Change. Developing Managerial Competencies for a Turbulent World.* San Francisco: Jossey-Bass.

Morrison, R.F. and Hock, R.R. (1986). Career building: Learning from cumulative work experience. In D.T. Hall et al., *Career development in organizations.* San Francisco: Jossey-Bass, 1986.

Mouzelis, N.P. (1973). *Organisation and Bureaucracy: An Analysis of Modern Theories.* Chicago: Aldine.

Naugle, D.G. and Davies, G.A. (1987). Strategic-skill pools and competitive advantage. *Business Horizons, 30,* 35–42.

Nelson, R.R. and Winter, S.G. (1982). *An Evolutionary Theory of Economic Change.* Cambridge, MA: Harvard University Press.

Newman, M. (1979). *The Poor Cousin: A Study of Adult Education.* London: Allen & Unwin.

Nordhaug, O. (1982). *Utbytte av voksenopplæring* (Participants' Benefits from Adult Education). Bergen: SFU, University of Bergen.

Nordhaug, O. (1985). *Effekter av personalopplæring* (Outcomes from Personnel Training). Trondheim: Tapir/Norwegian Institute of Adult Education Reseach.

Nordhaug, O. (1987). Adult education and social science: A theoretical framework. *Adult Education Quarterly, 38,* 1–13.

Nordhaug, O. (1989). Reward functions of personnel training. *Human Relations, 42,* 373–388.

Nordhaug, O. et al. (1990a). *Strategisk personalledelse.* (Strategic Human Resource Management.) Oslo: TANO.

Nordhaug, O. et al.(1990b). *Kompetansestyring.* (Competence Governance.) Oslo: TANO.

Nordhaug, O. et al. (1990c). *Læring i organisasjoner.* (Learning in Organizations.) Oslo: TANO.

Nordhaug, O. (1991a). *The Shadow Educational System.* Oslo: Norwegian University Press & Oxford University Press.

Nordhaug, O. (1991b). Human resource provision and transformation: The role of training and development. *Human Resource Management Journal, 1,* 17–26.

Nordhaug, O. (1991c). Organizational effects of training: Aggregation and transformation. *Scandinavian Journal of Management, 7,* 134–149.

Nordhaug, O. and Grønhaug, K. (1992). Competence as resources in firms. *Journal of General Management* (forthcoming).

Normann, R. (1983). Image och intern marknadsforing i serviceforetagets strategi. (Image and internal marketing in service companies' strategy.) I J. Arndt and A. Friman (Eds.), *Intern marknadsforing.* (Internal Marketing.) Malmo: Liber.

Normann, R. (1985). Developing capabilities of organizational learning. In J.M Pennings et al., *Organizational Strategy and Change.* San Francisco: Jossey-Bass.

Northrup, H.R. and Malin, M.E. (1986). *Personnel Policies for Engineers and Scientists. An Analysis of Major Corporate Practice.* Manpower and Human Resources Studies No.11. Philadelphia: Industrial Research Unit, The Wharton School, University of Pennsylvania.

Okun, A. (1980). The invisible handshake and the inflationary process. *Challenge, 22* (January-February), 5–12.

Okun, A. (1981). *Prices and Quantities: A Macroeconomic Analysis.* Washington, D.C.: Brookings Institution.

Olson, L. (1986). Training trends: the corporate view. *Training and Development Journal,* September, 32–35.

Ouchi, W.G. (1980a). Markets, bureaucracies, and clans. *Administrative Science Quarterly, 25,* 120–142.

Ouchi, W. (1980b). Efficient boundaries. Mimeo. Los Angeles: University of California, Los Angeles.

Packer, A.H. (1991). The demographic and economic imperative.

In D.W. Hornbeck and L.M. Salamon (Eds.)(1991). *Human Capital and America's Future*. Baltimore: Johns Hopkins University Press.

Parsons, T. (1960). *Structure and Process in Modern Societies*. Glencoe, IL: Free Press.

Pavett, C.M. and Lau, A.W. (1983). Managerial work: The influence of hierarchical level and functional specialty. *Academy of Management Journal*, March, 170–177.

Pearn, M. (1992). A competency approach to role and career management restructuring. In R. Boam and P. Sparrow (Eds.), *Designing and Achieving Competency*. London: McGraw-Hill.

Pelz, D. and Andrews, F. (1966). *Scientists in Organizations*. New York: Wiley.

Perry, L.T. (1986). Least-cost alternatives to layoffs in declining industries. *Organizational Dynamics*, *14*, 48–61.

Pfeffer, J. (1981). *Power in organizations*. Marshfield, MA: Pitman.

Pfeffer, J. and Cohen, V. (1984). Determinants of internal labor markets in organizations. *Administrative Science Quarterly*, *29*, 550–572.

Pfeffer, J. and Salancik, G.R. (1977). Organization design: The case for a coalitional model of organizations. *Organizational Dynamics*, *6*, 15–29.

Phillips, J.J. (1987). *Recruiting, Training, and Retaining New Employees*. San Francisco: Jossey-Bass.

Pines, M. and Carnevale, A.P. (1991). Employment and training. In D.W. Hornbeck snf L.M. Salamon (Eds.)(1991). *Human Capital and America's Future*. Baltimore: Johns Hopkins University Press.

Polanyi, M. (1962). *Personal Knowledge: Toward a Post-Critical Philosophy*. New York: Harper Torchbooks.

Ponalyi, M. (1964). *The Tacit Dimension*. Garden City, NY: Doubleday Anchor.

Porter, M.E. (1980). *Competitive Strategy: Techniques for Analyzing Industries and Competitors*. New York: Free Press.

Pottinger, P. and Goldsmith, J. (Eds.) (1979). *Defining and Measuring Competence*. San Francisco: Jossey-Bass.

Prahalad, C.P. and Hamel, G. (1990). The core competence of the firm. *Harvard Business Review*, May-June, 79–91.

Quinn, J.B. (1985). Managing innovation: Controlled chaos. *Harvard Business Review*, *63*, May-June, 73–84.

Quinn, R.P. and de Mandilovich, M.S.B. (1975). *Education and Job Satisfaction: A Questionable Payoff*. Ann Arbor: Survey Research Center.

Ralphs, L.T. and Stephan, E. (1986). Human resource development in the *Fortune* 500. *Training and Development Journal*, October.

Rasmussen, R.V. (1991). Issues in communication skills training. In J.D. Bigelow (Ed.), *Managerial Skills*. Newbury Park, CA: Sage.

Reve, T. (1990). *Bankkrisen: Hva gikk galt?* (The Banking Crisis: What Went Wrong?) Report No. 3/90. Bergen: SNF.

Reve, T. and Stavseng, T. (1984). Samarbeid som strategisk virkemiddel. In

J.Holbek (Ed.), *Foretaksstrategi.* (Corporate Strategy.) Oslo. Bedriftsøkonomen.

Reve, T. and Johansen, E. (1982). Offshore markeder krever samarbeid. (Offshore markets require cooperation.) *Norges Industri*, No.2, 17–19.

Robbins, S.P. (1989). *Training in interpersonal skills.* London: Prentice Hall International.

Roethlisberger, F.I. and Dickson, W.I. (1939). *Management and the Worker.* Cambridge, MA: Harvard University Press.

Roth, L. and Devanna, M.A. (1983). *A Career Development Study.* New York: Center for Research in Career Development, Columbia University.

Rowan, R.L. and Barr, R.E. (1986). *Employees Relations and Trends and Practices in the Textile Industry.* Philadelphia, PA: IRU, University of Pennsylvania.

Rummel, R.J. (1979). *Applied Factor Analysis.* Evanston, IL: Northwestern University Press.

Ryan, P. (Ed.) (1991a). *International Comparisons of Vocational Education and Training for Intermediate Skills.* Lewes: Falmer Press.

Ryan, P. (1991b). Adult learning and work: Finance, incentives and certification. Paper presented at conference on "Adult Learning and Work: A Focus on Incentives", arranged by OECD and the University of Pennsylvania, Philadelphia, November 4–5, 1991.

SCANS (1991). *What Work Requires of Schools. A SCANS Report for America 2000.* Washington, D.C.: U.S. Department of Labor, Secretary's Commission on Achieving Necessary Skills.

Sackmann, S.A. (1991). *Cultural Knowledge in Organizations: Exploring the Collective Mind.* Newbury Park, CA: Sage.

Saha, A. (1987). Training as a major factor in Japanese economic success. *European Journal of Industrial Training*, *11*, 11–16.

Sanger, D.E. (1991). Apple and Sony may become allies. *New York Times*, October 10, pp.D1, D6.

Scarpello, V.G. and Ledvinka, J. (1988). *Personnel/Human Resource Management. Environments and Functions.* Boston: PWS Kent.

Schein, E.H. (1985). *Organizational Culture and Leadership.* San Francisco: Jossey-Bass.

Schuler, R.S. and Jackson, S.E. (1987). Linking competitive strategies with human resource management practices. *Academy of Management Executive*, *1*, 207–219.

Schuler, R.S. and MacMillan, I.C. (1984). Gaining competitive advantage through human resource management practices. *Human Resource Management*, *23*, 241–256.

Schultz, T.W. (1961). Investment in human capital. *American Economic Review*, *51*, 1–17.

Schultz, T.W. (1981). *Investing in People. The Economics of Population Quality.* Berkeley, CA: University of California Press.

Schwenk, C.R. (1984). Cognitive simplification processes in strategic decision-making. *Strategic Management Journal, 5,* 111–127.

Scott, W.R. (1987). *Organizations. Rational, natural, and open systems.* Englewood Cliffs, NJ: Prentice-Hall.

Selznick, P. (1957). *Leadership in Administration.* New York: Harper & Row.

Senge, P.M (1990). *The Fifth Discipline. The Arts and Practice of the Learning Organization.* New York: Doubleday Currency.

Shackleton, v. (1992). Using a competency approach in a business change-setting. In R. Boam and P. Sparrow (Eds.), *Designing and Achieving Competency.* London: McGraw-Hill.

Simon, H.A.(1957). *Models of Man.* New York: Wiley.

Smith, M. and Robertson, I. (1992). Assessing competencies. In R. Boam and P. Sparrow (Eds.), *Designing and Achieving Competency.* London: McGraw-Hill.

Sparrow, P. and Boam, R. (1992). Where do we go from here? In R. Boam and P. Sparrow (Eds.), *Designing and Achieving Competency.* London: McGraw-Hill.

Spencer, L.M.,jr. (1986). *Calculating human resource costs and benefits.* New York: Wiley.

Starbuck, W.H. and Hedberg, B.L.T. (1977). Saving an organization from a stagnating environment. In H.B.Thorelli (Ed.), *Strategy + Structure = Performance.* Bloomington, IN: Indiana University Press.

Starbuck, W.H. and Miliken, F.J. (1988). Executives' perceptual filters: What they notice and how they make sense. In D.Hambrick (Ed.)., *The Executive Effect: Concepts and Methods for Studying Top Managers.* Greenwich, CT: JAI Press.

Staw, B. (1980). Knee-deep in big muddy: A study of escalating commitment to a chosen course of action. *Organizational Behavior and Human Performance, 16,* 27–44.

Steers, R.M. and Porter, L.W. (1979). *Motivation and Work Behavior.* New York: McGraw-Hill.

Stinchcombe, A.L. (1990). *Information and Organizations.* Berkeley, CA: University of California Press.

Thompson, J.D. (1967). *Organizations in Action.* New York: McGraw Hill.

Thurow, L. C. (1979). Education and Economic Equality. In J. Karabel and A. H. Halsey (Eds.), *Power and Ideology in Education.* New York: Oxford University Press.

Thornton, G.C. and Byham, W.C. (1982). *Assessment Centers and Managerial Performance.* New York: Academic Press.

Thorsrud, E. and Emery, F.E. (1970). *Mot en ny bedriftsorganisasjon.* (Towards a New Organization of the Firm.) Oslo: Tanum.

Tichy, N.M., Fombrun, C.J., and Devanna, M.A. (Eds.) (1984). *Strategic Human Resource Management.* New York: Wiley.

Tosi, H. and Tosi, L. (1986). What managers need to know about knowledge-based pay. *Organizational Dynamics, 14,* Winter, 52–64.

Tough, A. (1971). The adult's learning projects: An approach to theory and research in adult learning. Toronto: Ontario Institute for Studies in Education.

Tough, A. (1979). Major learning efforts: Recent research and Future Directions. *Adult Education, 28,* 250–263.

Tough, A., Abbey, D., and Orton, L. (1979). Anticipated benefits from learning. Unpublished manuscript, cited in Cross, 1982.

Training Commission (1988). *Classifying the Components of Management Competence.* Sheffield: Author.

Ulrich, D. and Lake, D. (1990). *Organizational Capability.* New York: Wiley.

Ultee, W.C. (1980). Is Education a Positional Good? *The Netherlands' Journal of Sociology, 16:* 135–153.

U.S. Department of Labor, U.S. Department of Education, and U.S. Department of Commerce (1988). *Building a Quality Workforce.* Washington, D.C.: Authors.)

van Houten, G. (1990). The implications of globalism: New management realities at Philips. In P.Evans, Y.Doz, and A.Laurent (Eds.), *Human resource management in international firms.* New York: St.Martin's Press.

van Maanen, J. (1976). Breaking in: socialization to work. In R.Dubin (Ed.), *Handbook of Work, Organization, and Society.* Chicago: Rand McNally.

Van Maanen, J. and Schein, E.H. (1979). Toward a theory of organizational socialization. *Research in Organizational Behavior,* vol.1: 209–264.

von Hippel, E. (1988). *The Sources of Innovation.* New York: Oxford University Press.

Wachter, M.L. and Wright, R.D. (1990). The economics of internal labor markets. In D.J.B. Mitchell and M.A. Zaidi (Eds.), *The Economics of Human Resource Management.* Oxford: Basil Blackwell.

Walker, J.W. (1981). *Human Resource Planning.* New York: McGraw-Hill.

Walker, J.W. (1992). *Human Resource Strategy.* New York: McGraw-Hill.

Walsh, J.P and Ungson, G.R. (1991). Organizational memory. *Academy of Management Review, 16,* 57–91.

Weick, K.E. and Gilfillan, D.P. (1971). Fate of arbitrary traditions in a laboratory microculture. *Journal of Personality and Social Psychology, 17,* 179–191.

White, R. (1959). Motivation reconsidered: The concept of competence. *Psychological Review, 66,* 297–323.

Whitley, R. (1989). On the nature of managerial tasks and skills: Their distinguishing characteristics and organization. *Journal of Management Studies, 26,* 209–224.

Williamson, O. E. (1981). The economics of organization: The transaction cost approach. *American Journal of Sociology, 87,* 548–577.

Williamson, O.E. (1983)(1975). *Markets and Hierarchies.* (Paperback edition.) New York: Free Press.

Williamson, O.E. (1985). *The Economic Institutions of Capitalism.* New York: Free Press.

Winter, S.G. (1985). Knowledge and skills as strategic assets. In D.J. Teece

(Ed.), *The Competitive Challenge*. Cambridge: Ballinger.

Woodruffe, C. (1992). What is meant by a competency? In R. Boam and P.Sparrow (Eds.), *Designing and Achieving Competency*. London: McGraw-Hill.

Yates, D., jr. (1985). *The politics of management*. San Francisco: Jossey-Bass.

Yellen, J. (1984). Efficiency wage models of unemployment. *American Economic Review, 74* (2), 200–205.

Yukl, G.A. (1989). *Leadership in organizations*. (2nd edition.) Englewood-Cliffs, NJ: Prentice Hall.

Zimmerman, M.B. (1982). Learning effects and the commercialization of new energy technologies: The case of nuclear power. *Bell Journal of Economics, 13*, 443–464.

Index

cultural knowledge 65, 66

decentralization 105, 139, 182, 219
decision-making capacity 177, 182, 183
defensive mechanisms 197, 217
deferred compensation 97
delearning 108, 126, 186, 199, 218
demographic analysis 29
demography 140
deskilling 242
despecialization 39, 41, 191
distinctive competence 80, 104, 107, 116, 243
distinctiveness 79, 106, 106, 107, 113
diversity 79, 87, 92, 93
division of labor 39, 40, 135, 190, 208, 218
division of competence 219
durability 79, 91, 92, 110

economies of scale 33
effectiveness 111, 245
efficiency 86, 110, 111, 245
efficiency wages 97
efficient boundaries 149
emancipatory knowledge 53
employee-competence matrix 82, 83
employee-customer fits 102
employee stockownership 234
employment relationship 238
entrepreneurship 41
entry barriers 107
environmental heterogeneity 136
environmental stability 136
evaluation (of training) 85, 192, 198
executive development 66, 110
executive teams 206
executive training 179
exit barriers 103, 107, 241
expert knowledge systems 242
expertise 125
extended internal labor market 31
extensibility 79, 105, 106, 113
external environment 122, 125, 136, 155, 179, 184, 219
external labor market 30, 31, 56, 57, 98, 100, 103, 152, 185, 202, 233
external training 144, 146, 150
extrinsic rewards 43, 234, 236